Report on the State of the European Union

AF798859

Jérôme Creel • Éloi Laurent
Jacques Le Cacheux
Editors

Report on the State of the European Union

Volume 5: The Euro at 20 and the Futures of Europe

palgrave
macmillan

Editors
Jérôme Creel
OFCE, Sciences Po
Paris, France

Éloi Laurent
OFCE, Sciences Po
Paris, France

Jacques Le Cacheux
Université de Pau et des Pays de l'Adour
Pau, France

ISBN 978-3-030-40478-9 ISBN 978-3-319-98364-6 (eBook)
https://doi.org/10.1007/978-3-319-98364-6

Library of Congress Control Number: 2004057663

© The Editor(s) (if applicable) and The Author(s), under exclusive license to Springer Nature Switzerland AG, part of Springer Nature 2018
This work is subject to copyright. All rights are solely and exclusively licensed by the Publisher, whether the whole or part of the material is concerned, specifically the rights of translation, reprinting, reuse of illustrations, recitation, broadcasting, reproduction on microfilms or in any other physical way, and transmission or information storage and retrieval, electronic adaptation, computer software, or by similar or dissimilar methodology now known or hereafter developed.
The use of general descriptive names, registered names, trademarks, service marks, etc. in this publication does not imply, even in the absence of a specific statement, that such names are exempt from the relevant protective laws and regulations and therefore free for general use.
The publisher, the authors and the editors are safe to assume that the advice and information in this book are believed to be true and accurate at the date of publication. Neither the publisher nor the authors or the editors give a warranty, express or implied, with respect to the material contained herein or for any errors or omissions that may have been made. The publisher remains neutral with regard to jurisdictional claims in published maps and institutional affiliations.

This Palgrave Macmillan imprint is published by the registered company Springer Nature Switzerland AG
The registered company address is: Gewerbestrasse 11, 6330 Cham, Switzerland

Contents

List of Contributors

Guillaume Allègre OFCE, Sciences Po, Paris, France

Christophe Blot OFCE, Sciences Po, Paris, France
Université Paris Nanterre, Nanterre, France

Jérôme Creel OFCE, Sciences Po, Paris, France
ESCP Europe, Paris, France

Paul Hubert OFCE, Sciences Po, Paris, France

Fabien Labondance CRESE Université de Besançon, Besançon, France

Gissela Landa Rivera OFCE, Sciences Po, Paris, France

Éloi Laurent OFCE, Sciences Po, Paris, France
School of Management and Innovation Sciences Po, Paris, France
Stanford University, Stanford, CA, USA

Jacques Le Cacheux Université de Pau et des Pays de l'Adour, Pau, France
Ecole Nationale des Ponts et Chaussées, Marne-la-Vallée, France
Sciences Po, Paris, France

Paul Malliet OFCE, Sciences Po, Paris, France

Maxime Parodi OFCE, Sciences Po, Paris, France

Hélène Périvier OFCE, Sciences Po, Paris, France
PRESAGE, Sciences Po, Paris, France

Frédéric Reynès NEO – Netherlands Economic Observatory, Rotterdam, Netherlands
OFCE, Sciences Po, Paris, France
TNO – Netherlands Organisation for Applied Scientific Research, The Hague, Netherlands

Francesco Saraceno OFCE, Sciences Po, Paris, France
LUISS, Rome, Italy

Aurélien Saussay OFCE, Sciences Po, Paris, France

Grégory Verdugo OFCE, Sciences Po, Paris, France
Université d'Evry, Évry, France

List of Figures

List of Tables

1

Introduction: Once More unto the Breaches

Jérôme Creel, Éloi Laurent, and Jacques Le Cacheux

After the French presidential election in May of 2017, which saw the decisive victory of Emmanuel Macron over Marine Le Pen, a sigh of relief could be heard in all European capitals and Brussels headquarters: the

J. Creel (✉)
OFCE, Sciences Po, Paris, France

ESCP Europe, Paris, France
e-mail: jerome.creel@sciencespo.fr

É. Laurent
OFCE, Sciences Po, Paris, France

School of Management and Innovation Sciences Po, Paris, France

Stanford University, Stanford, CA, USA
e-mail: eloi.laurent@sciencespo.fr

J. Le Cacheux
Université de Pau et des Pays de l'Adour, Pau, France

Ecole Nationale des Ponts et Chaussées, Marne-la-Vallée, France

Sciences Po, Paris, France
e-mail: jacques.lecacheux@sciencespo.fr

© The Author(s) 2018

J. Creel et al. (eds.), *Report on the State of the European Union*,
https://doi.org/10.1007/978-3-319-98364-6_1

worse had been avoided, the European Union (EU) would survive. A visibly rejoiced European Commission President Jean-Claude Juncker would even go on declaring on 13 September 2017 that "the wind" was "back in Europe's sails". A little more than a year later, the gentle breeze has turned, once more, into a fierce tornado.

Weakened by a decade of economic crisis and shaken by the awakening of populism, the European project actually faces four disintegrations: the Brexit, democratic disaffection, monetary and financial fragmentation, and territorial dislocation. If EU Member States want to escape those looming risks, they must, as they always have in the last five decades, reinvent Europe in order to save it.

To begin with, after 60 years of continuing enlargement, the EU will face its first shrinking when the UK leaves at 11 pm (UK time) on Friday 29 March, 2019. It probably means that any significant progress in European defense integration will be stalled for the foreseeable future. Yet, this European disintegration is the most favorable for the EU, as it provides remaining member states a golden opportunity to rethink the terms of their alliance and finally spell out what exactly they plan on achieving together. What they should do according to us is to address the other three disintegrations before they are out of hand.

Regarding monetary union, the worse has been avoided since the critical intervention of the European Central Bank (ECB) in July 2012 to save the euro and the chaotic but eventually stabilizing summer of 2015 (when Greece almost exited from the euro area [EA]), but very little has been actually changed in the EA governance since 2008. Different initiatives including those unveiled by Emmanuel Macron in La Sorbonne on 26 September 2017 have not (yet?) delivered any concrete or decisive result.

The overall prospect for the economic performance of the EU might be the sign that the region is finally exiting the "great recession" that started a decade ago. But the issue has been in the past not with the (misleading) average performance of EU and EA member states but with divergence between them. And this remains unaddressed.

Even more concerning: if "the wind" is indeed "back in "Europe's sails", EU citizens are still not on board. The Standard Eurobarometer 89 of 2018 (published in March 2018) indicates that 42% of EU citizens have trust in the EU. While this proportion has increased since 2015 when it was at 32%, it remains far from its level of 2007 when almost 60% of EU citizens expressed confidence in the EU. It was in 2011 that a large majority of citizens began to turn away from the EU, at a time, one might think, when the EU Member States were proving resolutely incapable of proposing a coordinated and effective strategy to get out of the crisis and when the bloc was once again plunging into recession. The divide between the core and the periphery of the EA is clearly visible in national responses to the survey: while the Germans and the Dutch show relatively high confidence—with 50% of their citizens trusting the EU—, the Greeks, the Italians, the Cypriots and also the French are much more skeptical. While the discontent *vis-à-vis* the EU seems uneven between the Member States, it translates quite uniformly into the well-documented rise of right and left populist parties throughout the continent, the latest episode of which has shaken Italy for the last months.

The relief brought by the defeat of Marine Le Pen has in fact been quickly clouded by the view of 93 far-right MPs making their entry into the German Bundestag on 24 October 2017. The general trend is very clear and far from reassuring, as shown by the data from TIMBRO Authoritarian Populism Index 2017: on average, 20% of Europeans now vote for a populist party, a share that has roughly doubled since the early 2000s. In the latest rounds of general elections, 55 million Europeans have voted for a populist party (more than 21%).

Finally, the EU faces a risk of territorial dislocation. The success of the single market inherited from the Treaty of Rome (1957) has been paradoxical: it brought countries closer together but led to divergence between the regions (and more generally local jurisdictions or territories). It can for instance be shown that in the EU the gap in economic development between regions is stronger than the gap between countries. This spatial fracture within Europe's countries, which is found in other countries outside Europe but which the single market has undoubtedly accentuated by the powerful agglomeration effects it generates, has two perilous consequences for the unity of Nation states: it fosters secession temptations of rich regions; it segregates and polarizes the electorate. While Catalogna might not succeed in its attempt to escape the authority of Madrid, it is the symptom of how cultural identity and economic separatism combined can fracture the EU. As for spatial polarization, one only needs to look at the map of votes in recent elections or referenda in UK, France or Austria to see that because European citizens do not live in the same area, they might end up not living the same era.

Twenty years after the completion of monetary union, the European project thus needs new positive narratives to survive. This reinvention should start by a re-visitation: how was the euro actually achieved? What are today its biggest challenges? How can it inspire future European endeavors? The different chapters in this volume intend to answer these questions.

Chapter 2 by Jacques Le Cacheux reviews the various, and sometimes contradictory, economic ideas and doctrines that have influenced the design of the European Monetary Union (EMU). Among these, quite importantly the macroeconomic and monetary framework adopted in Germany under the influence of ordo-liberalism, and the New Classical views about the functioning of market economies, with a clear distrust of political interferences and a strong aversion toward inflation. The European treaties have embedded very specific economic doctrines into institutional and stringent policy rules. The Great Recession and the subsequent sovereign debt crisis in the EA have shaken these certainties and require new thinking of macroeconomic and monetary matters.

Chapter 3 by Jérôme Creel recalls that the history of the euro is intrinsically related to the Maastricht Treaty, which defined the objectives and statutes of the ECB that shaped the institutional architecture of EA economic policies—the dominance of monetary policy over fiscal policies—, the characteristics of the implemented monetary policy—a form of inflation-targeting—and its performances that have been rather disappointing, most certainly since the global financial crisis. While the objectives and statutes were prepared for a stable environment, the upheaval following the crisis required many changes in the implementation of monetary and fiscal policies, which have taken time to emerge and enhance the EA performance.

Bridging the history and the current challenges of the EA, Chap. 4 by Jacques Le Cacheux analyzes the intrinsic risk of building a monetary union. For those who supported the project, monetary union was seen as the completion of economic integration and of the single market. This combination was expected to boost economic growth and foster economic convergence among EU economies. It has led to a significant intensification of economic and financial integration: trade in goods and services has increased, cross-border provision of services and labor commuting too; labor and capital have become more mobile. But for the lack of significant progress in political integration and collective decision-making, member state governments have been prone to resort to tax competition and other non-cooperative strategies. Although this has tended to increase economic inequalities and asymmetries among EU member states, the outlook for more cooperative strategies is not mixed: tensions tend to exacerbate and public opinions are expecting collective action, but agreement on common policies is made more difficult by existing differences in economic situations and performance.

Chapter 5 by Jérôme Creel and Francesco Saraceno goes on to argue that the *design* of constraints on the fiscal policy in the EMU is not intrinsically linked to the implementation of the single currency, but it is the result of the dominant New-Keynesian macroeconomic framework at the time of the Maastricht treaty. This framework gives almost no role to fiscal policy, viewed as a disturbance to market adjustments. The *application* of fiscal rules in the Stability and Growth Pact and the recent Fiscal Compact fare rather poorly in terms of the classic criteria for the optimality of fiscal rules though. This is due to the fact that the existence of these rules has produced a poor performance of the EA economy including during the recent crisis. The current reform debate should thus take stock of the recent theoretical and empirical developments, most notably on the size of multipliers, to revamp the rules and improve counter-cyclicality. Meanwhile, fiscal reforms should not underestimate the possible role of fiscal policy on potential output.

Chapter 6 by Christophe Blot, Paul Hubert and Fabien Labondance analyzes the deep reforms of the ECB, in terms of its prerogatives and objectives, since the subprime and sovereign debt crises. The ECB has taken over the objective of financial stability, it has expanded the range of its instruments, and it is in charge of the supervision of significant banks within the Banking Union. Strikingly, these changes took place without a treaty change. The ECB has behaved pragmatically and adapted its operational framework to fix the many dimensions of the crisis. While some of its actions have had some fiscal consequences, the legality of its decisions was contested. Reforms are thus necessary to clarify the role of the ECB in terms of financial stability and possible interference with public finances. However, reforms should not only concern fiscal and institutional issues. There is also room to improve the governance of the ECB. Since 1999, the EA has grown from 11 to 19 members, which raises the question of the decision-making process.

Chapter 7 by Jacques Le Cacheux elaborates on economic convergence that used to be high on the agenda of European integration. But 25 years of functioning of the single market and 20 years of existence of the euro have increased, rather than decreased, national and regional differences in economic performance. Even before the crises, divergences were manifest, though largely ignored. Since then, real economic divergences have widened in the EA, whereas the member states in Central and Eastern Europe have apparently been catching up. At the regional level, divergence is more apparent. Among the underlying causes, the very poor productivity performance of some member states and regions, along with high unemployment. Very slow productivity growth itself seems to result from weak investment. In this context, the limited efficiency of cohesion policies implemented with the European budget seems significant. Current debates about the future and the financing of the EU budget are analyzed in the light of economic convergence. Particular attention is devoted to the proposal by the Commission for a new Multiannual Financial Framework that includes changes in the main EU common policies (Common Agricultural Policy and Cohesion Policy) and more minor changes on the revenue side of the EU budget.

Chapter 8 by Jérôme Creel and Francesco Saraceno concludes the part of the book dedicated to current challenges in the EA and highlight current reform proposals. Previous chapters have shown that the organization of economic policies in the EA is far from optimal. Far-reaching institutional reforms are needed in order to meet a number of key aims of a monetary union: boost economic development, improve upward convergence and increase stability. There is certainly no shortage of individual proposals on the table. It is helpful to group the proposals into two fundamental views, which have a contrasting philosophy and endorse quite different tools. The first view focuses on the compliance with agreed rules and places faith in market discipline to incentivize improved competitiveness and reduced public indebtedness. The second view highlights the requirements of solidarity and coordination between the EU Member States. While both views have their pros and cons, the on-going process of reforms has left the EA with minimal proposals by the Commission that does not clearly decide which of these two views would be the preferred one.

Beyond the single currency, many other economic challenges are crucial for the future of the EU. Chapter 9 by Guillaume Allègre deals with the factors contributing to inequality in developed countries (technological change, globalization, the decline of trade unions). It also deals with the EU's record and prospects. While inequality has grown less rapidly in the EU than in other world regions, European countries are heterogeneous in their level of within-country inequality due to differences in labor market institutions, which determine wage inequalities, and differences in the redistribution operated by the tax and benefit system. As for between-country inequality, data show that there has been convergence, but limited to the lowest-income countries. Overall, global inequality in the EU—measured between European citizens—is at the same level as in the United States. Tax competition over mobile tax bases certainly puts pressure on the progressivity of the overall tax system. In order to keep inequalities low, the EU needs to limit tax competition, notably through minimum tax rates on corporate income; it also needs to put an end to low wage growth strategies through a coordination of national wage policies.

Chapter 10 by Hélène Périvier and Grégory Verdugo then studies the evolution of the European labor markets with a gender perspective while distinguishing the structural evolutions from the cyclical dynamic explained by the crisis. In most countries, although female labor force participation increased dramatically over the last decades, the gender gap remains large. On the cyclical side, the gender impact of the crisis is well established. On the structural side, the increase in the level of education of women is a major factor of their growing participation in the labor market. Moreover, while the EU attempted to monitor the increase in female involvement on the labor market and the decrease of the gender gap, its strategy finally proved disappointing. By focusing on employment rate without considering part-time employment, the European

Employment strategy has limited the achievement in terms of gender equality, especially for countries with a high share of women working part-time. Last, Horizon 2020 contains no gender targets.

Chapter 11 by Aurélien Saussay, Paul Malliet, Gissela Landa Rivera and Frédéric Reynès strives to identify what role the EU can play to be most effective in fostering the implementation of ambitious energy transition policies. First, most energy transition related projects are best managed at the local or national level, making the European level better equipped to act as a fundraiser or a pilot of transnational energy and transportation network infrastructures. This is highlighted by an analysis of the projects financed by the European Fund for Strategic Investments. Second, coordination between national energy policies should be ensured at the EU level, which could more efficiently associate the different sources of funding, constitute a capacity market and even define a common carbon tax policy beside the Emissions Trading System. Despite a significant leading position in many R&D climate mitigation areas, the economic benefits that could be reaped are not sufficiently secured under the current frameworks. The near disappearance of the European photovoltaic manufacturing industry at the hands of their Chinese competitors should make European authorities acutely aware of the fragility of European temporary advantages. Once the R&D stage is complete, more efforts should be put toward the commercialization of innovative energy transition related products and technologies.

Chapter 12 by Éloi Laurent advocates a two-step approach to reenchant the European project: first, put well-being and sustainability, and not public finance discipline, growth or finance, at the center of European policy; second, build a social-ecological state calibrated for the early twenty-first century where the inequality and ecological crises feed one another. This approach would be consistent with the history of the EU, as it has built itself as a normative and post-materialistic power; in the current geopolitical context, it must also take its “fate into its own hands” and depart from the US where the obsession of growth, profit and finance is coincidental with the alarming degradation of inequality, health, trust in democracy and environmental quality. Yet, there is a real European paradox regarding well-being indicators since the great recession: on the one hand, the EU has tried to capitalize on the discontent with standard economics and to embrace the "beyond GDP" agenda. On the other, it has become even more rigid in applying its ill-advised targets.

Chapter 13 by Maxime Parodi argues that democracy at the EU level must account for the multiplicity of peoples, views, interactions and transnational conflicts that is so specific to this area. The neologism "demoicracy" was developed to insist precisely on the need to democratize relations between multiple democracies. In this context, the single currency poses a particular challenge because it forces to cooperate politically, an outcome that was not necessarily obvious when everyone had their currency and tried to use it to get an advantage against their neighbors. Henceforth, central institutions like the ECB are needed, but in light of the principle of non-domination, it is also necessary to give the countries some autonomy by relying more on voluntary cooperation that is aware of externalities and systemic risks than on a central authority lacking in legitimacy. In conformity with the demoicratic principle, the ultimate goal of the EU shall be to find the right institutional arrangement by bringing into our national debates the externalities and systemic risks that the States impose on their neighbors. These are the grounds on which the European Parliament and other means of mobilizing Europe's citizens can advance demoicracy.

This list of ambitious projects for the EU and EA is rather long and comprehensive, dealing with institutions, climate, energy, sustainability, gender, inequality, public and economic policies. Undoubtedly, it contrasts with the decisions taken at the European Council of June 2018 that mainly revolved around two topics: illegal migrations and securing EU external borders. Immigration and terrorism rank, respectively, first and second as the most important issues facing the EU according to the responses to the Eurobarometer 89. While dealing with the issues that are important to the people is certainly important in itself, it may also reveal the lack of an ambitious and well-structured project for the EU by its current authorities: they give the impression of lagging behind people's perceptions of key challenges rather than leading the people toward a prosperous, equal and sustainable EU. We hope that this volume can contribute to grasping and then meeting these challenges so that, 20 years after the euro, the European project is again engaged with the future.

Part I

Ideas and Achievements

2

Ideas That Made the Euro (and Those That Did Not Make It)

Jacques Le Cacheux

Practical men who believe themselves to be quite exempt from any intellectual influence, are usually the slaves of some defunct economist. Madmen in authority, who hear voices in the air, are distilling their frenzy from some academic scribbler of a few years back.
(Keynes 1936, 383)

The eurozone does not look like any of the existing or past currency areas. It is a very peculiar institutional construct in which discretionary policy actions are strictly limited and policy rules dominate, thus defining a policy regime of "monetary dominance" (Woodford 2001) in which an independent central bank sets monetary policy according to an inflation target, while (aggregate) fiscal policy is the outcome of decentralized

J. Le Cacheux (✉)
Université de Pau et des Pays de l'Adour, Pau, France

Ecole Nationale des Ponts et Chaussées, Marne-la-Vallée, France

Sciences Po, Paris, France
e-mail: jacques.lecacheux@sciencespo.fr

© The Author(s) 2018

J. Creel et al. (eds.), *Report on the State of the European Union*,
https://doi.org/10.1007/978-3-319-98364-6_2

decisions by national governments constrained by a set of fiscal policy rules and, in principle, submitted to a "no bail-out" clause on the debt they emit.

The ideas that inspired this institutional setting and the process by which it was progressively brought into existence were the dominant ideas among decision-makers and "technocrats" involved in the decision-making process at the time: ideas become enshrined in institutions. In the case of the European Union (EU), and even more so in the case of the Euro Area (EA), this embodiment is all the more persistent, as many of the economic and monetary institutions and policy rules have been written in the treaties, having constitutional value and that cannot be changed except by unanimous consent of all member states.[1] After briefly recalling the history of the first attempts at monetary integration, this chapter reviews the intellectual influences inspiring the monetary arrangements written in the Maastricht Treaty, starting with the combination of German ordo-liberalism with the dominant macroeconomic school of New Classical Economics. The way in which the theory of Optimal Currency Areas has been read selectively is then analysed in Sect. 4. Section 5 attempts at synthesizing the main intellectual ingredients of the "Brussels-Frankfurt consensus" that have dominated economic and monetary policy-making in the EU over the past two decades. In Sect. 6, some reflections on the blatant weaknesses of this underlying analytical framework are offered.

1 A Kick-Start in 1969

Monetary union was not an option in the Rome Treaty instituting the European Economic Community in 1957: the six founding states were then all members of the international monetary system of fixed exchange rates that had been adopted in 1944 in Bretton Woods, and they all had almost inconvertible currencies, combining exchange controls and numerous restrictions on financial transactions and capital mobility. The first signs of fragility in the international system in the early 1960s did ignite reflections on specifically European monetary arrangements, but the idea that economic integration could be seriously hampered by exchange-rate instability surfaced in European debates only in 1969, after the devaluation of the French franc and the revaluation of the Deutsch Mark, a more than 20% change in the bilateral parity that caused enormous damage to the main pillars of European integration at the time, the Common Market and, even more so, the Common Agricultural Policy (CAP).

Submitted to the European Council in 1971, the "Werner Plan" (Werner 1970) is the first detailed roadmap for the completion of economic and monetary union (EMU) in the European Community. The aim was to reach "immutable fixed exchange rates or, preferably, a single Community currency", and it was proposed to do it progressively over a period of ten years starting on 1 January 1971: the process would have started from the existing fixed exchange-rate regime, reinforced economic and fiscal policy coordination, and narrowed exchange fluctuation bands, thereby smoothly achieving EMU by the end of the decade.

As is well known, it was not smooth, and never reached the aim. Only months after the Werner Plan had been adopted, President Nixon officially announced the end of the US dollar gold-convertibility, one of Bretton Woods' central pillars, and soon the dollar started freely floating, later followed by all other major currencies. Europe's initial reaction was to try and set up the first EC fixed exchange-rate system, the European Snake, an implementation of the first stage of the Werner Plan officially launched in April 1972. It included all six member states of the EEC, as well as the currencies of the three countries that were soon to join the EEC (Denmark, Ireland and the UK), and was designed as a European Bretton Woods system, with the Deutsch Mark in practice serving as the leading currency. But the financial turmoil created by the depreciation of the dollar, soon to be followed by the first oil shock and its deflationary consequences on oil-dependent European economies set the stage for a rapid dismantling of the Snake: the British pound left to Snake in June 1972, immediately followed by the Irish pound and, a few days later, the Danish crown; less than one year later, as the US dollar was forced to float, the Italian lira also had to float; and in 1975, it was the turn of the French franc, so that by 1976, the Snake had shrunk into mini-Deutsch Mark zone and was no longer a genuine European fixed exchange-rate system. A new, more flexible system, the European Monetary System

(EMS), was soon to be adopted, and its Exchange Rate Mechanism (ERM) started operating in March 1979, without the British pound.

The failure of the Snake, and the stagflation that prevailed in many developed economies—with the notable exception of Germany—in the aftermath of the first oil shock led to new thinking on the monetary integration. The surge of inflation and the relative failure of Keynesian demand-management policies in the fight against unemployment, as well as the remarkable performance of the German economy, brought increasing support to the Monetarist tenets, in particular the idea that monetary policy could do little to cure unemployment, and that the steady growth of money supply could tame inflation and stabilize exchange rates.

A brand of monetarism, Hayekian rather than Friedmanian, was the source of inspiration of the "Optica Report" (Basevi et al. 1976).[2] As a remedy against monetary and exchange-rate instability, the report proposed the creation of a parallel, European currency, managed by an independent, private central bank with the exclusive objective of price stability; this parallel currency would then freely compete with existing national currencies and progressively replace them, as private agents would spontaneously choose this stable money for their economic and financial transactions. Although the report received a lot of attention, its proposals were never seriously contemplated by European decision-makers.

At the opposite end of the intellectual spectrum, the idea that EMU had to be accompanied by fiscal integration was forcefully exposed in another report, under the auspices of the EC Commission: the MacDougall Report (1977). Inspired by Fiscal Federalism, a branch of economic analysis dedicated to the study of multilevel governments, and the Musgravian view of the functions of the state, the report proposed a reallocation of fiscal competences between the national and the supranational (European) levels based on the concept of spillovers, leading to an economic equivalent of the subsidiarity principle: an adaptation in the European institutional of Olson's (1969) "Principle of Fiscal Equivalence", based on the idea that all competences that generate significant spillovers among European member states ought to be centralized. This led the study group to recommend a European budget of significant size in order to provide European public goods, perform significant redistribution across regions and achieve necessary macroeconomic stabilization in the

EMU. The report proposes that the EU budget be increased up to 2% of EC GDP immediately, eventually to reach 5–7% of GDP and even 7.5–10% of GDP if a common European defense were adopted. The view of an EMU standing on two legs—monetary and fiscal—was thus set forth in the early stages of thinking about monetary union; needless to say, it did not prevail.

2 The Economic and Intellectual Context of the Late 1980s in Europe: The Delors Report

The success of the EMS in terms of monetary stability—most EC countries had returned to low inflation by the mid-1980s and parities had been kept unchanged after 1987—induced those member states that were not yet in the ERM to join: Spain entered in 1989, Portugal and even the UK in 1990. Building on this success, the Delors Committee, grouping European central bankers under the chairmanship of the President of the EC Commission, decided to revive the objective of completing EMU. Adopted in 1986, the Single European Act had set the process of completing the Single Market in motion and the abolition of physical borders was to be accomplished on 1 January 1993. Hence, with economic integration well on the way and monetary stability practically achieved, progress toward monetary unification could be resumed; high economic growth in the last years of the 1980 seemed to make it easier by reducing public deficits and debt ratios in many European countries.

The Delors Report is a blueprint for EMU, written by central bankers; it precisely describes the institutions necessary for its final stage as well as the three major phases of the process by which it ought to be achieved; and the part of the Maastricht Treaty, adopted in 1992, that deals with EMU will be almost a copy-paste of its recommendations. Given the recent experience of high inflation in many countries contrasting with monetary stability in Germany, it wholeheartedly embraces the postulate of central bank independence and the idea that monetary stability ought to be the overriding objective of monetary policy, both during the phases leading to

EMU and in the future European monetary union. It also insists on the necessity to impose binding rules on national fiscal policies and on the ban on monetary financing of budget deficits by the central bank. However, it also pleads in favor of fiscal coordination in order to achieve an appropriate macroeconomic policy mix whose "*broad objective would be to promote growth, full employment and external balance in an environment of price stability and economic cohesion*" (Delors et al. 1989, 24).

3 Rules Rather than Discretion: Ordo-liberalism Plus New Classical Economics

The analytical and doctrinal foundations of the institutional design recommended by the Delors Report and, for the most part, enshrined in the Maastricht Treaty are an idiosyncratic synthesis of two major intellectual strands: ordo-liberalism, the doctrine that inspired the economic institutions and policies of post–Second-World-War Germany, and the school of New Classical Economics that came to dominate macroeconomics in the late 1970s and 1980s. Though differing in a number of ways, these two doctrines share a common distrust of discretionary policy-making, hence a common plea in favor of policy rules.

Initially exposed in the 1930s by three German intellectuals from Freiburg,[3] the ordo-liberal doctrine was clearly a reaction to the disastrous economic and monetary developments in Germany during the 1920s and early 1930s, specifically the hyperinflation of 1923 and the Great Depression. It is distinct from classical economic liberalism in that it emphasizes the necessity of a strong legal and institutional setting in order for a market economy to perform. In particular, competition policy is regarded as an essential ingredient, whereas state interferences with economic activity are to be banned.[4] A balanced budget and a monetary policy geared at price stability complete the ordo-liberal policy recommendations.[5]

The idea that rules ought to be preferred to discretion in the conduct of economic policies, and in particular macroeconomic policy, also happens to be one of the major implications of the New Classical Economics, thus providing intellectual support and academic legitimacy to the main tenets of ordo-liberalism. Built upon the rational-expectations hypothesis, New

Classical Economics postulates a perfectly competitive environment in which markets clear, except when some hindrance affects the price adjustment mechanism, as may be the case on labor markets due to imperfectly flexible wages and/or misperceptions by workers of the price signals. In such an environment, the Phillips curve, which had for long been interpreted as a stable relationship between inflation and unemployment, is vertical in the long-run, and at best holds in the very short run; put differently, there exists a "natural" rate of unemployment that cannot be altered by macroeconomic policies. These policies are therefore at best impotent, and may even be detrimental, if governments try to systematically exploit the short-run inflation-unemployment trade-off: in a widely cited paper, Kydland and Prescott (1977) establish that policy rules always dominate discretion in such an economic environment.[6]

A distinct strand of macroeconomic analysis, though resting on similar assumptions, has also influenced the Euro Area institutional design, and may even be regarded as the missing link between ordo-liberalism and New Classical Economics: Sargent's and Wallace's (1981) "unpleasant monetarist arithmetic", in which the authors demonstrate the inescapable relationship between monetary policy and public finance: because monetary policy influences real interest rates, it has an impact on public debt sustainability, with the risk of a feedback on monetary policy when public debt becomes unsustainable and a bail-out is required.[7]

These ideas have been translated into the Maastricht Treaty and the conditions imposed on countries wanting to join the EMU: the independence of national central banks, a set of criteria on nominal variables (inflation rates, long-term nominal interest rates, exchange rate) and on public finances (3%-of-GDP ceiling on public deficit, 60%-of-GDP ceiling on gross public debt).

4 Optimal Currency Area Theory: Selective, Non-Keynesian Reading

In addition to developments in the field of macroeconomic theory, one of the fundamental sources of inspiration for EMU has always been the theory of OCA, though the way in which it has been interpreted has varied over time, and its influence on the final institutional design of the Euro Area is arguably limited. In his original article, Robert Mundell (1961)[8] does cite the European Community as one of the possible experimental fields of OCA analysis, though what he has in mind is clearly the choice of exchange regimes in general. Mundell's analysis stresses the importance of various adjustment channels in the face of asymmetric shocks hitting the currency area, i.e. shocks that differently affect the countries forming the union and that could have been dealt with by changing parities had the member countries retained their national currencies instead of sharing a single currency. Production factor (labor and capital) mobility and price flexibility are singled out as the most important channels of adjustment to such shocks: flexible factor prices will soon have relative prices converge to the new market clearing equilibrium; and in case of imperfectly flexible prices, factor movements from the negatively hit to the positively affected countries will restore equilibrium.

Further developments in the theory of OCA have emphasized other important aspects of currency unions, such trade openness and interdependence, similarity or complementarities of national production structures, and the existence a significant central budget acting as an automatic stabilizer in the face of asymmetric shocks.

How much has the OCA inspired the institutional design of the Euro Area? Promoting factor mobility is one of the major objectives of completing the Single Market and the "four freedoms" (goods, services, capital and people) are at the forefront of the Single European Act. Indeed, the complete liberalization of international capital movements was recommended by the Delors Report, and has in fact been the first step taken in July 1990 on the way toward monetary union. Similarly, free mobility of people within the Single Market is one of the fundamental liberties; the Schengen Agreements, signed in 1985 and effective since 1995 among 26 countries, guarantee the free circulation of EU citizens and of non-EU citizens legally admitted in any of the participating member states[9]; in addition, a number of directives in the field of labor law have been adopted since the completion of the Single Market in order to facilitate intra-EU labor mobility.[10] And EU institutions, in particular, the European Commission, have been actively promoting the notion of "structural reform", in effect meaning more flexibility, in theory in all markets, but in practice mostly labor market flexibility.

That the Euro Area is not an optimal currency area is not surprising, in spite of the sometimes painful convergence process that was imposed on states wanting to join; that a number of EU policies aim at promoting those mechanisms that would bring it closer to satisfying the optimality criteria put forward in this literature is also to be expected.[11] But the main implications of a non-optimal currency area, that is that policies should be implemented to remedy the insufficient adjustments in the face of shocks, has been mostly ignored in the conception of Euro Area institutions. In particular, many contributors to OCA analysis have emphasized the important role played by fiscal arrangements in existing currency unions, either the aforementioned existence of a sizable central budget that automatically cushions at least part of asymmetric shocks or some form of fiscal policy coordination in the face of symmetric shocks[12]; and even though the Delors Report explicitly recommended fiscal policy coordination in order to achieve the appropriate macroeconomic policy mix in the face of common shocks, there has been a clear bias in favor of rules, whereas little effort has been devoted to coordination in an institutional setting that is more conducive to non-cooperative national strategies.[13]

5 The Analytical Foundations of the Brussels-Frankfurt Consensus

What has crystallized in the Maastricht Treaty, the Stability and Growth Pact adopted in 1997 as a protocol to the Amsterdam Treaty and, more recently, in the "Fiscal Compact" of 2012[14] is a set of institutions and economic policy rules that may be summarized as the "Brussels-Frankfurt consensus" (Sapir et al. 2003): the prominence of stability objectives, in line with the sources of inspiration analyzed above; but it appears much more stringent and precise than whatever had been experienced before, even in Germany, where there are forms of political accountability of independent institutions and where, until recently at least, fiscal policy rules were generic. In the EU, policy rules have been specified in detail, often with precise figures.

This "consensus" has a distinctly non-Keynesian or even anti-Keynesian bias: provided competition policies are properly conducted and monetary stability is achieved, markets will, in most circumstances, reach satisfactory equilibriums and will be able to adjust to shocks; fiscal policies should not, in general, try to stabilize economic activity and only automatic stabilizers should, within limits, be allowed to operate. Underlying this set of rules is the hypothesis, consistent with a large fraction of the literature in New Classical Economics, that fiscal policy is at best ineffective—the so-called "Ricardo-Barro equivalence hypothesis"—and may even prove harmful—if, as suggested by some empirical studies of fiscal consolidations in the 1990s, fiscal policy has anti-Keynesian effects (i.e. the fiscal multiplier is negative).[15] Of course, there may be "exceptional circumstances" in which EA institutions or national governments may dispense with the rules; but experience in the 2009 Great Recession and the subsequent "sovereign debt crisis" has shown that, at least with regard to fiscal policy, their definition is rather restrictive and return to the rule soon prevails.[16]

6 The State of Macro Is Not Good

The institutional setting in which monetary and fiscal policies are conducted in the Euro Area may be summarized as follows: an inflation-targeting monetary policy that should roughly follow a Taylor rule, whereby the main monetary policy instrument (the short-term interest rate) is set by the central bank according to a formula that relates it to deviations of observed inflation from target inflation and deviations of observed output from potential output, as well as some target "natural" real interest rate; and national fiscal policies are geared by a target of "structural balance". Both policy rules are anchored in the theoretical macroeconomic framework of New Classical Economics; more precisely, both rely on the notion of "potential output". Indeed, the Taylor rule includes it twice: in the "natural interest rate", implicitly referring to the level of the real interest rate compatible with macroeconomic equilibrium; and in the target output level against which deviations are calculated. And the definition of "structural deficits" is itself based on the estimation of an "output gap", the deviation of observed GDP from its "potential" level. Crucial in this specification of economic policy rules is the assumption that such "potential output" exists and is invariant to macroeconomic policies.[17]

Contemporary standard macroeconomic theory, New Classical and New Keynesian alike,[18] rests on this hypothesis: "Potential output" refers to a macroeconomic equilibrium level—and "potential growth" to a macroeconomic equilibrium path—that would prevail and be observed in the absence of macroeconomic, stochastic (demand or supply) exogenous shocks that hit the economy, much like the Newtonian pendulum. The equilibrium is determined by production techniques and available production factors, and usually specified as a standard macroeconomic production function. The existence and invariance of "potential output" thus requires that both techniques and the available quantities and qualities of production factors (capital and labor) are affected neither by exogenous shocks nor by macroeconomic policies. These assumptions are obviously highly questionable. First, macroeconomic policies are not aggregates: monetary policy operates through changes in relative asset prices; fiscal policy—and especially discretionary changes on the revenue side of the budget—does affect relative prices and/or relative returns; they cannot be assumed to leave "potential output" unchanged. In a similar vein, macroeconomic shocks are seldom exogenous: hence for instance, the subprime crisis that erupted in 2007 may be traced backed to previous US policies.

Provided it effectively exists, measuring "potential output", and hence the "output gap", and the "structural deficit" that so prominently constrains national fiscal policies, may mobilize various econometric techniques and necessitate data on the available stock of productive capital and the "equilibrium" employment level, all variables that are at best poorly measured in national accounts, and often derived from the very same theoretical framework that is to be empirically implemented by use of these data.

In short, the rigid macroeconomic policy rules that dictate or constrain policies in the Euro Area are defined in reference to a hypothetical construct whose empirical counterpart is shaky. Indeed, divergences among international and national institutions as to the precise estimates of "potential output" and their variability over time[19] raise serious doubts about its relevance and reliability as a guide for macroeconomic policies. Of course, the intention behind the choice of "structural deficit", rather than observed deficit, as a criterion for fiscal policy is sound: relying on observed deficit induces a strong pro-cyclical bias in fiscal policy, which would make it destabilizing.

But excessive reliance on the standard macroeconomic analytical framework may not be warranted, given the theoretical and empirical weaknesses that have been revealed during the 2009 Great Recession and its aftermath. Contrary to what Blanchard (2009) asserted (in a paper written before the 2008 crisis, and published after), the state of macro is not good: in times of rapid technical and institutional change, in times of significant shocks hitting the economy, the standard framework is probably not appropriate. Attempts to propose new foundations have been made by several authors[20]; but no convincing full-fledged alternative is available yet. In the meantime, it would probably be reasonable to act pragmatically, and not to stick too closely to rigid rules that have such fragile foundations.

Notes

1. Of course, all countries have constitutions that include provisions concerning economic policy. But national constitutions are interpreted and can be amended following a well-specified process. In this, the EU is unique. On the inconveniencies of writing detailed policy rules into treaties, see Laurent and Le Cacheux (2006).
2. The first Optica Report had been preceded by the publication in 1975 in *The Economist* of the "All Saints Day Manifesto" ("A Currency for Europe"), a plea in favor of monetary unification, signed by a few European economists along with some of the authors of the Optica Report. A second Optica Report was published in 1977.
3. Walter Eucken, an economist, and two lawyers, Franz Böhm and Hans Grossmann-Dörth.
4. This "free and undistorted competition" is to be found as a leading objective in the Rome Treaty (1957) already, and in all European treaties since then.

5. In fact, the ordo-liberal doctrine did not take hold of German economic policy-making until after the Second World War, partly under the influence of the US. Indeed, the economic aspects of the German constitution, the monetary reform of 1948, and the law instituting the independence of the Bundesbank in 1957 were dictated by US economists.
6. The application of this result in the field of monetary policy was later published by Barro and Gordon (1983) in a paper that apparently exerted a major influence on the design of monetary institutions in the Euro Area.
7. The relationship between monetary and fiscal policies is of course a longstanding theme in macroeconomic analysis. It is the main message of many of Sargent's contributions, in particular on policies to fight high inflations (Sargent, 1982). It is also central in the notion of "regimes" developed by Woodford (see, e.g. Woodford 2001).
8. Many contributions have followed suit after Mundell's 1961 path-breaking paper, including by such authors as Peter Kenen, Ronald McKinnon, and so on. A very useful critical synthesis is provided by De Grauwe (2018, ch. 2) in his classic text on monetary unions.
9. Five EU member states are not in the Schengen space: Ireland and the UK, who have refused to participate, and Bulgaria, Croatia and Romania, not yet deemed legally ready to join. Three non-EU European countries are included in the Schengen space: Iceland, Norway and Switzerland.
10. One of the most popular EU policies, Erasmus, aimed at facilitating intra-EU student mobility, may also be regarded as a means of enhancing people mobility. More on mobility in Chap. 4.
11. There is a significant body of literature on the endogeneity of optimality criteria in OCA analysis. For a recent contribution including many relevant references, see Schiavo (2008).
12. See the critical review offered by De Grauwe (2018) and the references therein.
13. The incentives arising from the EA institutional setting have been analyzed in the previous installments of this series, in particular in Le Cacheux and Laurent (2015).
14. The Fiscal Compact is the Treaty on Stability, Coordination and Governance in the Economic and Monetary Union (TSCG) signed by 25 member states in 2012. More on the TSCG: https://ec.europa.eu/info/publications/fiscal-compact-taking-stock_en. See also Chap. 5.

15. See the developments on this point in Le Cacheux and Laurent (2015) and the references provided therein.
16. The Commission was quick to reinstate the "excessive deficit procedure" after the 2009 Great Recession and to enforce relatively rapid fiscal consolidation in the aftermath of the "sovereign debt crisis" of 2010–2012. The experience of the European Central Bank with non-conventional monetary policies may be an exception. See Chap. 6.
17. Implicit in the insistence of the Commission on the necessary "structural reforms" is the hypothesis that such reforms, in the direction of more flexibility in market mechanisms, do raise potential output. On the hypothesis of invariance of "potential output" and its theoretical foundations, see Le Cacheux (2017).
18. The characteristics of this convergence, sometimes called the "New Macroeconomic Synthesis", are convincingly described and analyzed by Blanchard (2009).
19. An illustration of the variability of estimates of "potential output" carried out by the Commission is provided in Le Cacheux and Laurent (2015).
20. One such attempt, among others, is described by Stiglitz (2015).

References

Barro, Robert J., and David B. Gordon. 1983. A Positive Theory of Monetary Policy in a Natural Rate Model. *The Journal of Political Economy* 91 (4): 589–610. http://www.networkideas.org/feathm/sep2006/pdf/Barro_%20Gordon.pdf.

Basevi, Giorgio, Emil Claassen, Pascal Salin, and Niels Thygesen. 1976. *Optica Report 75. Towards Economic Equilibrium and Monetary Unification in Europe.* https://www.cvce.eu/content/publication/2012/5/29/1403ebca-0839-4eca-9423-c9fcb7452555/publishable_en.pdf.

Blanchard, Olivier J. 2009. The State of Macro. *Annual Review of Economics* 1: 209–228.

De Grauwe, Paul. 2018. *Economics of Monetary Union.* 12th ed. Oxford: Oxford University Press. https://academic.oup.com/cesifo/article/59/3/520/281810.

Delors, Jacques, et al. 1989. *Report on Economic and Monetary Union in the European Community*. Brussels. http://aei.pitt.edu/1007/1/monetary_delors.pdf.

Keynes, John Maynard. 1936. *The General Theory of Employment, Interest and Money*. London: Palgrave Macmillan.

Kydland, Finn E., and Edward C. Prescott. 1977. Rules Rather than Discretion: The Inconsistency of Optimal Plans. *The Journal of Political Economy* 85 (3): 473–492. http://www.finnkydland.com/papers/Rules%20Rather%20than%20Discretion%20The%20Inconsistency%20of%20Optimal%20Plans.pdf.

Laurent, Éloi, and Jacques Le Cacheux. 2006. *Integrity and Efficiency in the EU: The Case Against the European Economic constitution*. Harvard CES Working Papers 130. https://hal-sciencespo.archives-ouvertes.fr/file/index/docid/972707/filename/laurent-lecacheux.pdf.

Le Cacheux, Jacques. 2017. Croissance potentielle : la politique macroéconomique au royaume des aveugles? *Revue économique* 68 (HS1): 29–39.

Le Cacheux, Jacques, and Éloi Laurent. 2015. *Report on the State of the European Union. Is Europe Sustainable*. Vol. 4. London: Palgrave Macmillan.

MacDougall, Donald (Sir), et al. 1977. *Report of the Study Group on the Role of Public Finance in European Integration*. https://www.cvce.eu/content/publication/2012/5/31/c475e949-ed28-490b-81ae-a33ce9860d09/publishable_en.pdf.

Mundell, Robert A. 1961. A Theory of Optimal Currency Areas. *The American Economic Review* 51 (4): 657–665.

Olson, Mancur. 1969. The Principle of "Fiscal Equivalence": The Division of Responsibilities Among Different Levels of Government. *The American Economic Review* 59 (2): 479–487.

Sapir, André, et al. 2003. *An Agenda for a Growing Europe: Making the EU Economic System Deliver*. Report of an Independent High-Level Study Group Established on the Initiative of the President of the European Commission. Brussels. http://citeseerx.ist.psu.edu/viewdoc/download?doi=10.1.1.620.4948&rep=rep1&type=pdf.

Sargent, Thomas J. 1982. The Ends of Four Big Inflations. In *Inflation: Causes and Effects*, ed. Robert E. Hall. Chicago: Chicago University Press. http://www.nber.org/chapters/c11452.pdf.

Sargent, Thomas J., and Neil Wallace. 1981. Some Unpleasant Monetarist Arithmetic. *Federal Reserve Bank of Minneapolis Quarterly Review* 5: 1–17.

Schiavo, Stefano. 2008. Financial Integration, GDP Correlation, and the Endogeneity of Optimal Currency Areas. *Economica* 75 (297): 168–189. https://hal-sciencespo.archives-ouvertes.fr/file/index/docid/1022326/filename/schiavo-economica.pdf.

Stiglitz, Joseph E. 2015. Reconstructing Macroeconomic Theory to Manage Economic Policy. In *Fruitful Economics, Papers in Honor of and by Jean-Paul Fitoussi*, ed. Éloi Laurent and Jacques Le Cacheux. London: Palgrave Macmillan.

Werner, Pierre. 1970. *Report to the Council and the Commission on the Realization by Stages of Economic and Monetary Union in the Community*. http://aei.pitt.edu/1002/1/monetary_werner_final.pdf.

Woodford, Michael. 2001. *Fiscal Requirements for Price Stability*. NBER Working Papers 8072, January. http://www.nber.org/papers/w8072.

3

The First Twenty Years: Institutions, Policy and Performance

Jérôme Creel

1 Introduction

The adoption of the euro on 1 January 1999 was a new step in the process of European integration, leading to the advent of the European Monetary Union (EMU). While the Maastricht Treaty (1991) laid down the institutional setting of the EMU, its content also revealed the dominance of monetary policy on fiscal policy, later enhanced by the introduction of fiscal rules in the Stability and Growth Pact (SGP) of 1997.

The Maastricht Treaty forged the institutional framework which helped enforce the credibility of the euro area. To reach this goal, an independent European Central Bank (ECB) was set up with curbing inflation as its major objective; public deficits were capped, yet no coordination strategy between monetary and fiscal policy was imposed. Even so, the euro area was then deemed to be ready to become an area of monetary and financial

J. Creel (✉)
OFCE, Sciences Po, Paris, France

ESCP Europe, Paris, France
e-mail: jerome.creel@sciencespo.fr

© The Author(s) 2018

J. Creel et al. (eds.), *Report on the State of the European Union*,
https://doi.org/10.1007/978-3-319-98364-6_3

stability generating investment and economic growth. Unfortunately, mere compliance with this academic diktat did not deliver the expected results.

The Maastricht institutional framework matched a stable macroeconomic environment where GDP would smoothly tend towards its potential level at a stable inflation rate. The nominal convergence criteria, also embedded in the Maastricht Treaty, would lead to real convergence towards that stable environment and the euro area would be optimal (see discussion on optimum currency areas in Chap. 2). This institutional framework did not prove particularly optimal, even in good times, because it was unbalanced between a single discretionary monetary policy and several governments which had only constrained fiscal instruments at their disposal and were deprived from their monetary sovereignty.

The global financial crisis (GFC) tore the Maastricht framework apart. The Great Recession revealed the sensitivity of euro area Member States to three different factors: external financial shocks, growing public debts and internal competitiveness. The financial crisis in the USA spread to the euro area and required a substantial change in the implementation of monetary policy. Fiscal policy has had to come to the rescue, leading to substantial increases in deficits and debts. The early years of the euro area also showed the weaknesses of the institutional framework: it did not pay attention to real divergence—taking for granted that nominal convergence would be a sufficient condition to achieve it—that spurred banking and financial crises in the so-called peripheral countries of the euro area (on this issue, see Chap. 7).

This chapter concentrates on the features of ECB's monetary policy since the creation of the euro and more precisely, on the modifications introduced after the GFC which have questioned a possible reversal in the macroeconomic paradigm in the euro area.

2 The Institutional Framework of the Euro Area

While 11 countries adopted the euro in a first stage (Austria, Belgium, Finland, France, Germany, Ireland, Italy, Luxembourg, the Netherlands, Portugal and Spain), there were 19 out of 28 EU Member States for the

20-year birthday of the euro. Greece joined in 2001, Slovenia in 2007, Cyprus and Malta in 2008, Slovakia in 2009, Estonia in 2011, Latvia in 2014 and Lithuania in 2015.

To a very large extent, EMU institutional provisions, applicable since 1 January 1999, were laid out in the Maastricht Treaty, signed on 9–10 December 1991. The Amsterdam Treaty in 1997 introduced additional provisions, mostly related to fiscal policymaking after the adoption of the euro (two regulations on the SGP). The Lisbon Treaty in 2007 amended the Maastricht Treaty or Treaty on the European Union (TEU), for example by establishing the euro in Article 3. The Lisbon Treaty also amended the former Treaty of Rome, now Treaty on the Functioning of the European Union (TFEU), and consolidated the organizational and functional details of the EU. In the following, I refer to the number of the articles in treaties currently in force.

2.1 The Convergence Criteria

Among other provisions, the Maastricht Treaty laid out the EU Member States' objectives and tasks: "The Union shall establish an internal market. It shall work for the sustainable development of Europe based on balanced economic growth and price stability, a highly competitive social market economy, aiming at full employment and social progress, and a high level of protection and improvement of the quality of the environment" (Article 3, TEU).

Despite the explicit reference to employment, the treaty's marked preference for the fight against inflation is obvious: "(The activities of the Member States and the Union) shall include a single currency, the euro, and the definition and conduct of a single monetary policy and exchange-rate policy the primary objective of both of which shall be to maintain price stability and, without prejudice to this objective, to support the general economic policies in the Union, in accordance with the principle of an open market economy with free competition" (Article 119, TFEU).

The treaty also laid out the prerequisites to EMU entry. Countries on their way of adopting the euro have also to fulfil four convergence criteria (Article 140, TFEU):

- the achievement of a high degree of price stability;
- the sustainability of the government financial position;
- the observance of the normal fluctuation margins provided for by the exchange-rate mechanism of the European Monetary System, for at least two years, without devaluing against the euro;
- the durability of convergence achieved by the Member State with a derogation and of its participation in the exchange-rate mechanism being reflected in the long-term interest rate levels.

Details regarding these convergence criteria are left to Protocol 13. The criterion on price stability means that a Member State has an average rate of inflation, observed over a period of one year before the examination, that does not exceed by more than 1 ½ percentage point that of, at most, the three best performing Member States in terms of price stability. The criterion on the convergence of interest rates means that, observed over a period of one year before the examination, a Member State has had an average nominal long-term interest rate that does not exceed by more than 2 percentage points that of, at most, the three best performing Member States in terms of price stability. The criterion on government financial position means that at the time of the examination, the Member State is not the subject of a Council decision under Article 126(6) of the TFEU that an excessive deficit exists.

Some ambiguity remains as regards the latter criterion. As it stands, it excludes a reference value for the public-debt–to–GDP ratio. Nevertheless, Article 126 also defines compliance with budgetary discipline on the basis of two criteria: (a) whether the ratio of the planned or actual government deficit to gross domestic product exceeds a reference value, unless either the ratio has declined substantially and continuously and reached a level that comes close to the reference value, or alternatively, the excess over the reference value is only exceptional and temporary and the ratio remains close to the reference value; and (b) whether the ratio of government debt to gross domestic product exceeds a reference value, unless the ratio is sufficiently diminishing and approaching the reference value at a satisfactory pace. The reference values are specified in the Protocol 12 on the excessive deficit procedure annexed to the TEU and TFEU: 3% of GDP for the public deficit and 60% of GDP for the public debt.

The underlying idea was that all countries had to prove they could abide by certain sound management criteria before joining the EMU. Launching the single currency at a much earlier date and leave it to EMU in-built mechanisms to produce convergence could have been possible, but this reversed alternative was rejected.

2.2 Monetary Policy

The European system of central banks (ESCB) is composed of the ECB and the national central banks of the 28 EU Member States. It is entrusted with the euro area's monetary policy whose prime objective is "to maintain price stability" (Article 127, TFEU). Article 127 adds a secondary objective: "without prejudice to the objective of price stability, the ESCB shall support the general economic policies in the Union with a view to contributing to the achievement of the objectives of the Union".

The tasks of the ESCB are not limited to the implementation of monetary policy for the design of which the ECB retains full independence of means. They also include foreign-exchange operations, the operation of the payment systems and *contributions* to the prudential supervision of credit institutions and the stability of the financial system. In the latter case, one will have to wait after the GFC to see a Banking Union emerge, with a single supervision mechanism left to the ECB.

All EU Member States must ensure that the ECB and their national central banks are independent from "Union institutions, bodies, offices or agencies, from any government of a Member State or from any other body" (Article 130, TFEU).

Moreover, the TFEU forbids monetary financing of public debt: "overdraft facilities or any other type of credit facility with the ECB or with the (national) central banks in favour of (…) public authorities (…) shall be prohibited, as shall the purchase directly from them by the ECB or national central banks of debt instruments" (Article 123, TFEU). Consequently, this provision helps ensure that political pressures from euro area governments to refinance their debts do not interfere with ECB policies.

The TFEU also adds a "no bail out" provision that shall entirely limit risk-sharing between the EU Member States: "The Union (or a Member

State) shall not be liable for or assume the commitments of central governments, regional, local or other public authorities, other bodies governed by public law, or public undertakings of any (or another) Member State, without prejudice to mutual financial guarantees for the joint execution of a specific project" (Article 125, TFEU).

While the ESCB is given the task of implementing foreign-exchange operations, it shares with the Council the responsibility of exchange-rate policy: "In the absence of an exchange-rate system in relation to one or more currencies of third States (…), the Council, either on a recommendation from the Commission and after consulting the European Central Bank or on a recommendation from the European Central Bank, may formulate general orientations for exchange-rate policy in relation to these currencies. These general orientations shall be without prejudice to the primary objective of the ESCB to maintain price stability" (Article 219, TFEU). Strictly speaking, this provision is a thorn in the ECB's independence.

ECB's independence is limited for at least three additional reasons. First, its objectives and tasks are embedded in the functioning of the general principles of EU law via the TFEU (Cafaro 2018). Second, though it has some discretion in policymaking, its mandate is clear and compelling: price stability. Third, the TFEU has introduced some accountability provisions, for example a monetary dialogue between the ECB, on the one hand, and the European Parliament, the Council, the Commission and the European Council, on the other hand (Article 284, TFEU).

2.3 Fiscal Policy

Beyond the provisions on fiscal policy in the TFEU, the SGP prevents and corrects deviations of public deficits from its reference value. The SGP consists of the Council Resolution of 17 June 1997 and Council Regulations 1466/97 and 1467/97. Derived from the Maastricht Treaty, these instruments complete the treaty's provisions on government deficits and strengthen fiscal policy surveillance and coordination. The resolution details prevention and deterrence, SGP's two fundamental objectives: the former is developed in the first regulation, the latter together with its repressive corollary in the second.

The first regulation intensifies the economic policy surveillance procedures introduced by the Maastricht Treaty as each Member State has to publish a yearly "stability programme" (for euro area countries) or a "convergence programme". The programmes present medium-term macroeconomic forecasts with forthcoming trends in public expenditure and revenue. They clearly aim at overall fiscal positions "close to balance or in surplus", so that the positions leave the automatic stabilizers full room to manoeuvre and allow for amassing sufficient savings to finance the pensions of the future.

On the basis of the Commission's recommendation, the Council examines the stability or convergence programmes so as to detect any significant divergence from the medium-term objective. Since the regulation does not provide a strict definition of what must be understood by "significant divergence", the Commission has since then specified three criteria: to what extent the objective was missed, how much is due to discretionary causes and the probability risk of running excessive deficits. When significant divergence has occurred, the Commission can set off the "early warning" procedure, writing a proposal for the Council, which then may decide whether to send recommendations to the countries steering away from their programmes.

The second regulation strengthens the provisions of Article 126 of the TFEU on public deficits above 3% of GDP. The Commission must tell the Council whether the excess over 3% of GDP constitutes an excessive deficit or if it can come under the provisions for "unforeseen circumstances beyond the control of the Member State concerned". In that case, "the deviation from the reference value is judged temporary if the Commission's fiscal forecasts can establish that the deficit will fall below the reference value when the unforeseen circumstance or the severe recession vanishes". "In principle", the same logic applies when the excess is due to a severe recession, namely a yearly GDP fall of 2% and over. Apart from these mitigating circumstances, the country concerned will have to make up the deficit in the course of the following year. Otherwise, it may be subject to a non-interest-bearing deposit of 0.2% of GDP, plus one tenth of the amount in excess of 3%, up to a maximum of 0.5% of GDP. This can eventually be transformed into a fine if the deficit still endures after two years. Another sanction can be the suspension of all European Investment Bank operations with the country at fault.

However, this procedure is not set off systematically. The Council must indeed decide by qualified majority voting by all Member States (including the non-euro area countries) whether a deficit above 3% of GDP must be regarded as excessive. In view of the observations made by the country concerned, the Council may judge that a 2% GDP setback qualifies as a severe recession. "In principle", Member States pledged not to call upon the latter possibility unless they have suffered from a minimum 0.75% GDP setback. The pledge is legally non-binding, since it is mentioned in the Council resolution but not in the Council regulation. When the deficit is deemed excessive, the Council may address economic policy recommendations to the country at fault. If the recommendations are not acted upon, the Council may decide to impose penalties. Such a decision requires a two-third majority vote taken only by the euro area countries, excluding the country at fault.

2.4 An Incomplete and Asymmetric Framework

The original framework for monetary and fiscal policies in the euro area had an important weakness: the euro is a currency without a sovereign. The Member States issue debts in a currency they do not manage directly. It creates an asymmetry between a single non-democratic institution which must be accountable but has a technical role and 19 governments which continue to control (under constraints) tax and fiscal policies.

This situation makes euro area governments very sensitive to external shocks on creditors' trust. If the latter declines and generates liquidity and/or default risks, governments can neither issue money to pay interests on debts or repay debts nor shift the external value of their currency to alleviate the crisis.

Hence, it leaves the euro area vulnerable to what resembles a "balance-of-payment crisis". A lack of confidence in the solvency of the private sector might spark capital outflows, which, in turn, can generate a crisis. Substitute the private sector for the public sector in the previous sentence and one obtains a euro area "sovereign debt" crisis. The mere fear that a government might be illiquid or might default would destabilize the euro area as a whole because forbiddance of monetary financing of public debts by the ECB has not been accompanied by the creation of new tools to prevent the crisis via some risk-sharing mechanisms. According to the TFEU, the euro area has neither a lender of last resort for governments nor an *ex ante* debt restructuring mechanism.

The euro area framework faces a contradiction: it makes the occurrence of a crisis more likely and, meanwhile, develops no tools to cope with a crisis. Hence, the euro area draws heavily on market discipline: it foresees that markets will prevent, signal and solve a crisis. This is much too confidence allocated to financial markets, as the second decade of the euro showed.

The absence of risk-sharing mechanisms goes hand in hand with the assumption that fiscal policy is mostly ineffective at stabilizing the economy, hence with the reluctance towards high debts and deficits. The euro area framework thus gives the priority to monetary dominance. The decision to cap government debt and deficits can be illustrated by the outcomes of the "game of chicken" between governments, on the one hand, and the ECB, on the other hand.

The latter has price stability as its primary objective, whereas one may assume that the former have economic growth (or declining unemployment) as their primary objective. The ECB will usually opt for a tight policy with high interest rates and an appreciating euro while governments opt for a loose policy with high deficits. The loose/tight policy mix leads to constant outbidding between high interest rates and over-large deficits, for both authorities are trying to cancel out each other's harmful impact on their own policy. The higher the inflation-boosting government deficits, the tighter the monetary policy and the higher the growth-depressing interest rates, the looser the fiscal policy. This model of policy mix comes to what is usually referred to as a lack of dominant strategy for both authorities. The lack of dominant strategy requires that the two authorities cooperate if they wish to achieve a stable equilibrium, but two coordinated equilibria are possible. Yet, given their different sets of preferences, each authority will try to impose their own preferences on each other. Hence, the "game of chicken": the first authority that overthrows its opponent is left free to impose its own policy and to decide de facto what the other authority's policy shall be. The first is called a "conservative" equilibrium, whereby both the ECB and the national governments run tight policies. In this case, the ECB is said to exert domination. The second is called a "social" equilibrium, whereby both authorities run loose policies; national governments are then said to exert domination.

To put the matter at rest, the Maastricht and Amsterdam Treaties set out that the preferences of the ECB should prevail over the European policy mix: fiscal policy was capped and thus the coordination between the Members States' fiscal policies and ECB monetary policy had to emerge somewhat by default. The objective of fiscal policy is balancing the budget, which gives it only a small part in macroeconomic management, whereas the independence of monetary policy is clearly asserted. Monetary dominance is the clear outcome of the TFEU.

3 The Euro Area Economy: A Brief Assessment

In 1998, the ECB announced an operational definition of price stability: it is defined as "a year-on-year increase in the Harmonised Index of Consumer Prices (HICP) for the euro area of below 2%". To achieve this goal, two analytical pillars were added: one giving a reference value to the growth of the money supply, while the second takes into account several indicators of inflationary pressures (GDP growth, labour costs, exchange rates, tensions on production capacities). The ECB finally merged these two pillars into a single one in 2003. It also restated its price objective: the targeted inflation rate shall be "below, but close to, 2% over the medium term". By so doing, it avoided misunderstandings about its policy strategy when the inflation rate was below 2%.

As far as this objective is concerned, the ECB performance has been mixed as evidenced in Fig. 3.1. It took more than a year for the ECB to reach a 2% inflation rate. Then and until 2007, the inflation rate remained close to but above 2%. It peaked at more than 3% after an oil shock before plummeting in the recession year of 2009. Since 2013, the inflation rate has remained substantially below its target. The inflation swings reveal either a strong external component or real downward determinants. They show that the ECB has not been able to prevent or dampen shocks rapidly.

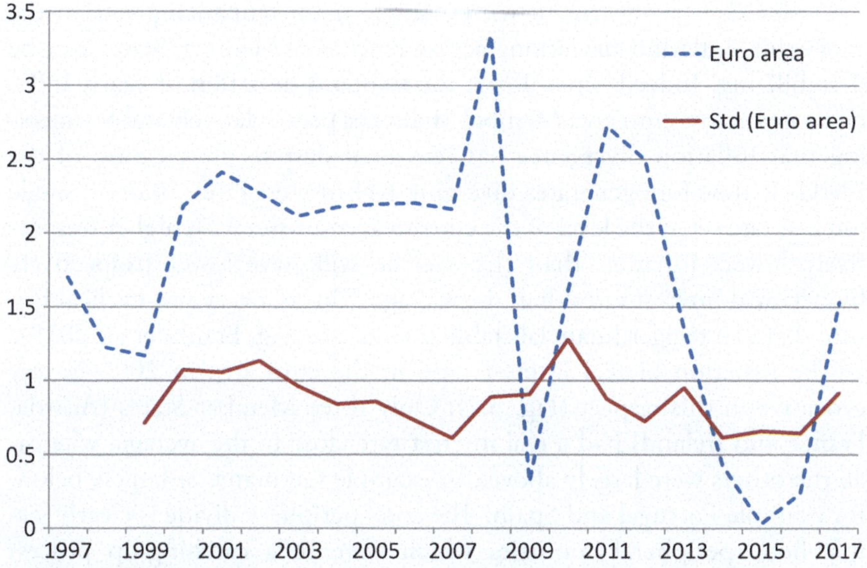

Fig. 3.1 The inflation rate of the euro area, in percent. (Source: Ameco)

The ECB uses three "conventional" instruments to guide the interbank market so that commercial banks have liquidity at a rate close to the main interest rate. Through this interest rate channel, the ECB seeks to control economic activity and, ultimately, inflation. The ECB decides on three key interest rates. First there is the main rate of weekly refinancing operations (MRO for Main Refinancing Operations). The ECB provides liquidity each week to banks in exchange for public or private securities used as collateral. This liquidity has a maturity of one week. This procedure is called "open market operations". Thus, the ECB controls both the quantities and the price of the liquidities it injects into the interbank system. On both sides of the MRO rate, there are permanent facilities. They provide additional credits (called marginal) to commercial banks that do not have sufficient liquidity or make marginal deposits with the ECB in the event that commercial banks have excess liquidity. The marginal deposit rate is below the MRO rate and the marginal lending rate is higher than the MRO rate. While there are three key interest rates, each one is unique to the whole euro area.

Under such a framework with a single main refinancing rate in the short-run, inflation deviations across euro area Member States can be destabilizing. Indeed, since 1999, the standard deviation of yearly inflation rates across euro area Member States has been relatively stable, meaning that inflation divergence has remained despite the creation of the EMU. It therefore generates diverging real interest rates: under a single interest rate set at the level of the euro area, countries with higher (respectively lower) inflation than the average will have lower (respectively higher) real interest rates than the average. This is a very pro-cyclical feature that can trigger financial stability risks (see, e.g. Franks et al. 2018).

The situation of real interest rates in the euro area in 2006 is very evocative in this respect (Fig. 3.2). Only three Member States (Austria, France and Ireland) had a real interest rate close to the average, whereas all the others were largely above, for example Germany, or largely below, for example Portugal and Spain. The core–periphery divide is clearly visible here: peripheral countries which were in a catching-up process towards the core countries benefited from a positive monetary impetus

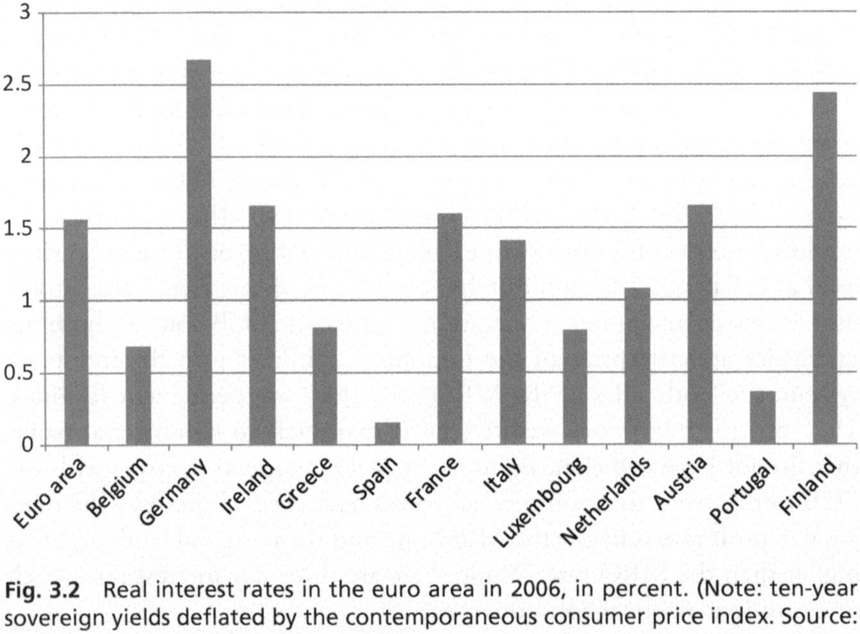

Fig. 3.2 Real interest rates in the euro area in 2006, in percent. (Note: ten-year sovereign yields deflated by the contemporaneous consumer price index. Source: Ameco, computations by the author)

which accelerated economic growth above potential, hence high inflation. In contrast, core countries had subdued economic conditions with low inflation while undergoing a negative monetary impetus.

Evidence reported in Fig. 3.3 confirms this original drawback of the euro area. While real long-term interest rates declined substantially between 1999 and 2008, the discrepancy across Member States remained stable. Figure 3.3 also highlights the consequences of the GFC on interest rates. Unlike in the USA, where the real long-term interest rate decreased rapidly after its peak in 2009, the euro area rate stayed long at a level higher than before the crisis. More importantly, the standard deviation rose sharply, but in contrast with the previous period, real interest rate hikes occurred in the periphery, not in the core. This is clear evidence of the continuous pro-cyclical feature of the ECB's monetary policy.

The performance of the euro area in terms of unemployment has also been mixed. The unemployment rate declined by 2 percentage points

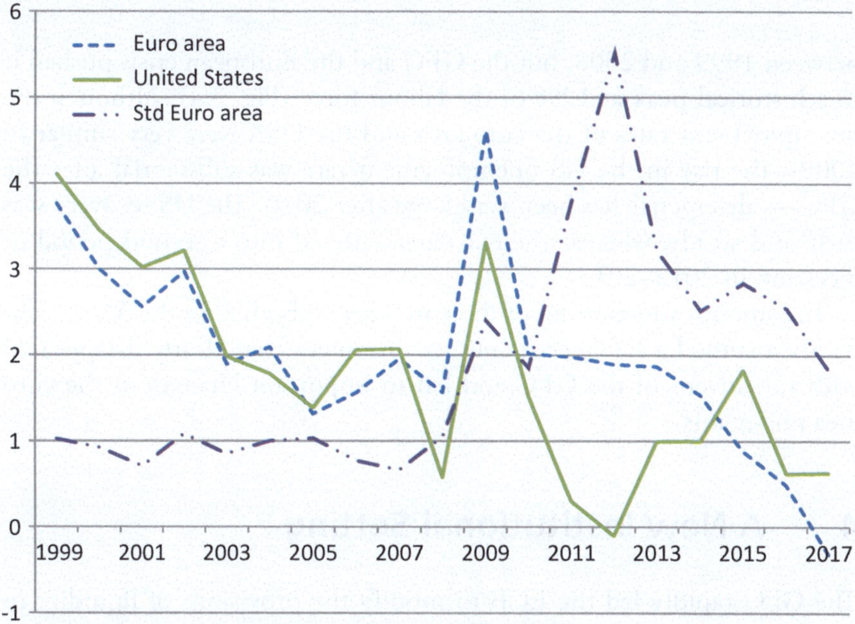

Fig. 3.3 The real long-term interest rate in the euro area, in percent. (Note: ten-year sovereign yields deflated by the contemporaneous consumer price index. Source: Ameco, computations by the author)

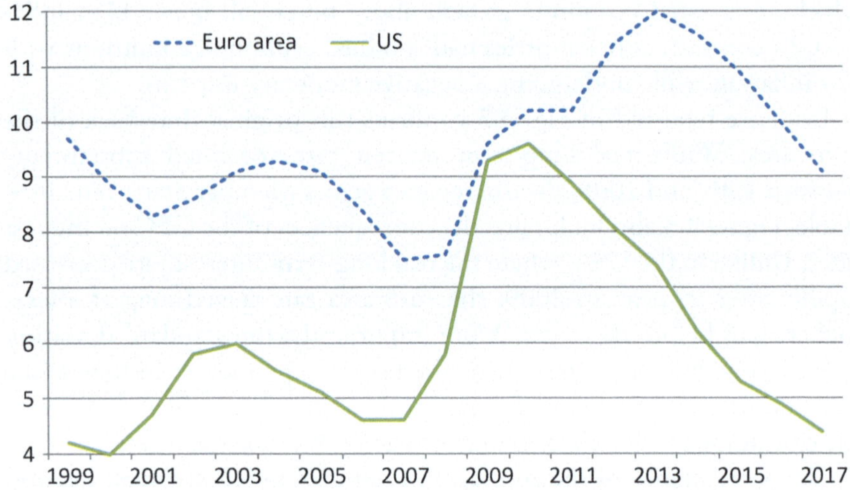

Fig. 3.4 Unemployment rate, in percentage points of the labour force. (Source: Ameco)

between 1999 and 2008, but the GFC and the European crisis pushed it to a historical peak at 12% of the labour force (Fig. 3.4). Although the unemployment rates of the euro area and the USA were very similar in 2009—the rise in the US unemployment rate was substantial after the GFC—, divergence has been very large after 2010. The US recovery was early and steady, whereas the euro area entered into a second period of recession in 2012–2013.

The smooth functioning of the euro area embodied in the Maastricht Treaty assumed a stable economic environment that clearly disappeared with the advent of the GFC and led to important changes in the euro area policy mix.

4 A New Institutional Setting

The GFC rapidly led the ECB to modify the provisions of liquidity to banks with the fixed-rate full-allotment MRO procedure since October 2008 and several longer-term refinancing operations since 2011. However, the recession in the euro area required more substantial changes.

Recession produced large increases in public deficits and debts and a temporary exemption of the fiscal rules. Shortly after, fiscal consolidation started, but before the economic recovery would be firm enough to compensate for the negative impact on aggregate demand. European fiscal policies did not close either output gaps or excessive public debt to GDP ratios.

Insufficient or ineffective fiscal policies—the macroeconomic stabilization properties of fiscal policies are discussed in Chap. 5—forced the ECB to react to the protracted crisis with unconventional instruments. During the summer of 2012 and following the contagion of Greek financial difficulties to other peripheral countries (Portugal, Spain and Ireland), the President of the ECB announced that the ECB "would do whatever it takes to preserve the euro" and he announced a new programme, Outright monetary transactions (OMT), of conditional purchases of government bonds (up to three-year maturity). Three years later, he announced the implementation of massive monthly purchases of public bonds (then private) at all maturities. Between the announcement of the extended Assets Purchase Programme (APP) in January 2015 and the end of 2017, the amounts of ECB's assets and liabilities expressed in percentage points of euro area GDP almost doubled to reach 40%. This substantial change in the size of ECB balance sheet raises several concerns.

First, it has been criticized for the inflation risk it could produce. Until 2018, this risk has not materialized though. Second, its effectiveness at fixing the issue of fragmented interest rate channels across euro area Member States remains disputable (see, e.g. Horvath et al. 2018, for a recent empirical investigation). Third, assuming these unconventional policies have been effective, without a fast and sharp reduction in the size of the balance sheet, the ECB would lack margins for manoeuvre if a new crisis occurs.

Finally, these policies interact with the financing of fiscal policies, since they aim at lowering interest rates on debts. The extended APP has had an impact on the real long-term interest rate of the euro area since 2013 and the negative value in 2017 (Fig. 3.3). In doing so, it may change the behaviour of governments, possibly less inclined to limit their public deficits. These interactions between monetary and fiscal policies therefore question the degree of independence of the ECB from European governments and raise concerns about policy dominance in the euro area: is it still monetary or has it become fiscal dominance? Legally speaking, it seems that monetary dominance still prevails.

The announcement of the OMT—this policy has never been implemented—earned the ECB legal proceedings before the German Constitutional Court. The European Court of Justice validated the OMT on the ground that the ECB complied with Article 123 (TFEU): it did not move from its price stability objective and conditionality removed an excessive issuance of public bonds (see more in Cafaro 2018). The provision on forbiddance of monetary financing of public debts would not be violated but only circumvented by intervention on secondary, not primary, markets.

However, interactions between monetary and fiscal policies could have an impact on risk-sharing between euro area Member States. By purchasing public bonds with a domestic (liquidity and/or default) risk premium, the ECB could socialize the costs of a liquidity or credit default crisis in a Member State to all euro area Member States. To avoid this, the ECB purchases bonds according to its capital key: it acquires larger volumes of German public debt than Portuguese public debt, for example. In addition, it transfers the risk to the national central banks of the states from which it acquired debts.

The protracted crisis in the euro area also gave rise to a new crisis management institution empowered to make loans between euro area Member States. The risk of default of the Greek government led in May 2010 to the development of an emergency plan, which revealed one of the shortcomings of European governance, namely the absence of a lender of last resort. To remedy this and to cope with the persistence of the Greek crisis, the euro zone set up a European Financial Stability Facility (EFSF), which has become the European Stability Mechanism (ESM). The latter has a conditional capacity of loans for the benefit of a State experiencing financial difficulties. A loan may be granted by the ESM provided it is accompanied by an International Monetary Fund (IMF) loan or the conditions for debt restructuring have been previously defined.

The ESM embodies the principle of solidarity set out in the TEU. It allows the *ex post* coordination of economic policies but does not have specific skills for crisis prevention. In this sense, the ESM is not an IMF dedicated to European countries. It therefore does not replace the SGP and adds to the complexity of the European institutional arrangements: the agreement on loans granted under the ESM involves the European Commission, the Eurogroup, the Council and, sometimes, the national parliaments. This mode of *ex post* coordination is therefore slow to emerge and to produce its effects.

The imperfect coverage provided by the ESM has also exacerbated moral hazard (Wyplosz 2017), that is systematic underestimation of risk by insured agents. Coordination failures can occur between lenders and borrowers, some for not being sufficiently aware of the quality of the borrowers and the others considering that the costs of risk taking would be socialized. The underestimation of the default risks may cause massive indebtedness and may contribute to self-fulfilling crises after a reversal of expectations or a sudden loss of confidence.

5 Conclusion

The euro area original institutional setting had its own flaws: while intensively relying on the newly born ECB, it lacked a fiscal leg. Consequently, the euro area economic performance was disappointing. It became worse after the GFC. First, the coordination of fiscal policies in the constrained framework of the SGP led to early recommendations in favour of fiscal consolidation, which generated a second phase of recession. Second, the absence of coordination with the ECB forced it to complement fiscal policies via massive unconventional measures, which raise the issue of future margins for manoeuvre for the ECB if a new crisis hit the euro area. Third, while a new institution, the ESM, emerged to cope with liquidity and default risks in the euro area, its functioning does not prevent moral hazard between euro area Member States and is not the solution to the potential risk of debt unsustainability.

It appears that the GFC has intensified the shortcomings of the TEU and TFEU as regards the management of monetary and fiscal policies in the EU. After the acute phase of the crisis, further reforms are needed.

References

Cafaro, S. 2018. The Evolving Role of the ECB During the Euro-Crisis. *Revue de l'euro* 52: 1–11.

Franks, J., B. Barkbu, R. Blavy, W. Oman, and H. Schoelermann. 2018. *Economic Convergence in the Euro Area: Coming Together or Drifting Apart?* IMF Working Paper 18/10, January.

Horvath, R., J. Kotlebova, and M. Siranova. 2018. Interest Rate Pass-Through in the Euro Area: Financial Fragmentation, Balance Sheet Policies and Negative Rates. *Journal of Financial Stability* 36: 12–21.

Wyplosz, C. 2017. A European Monetary Fund? *In-depth Analysis*. European Parliament, May.

Part II

The Euro at 20

4

Single Market and Single Currency: Intended and Unintended Effects

Jacques Le Cacheux

The combination of the European Single Market, instituted by the Single European Act of 1986 and officially launched on 1 January 1993, and the European currency union, adopted in the Maastricht Treaty (1992), and launched on 1 January 1999, forms the European Economic and Monetary Union (EMU), an economically and monetary integrated area grouping 19 countries and a population of about 340 million, and GDP totaling € 11,200 billion, an economic size roughly comparable, in 2017, to that of China, and second only to the US economy.[1]

But this large, open economy is in many ways far less integrated than the other two. The process of completing EMU is still incomplete, and the instruments in the hands of national governments are far more numerous and powerful than what may be observed in other economically and monetarily integrated areas. As a consequence, national

J. Le Cacheux (✉)
Université de Pau et des Pays de l'Adour, Pau, France

Ecole Nationale des Ponts et Chaussées, Marne-la-Vallée, France

Sciences Po, Paris, France
e-mail: jacques.lecacheux@sciencespo.fr

© The Author(s) 2018

J. Creel et al. (eds.), *Report on the State of the European Union*,
https://doi.org/10.1007/978-3-319-98364-6_4

governments tend to favor non-cooperative, competitiveness and attractiveness strategies, which exacerbate asymmetries and result in collectively inefficient outcomes. Section 1 recalls the main economic benefits and costs that were expected from the creation of EMU, and Sect. 2 reviews some of the evidence on the achievements so far in promoting the "four freedoms", namely freedom of movement of goods, services, persons and capital. Section 3 presents a brief analysis of strategies available to national governments and of the incentives existing in the current institutional setting. Section 4 documents the most popular strategies, namely tax and social competition. Section 5 offers some concluding remarks on the possibilities of promoting more cooperation.

1 Higher Mobility, Enhanced Competition

Economic and monetary union is not a goal of itself: it is predicated on the idea that economic integration will bring about efficiency gains as well as other benefits to producers and consumers, an objective already present in the Rome Treaty with its Common Market. Over two decades of experience with the latter had revealed the limits of a customs union: free trade, essentially in manufactured goods, had been a significant improvement over the interwar and immediate aftermath of the Second World War, when extreme forms of protectionism and highly interventionist states had been the dominant forms in Europe. Though somewhat debated today among economists and historians, the idea that protectionism could be held responsible for the depth and length of the Great Depression of the 1930s, and hence the war, was dominant in the post-war period and certainly in the minds of European integration Founding Fathers. But the experience of limited market integration combined with monetary instability in the 1970s and early 1980s had also revealed how weak and fragile free trade alone was.[2]

As made explicit by the various reports issued by the EU Commission trying to provide estimates of the potential benefits and costs of completing EMU (see, especially, Cecchini et al. 1988; Emerson et al. 1992), the main sources of gains were expected in enhanced market integration and competition. In addition to delivering the classical gains from trade predicted by Ricardian trade theory, fostering better specialization according to comparative advantage, the completion of the Single Market was supposed to open more sectors to competition and restrain the possibilities for national governments to distort it, reinforcing the tool of EU competition policy. "Free and undistorted competition" in a large market economy would bring forth static gains for consumers by way of a better allocation of resources and less market power, both yielding lower prices. It was also expected to induce dynamic gains, via scale economies and the positive pressure exerted by competition on innovation and technical progress. In addition, the completion of monetary union would reduce transaction costs and bring more transparency in price and cost comparisons across member states, facilitating arbitrage and restraining the possibilities for firms to "price to market"[3]; by eliminating exchange-rate uncertainty, it would also reduce the cost of capital, foster capital mobility and hence further improve resource allocation. In parallel, the Schengen agreements were geared at facilitating the mobility of persons among the countries that had signed them (i.e. 10 out of 12 member states at the time, the exceptions being the UK and Ireland). All this may not have resulted in higher mobility of persons in the absence of significant improvements in cross-border transport and communication infrastructures, such as Eurostar, Thalys, internet, roaming for mobile phone communications and so on.

2 The Four Freedoms in Practice

Free mobility of goods, services, capital and persons is an ambitious objective; in order to make it effective, it is not enough to abolish borders and remove the most conspicuous obstacles to movements. Just as non-tariff barriers have been shown to be at least as effective as tariffs in hindering trade flows, regulatory policies, procurement policies and many other petty aspects of the functioning of domestic economies play an equally, and sometimes even more, important role in impeding complete market integration.[4] Reaching a significant degree of mobility in all four domains is therefore a complex and lengthy process. It has implied to agree on a general principle of mutual recognition of national norms and standards,

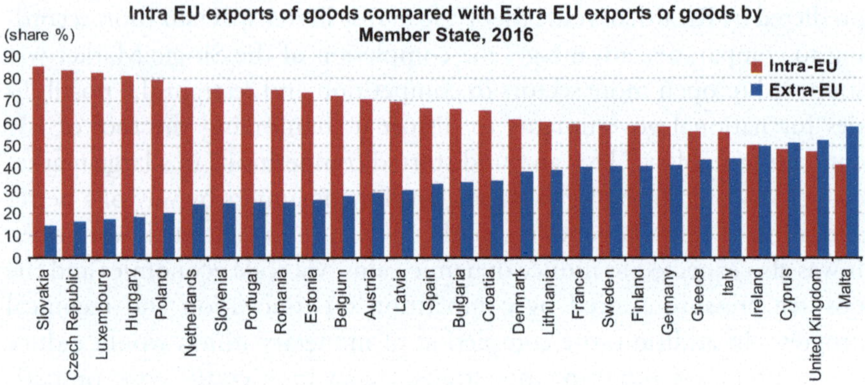

Chart 4.1 Intra- and extra-EU exports (as a share of total exports), 2016. (Source: Eurostat, Comext table DS-063319)

along with the adoption, over time, of a large number of directives defining common rules and minimum standards in such varied fields as safety regulations, health protection, consumer information, environmental protection and so on, but also labor laws and social protection.

The first and foremost achievement is clearly in the field of trade integration: 25 years after the abolition of physical borders for trade in goods within the Single Market, the effects of trade liberalization on trade flows is apparently significant, but with differences across EU member states, and there does not appear to be a specific effect of the euro on this dimension of market integration. Intra-EU trade on average represents about two thirds of total trade in goods for most of them; but some countries, mostly among those who join the EU in the latest enlargement wave (2004–2007), have much higher than average intra-EU trade ratios, while others—most notably the UK—have significantly lower ones (Chart 4.1). Similarly, EMU seems to have had differentiated impact on overall trade openness across EU member states: over the period 1995–2017, trade openness ratios display a very clear common upward trend, reflecting both the completion of EMU and the worldwide context of globalization[5]; but this movement has been much more limited in the large EU member states, with the notable exception of Germany (Chart 4.2).[6]

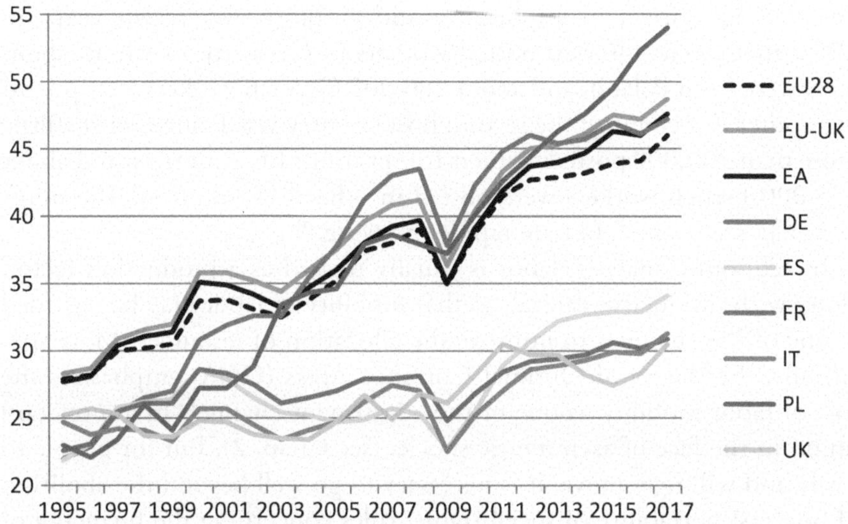

Chart 4.2 Trade openness ratios for selected EU countries, 1995–2017 (total exports to GDP ratios). (Source: Eurostat)

With regard to services, the situation is much more contrasted, and also more difficult to grasp empirically. Whereas a number of services, regarded as pertaining to the domain of "social services of general interest",[7] have been explicitly excluded from the principle of "free and undistorted competition", many others, in such sectors as public transport, postal services and telecommunications, have been liberalized or will be in the near future. Increasing trade in market services has been a common trend in the recent decades almost everywhere, be it in the EU or in the rest of the world. It has been fostered by liberalization and technical change, most notably in information technologies. Services trade flows within the EU have increased significantly, but apparently no more than elsewhere (EU Commission 2017).[8]

But exchange of services also includes direct provision by non-resident firms, not registered in the balance of payments statistics. This aspect includes the possibility for firms located in one member state to temporarily send dependent workers on a mission in another member state, the so-called system of "posted workers".[9] This type of service provision may be regarded as one of the dimensions of workers mobility, and one that has grown in importance and visibility over recent years: in 2016, there were 440,000 posted workers in Germany, of whom about 30% were from Poland, and about 260,000 German workers were posted in another EU country; the second host country was France, with a little more than 200,000 posted workers from various EU countries, and about 135,000 French workers were posted in other EU countries. The numbers may seem small, but are rapidly growing.[10]

In economic analysis, labor is usually treated as a production factor, along with productive capital, so that mobility of labor may be regarded as one of the channels to improve the allocation of resources. More specifically, the theory of Optimal Currency Areas (OCA) emphasizes the role of labor mobility as one of the adjustment channels in a monetary union in the face of asymmetric shocks (see Chap. 2). But for people to easily and willingly move, it is necessary to go well beyond the abolition of borders: portability of social rights, rules concerning the financing of these rights, recognition of diplomas and so on are among the many topics on which agreements have had to be found. Yet, for various reasons among which language and cultural barriers, but also various costs of mobility (in particular transaction costs in housing markets), mobility of persons is relatively limited in the EU, especially when compared to intra-country mobility, but it has been growing relatively fast. There is a significant cross-border, commuting population in some regions: about 1 million in the EU in 2017. And according to the latest published data, the number of EU citizens permanently residing in an EU member country other than that of origin reached almost 12 million in 2016,[11] of whom about 50% are hosted in Germany and the UK alone,[12] and this population of "EU movers" has been increasing by about 1 million per year over the past few years (EU Commission 2018a).

Just as for labor, the free movement of capital is a central ingredient for an efficient allocation of resources in economic analysis in general, and a major channel of adjustment to shocks according to the OCA theory. Increasing the degree of capital mobility and capital market integration has been one of the foremost objectives of EMU from the very beginning, but it is multidimensional and notoriously difficult to measure empirically. The complete liberalization of capital account transaction, not only within the EU, but "*erga omnes*", was indeed the first step in the process of economic and monetary unification as inscribed in the Maastricht Treaty (1992). But capital market integration is far from complete and the creation of a genuine "capital market union" is still an objective.[13]

Among capital movements, foreign direct investment is usually considered an essential dimension of economic integration. These flows are highly variable from year to year, but seem to have increased significantly in the EU over the past three decades, though decreasing in most recent years: inward foreign direct investment in the EU28 rose from US$ 21.7 billion in 1980 to US$ 95.6 billion in 1990, to US$ 680.3 billion in 2000, culminating at US$ 824.4 billion in 2007, to reach US$ 566.2 billion in 2016 (UNCTAD 2018).

Moreover, the nature of productive capital and the sources of value for firms have tended to change in recent years, among other things under the influence of technical change: indeed, the share of intangible assets (property rights, such as patents, registered trademarks, etc.) in firms' total capital stocks has been increasing considerably (Candau and Le Cacheux 2018) and the production of value relies more and more on the use of data; and intangibles and data are much easier to relocate than physical plants, making firms even more "footloose" than before.

3 Competitiveness and Non-cooperative National Strategies: From External to Internal Devaluations

In most blueprints issued by the European Commission in the late 1980s and early 1990s, EMU was presented as a means to reap large overall gains by boosting efficiency, reducing firms' market power and curtailing governments' interferences with market mechanism. Of course, these studies did foresee possible negative effects, notably in terms of regional imbalances and economic inequalities (e.g. Emerson et al. 1992, p. 12); but they usually recommended corrective policies to mitigate these negative consequences: in the tradition of Paretian reasoning, removing inefficiencies is Pareto improving, i.e. a positive-sum game, implying that at least part of the surplus thus generated may be redistributed from the gainers to the losers.

But redistribution implies taxation. And the consequences of EMU on national economic strategies and policy choices were unlikely to lead to more, or better, targeted redistribution unless changes in European institutions would make collective action on this point easier. Put differently, in the absence of progress in the political integration, non-cooperative national strategies are likely to prevail, especially among a large group of relatively heterogeneous countries of different sizes. And in parallel to the completion of EMU, with the successive EU enlargements—with Austria, Finland and Sweden joining in 1995, Cyprus, the Czech Republic, Estonia, Hungary, Latvia, Lithuania, Malta, Poland, Slovakia and Slovenia in 2004, Bulgaria and Romania in 2007, Croatia in 2013—the "club" of countries has almost doubled its membership, with mostly small and hence economically open countries among the newcomers.[14]

Non-cooperative, competitive strategies were already prevailing in the preceding decades, but in a different institutional and economic context, they had taken different forms: competitive currency devaluations in the 1970s and competitive disinflation in the 1980s, in the context of the European Monetary System (EMS). In EMU, these two modes of competing among national governments could no longer be resorted to, insofar as the single currency bars the possibility of changing parity, unless a government decides to exit the currency union, a rather extreme and risky strategy that has so far not been chosen; and monetary policy is uniform and decided by an independent institution, the European Central Bank (ECB).

The new forms of non-cooperative national strategies aim at precisely the same objective of gaining competitive advantages over partner countries, but national governments now use those instruments that have been left in their hands: tax policies, a competence that is submitted to unanimity decision-making in the European Council, hence with few European rules; and those policy instruments that impact labor costs, including wage policy and labor laws, and taxes and social contributions levied on labor earnings. These strategies may be regarded as "internal devaluations"; they have become all the more attractive for national governments, as increased mobility of goods, services, firms and capital have rendered them more powerful, and the absence of common policies in these areas leaves considerable margins of maneuver. And in the aftermath of the "sovereign debt crisis" of 2010–2012, the policies of fiscal consolidation imposed by the "Troïka" (European Commission, ECB and IMF) have tended to precisely promote these strategies, insofar as the countries hit by the crisis all had a clear problem of competitiveness, with labor costs having increased more than average in the decade preceding the crisis and external balances having been persistently negative as a consequence (see Chap. 7).

4 Tax Competition and the Outlook for EU Taxation[15]

For national governments pursuing essentially national objectives, competing by means of tax instruments is all the more tempting as tax bases are more mobile; and the literature on tax competition shows that this strategy will bring larger payoffs for small, open economies than for larger ones. Hence, it should not come as a surprise that tax competition, which of course exists in the wider context of economic and financial globalization, has been fiercer within the EU than elsewhere, at least until recently. In the EU, taxation matters cannot be collectively decided upon, unless there is unanimity in the European Council, effectively maintaining a veto power for every member state on these issues. Even though there were many discussions about tax cooperation and tax harmonization in the years following the adoption of the Single European Act, little progress has been accomplished, with a few exceptions.

With regard to Value Added Tax (VAT), basic principles governing the tax basis and structure of rates have been agreed upon; but contrary to what the European Commission had proposed in 1990, the destination principle has been maintained, so that sales to non-residents entities are treated as exports and tax exempt in the country of origin,[16] and only floors have been imposed on the main rates. Consequently, VAT increases have been one of the most favored strategies of national governments in recent years, especially in the context of forced fiscal consolidation, and most conspicuously in smaller countries: indeed, for member states who have a very high degree of trade openness, implying that most domestically produced goods are exported, hence VAT exempt, and that most domestically consumed goods are imported, VAT rate hikes are a very effective tool to improve the competitiveness of domestic producers, especially if (part of) the additional revenue is used to reduce labor costs by cutting employers social contribution rates.[17] Such "internal devaluations" have been common in recent years in the EU. They have resulted in a significant increase in the average standard VAT in the EU, from 19.5% in 2008 to 21.6% in 2017; and the countries posting the highest standard VAT are currently 27% in Hungary, 25% in Denmark, Croatia and Sweden, 24% in Finland and Greece, and 23% in Ireland, Poland and Portugal, all relatively small member states.[18]

Financial capital mobility has likely increased within the EU after the full liberalization of capital account transactions, and probably even more so in recent years after the completion of EMU. This mobility concerns both firms and individual asset holders. A number of EU directives have been adopted to limit the possibilities of tax evasion for multinational corporations and of tax fraud for individuals[19]: in particular, better tax cooperation with more automatic information exchanges among national tax authorities. Yet, the many cases revealed by publications such as *Luxleaks, Panama Papers, Paradise Papers* and so on clearly demonstrate that tax evasion and tax fraud are still quite widespread in the EU.

Due to higher mobility, and more specifically to the increasing reliance of multinational firms on "footloose" factors (intangible assets and data), tax competition seems to be particularly fierce in corporate taxation, where it may concern the statutory rate on corporate income or the definition of the tax base. Hence, for instance, the simple average of statutory tax rates on corporate income in the EU has come down from nearly 50% in the early 1980s to slightly less than 25% in 2017; and policy announcements in a number of member states suggest that it will soon be even lower.[20] And countries tend to compete on the definition of the tax base by displaying a wealth of deductions and tax credits for specific assets (foremost patents) or activities (R&D in particular), or even using specific tax rulings, in order to attract businesses, in a largely self-defeating and collective damaging game that essentially benefits the most mobile firms that are in a position to "bid" their location decisions to those countries offering the best tax-subsidy deal.

Even though tax competition may yield some benefits, by forcing governments to resort to more efficient forms of taxation and better uses of tax revenues, the literature on tax competition clearly establishes that, due to the existence of horizontal tax externalities, the decentralized equilibrium of tax competition games is collectively sub-optimal, leading to a situation of under-provision of public goods and under-taxation of the most mobile factors, with an unfair distribution of tax burdens bearing mostly on the least mobile tax bases, who often happen to be the least well-offs.

In recent years, under the pressure of public opinions, the Commission has moved to propose some improvements in EU taxation. In line with the OECD effort for more transparency, the automatic information exchange is one of the important changes promoted, especially in the much debated area of "tax rulings"; similarly, the Commission pursues its efforts to review specific tax treatments of multinational corporations that may fall under the ban of state aids.[21] It also, albeit with less and less support from member states, continues to propose a European Financial Transactions Tax (FTT). But even more importantly, the Commission has revived a directive proposal for the harmonization of corporate income tax bases: the CCCTB (Common Consolidated Corporate Tax Base) project, currently being discussed in the European Parliament, would fully unify the tax base definition in the EU and consolidate profits in the country of location of European headquarters for multinational firms operating in Europe. If adopted, the CCCTB directive would leave only statutory rates in the hands of national governments for them to compete; it would clearly open the way for the creation of an EU corporate income tax, though of course this would require a much more ambitious political move.[22]

5 Concluding Remarks: Social and Ecological Dumping? Can the EU Be More Than a Market?

The controversy about posted workers has revealed the potential for social dumping in a number of regulations currently in place in EMU. Though limited in scope, these disturbing signs have been growing in importance over time and they raise increasing political opposition. Given the large fraction of public expenditure dedicated to social protection in most EU member states, the pressure exerted by competition over labor costs may lead some national governments to cut social benefits in order to alleviate taxation on labor earnings.

A similar process may also be at work in the area of environmental regulation and taxation. Here too, competitive pressures tend to induce the adoption of beggar-thy-neighbor policies by national governments. Indeed, in addition to those described in this chapter, other negative consequences of EMU include the enormous increase in road transport of goods and persons, with very visible consequences on Green House Gas emissions, and other types of consequences of the natural environment. Even though common policies would clearly be warranted in these obvious collective or common goods cases, agreeing on them is, in the present institutional setting, hardly possible.

Generally speaking, the negative effects reported above clearly point to the incompleteness of EMU, not so much in the sense often emphasized by the Commission that the Single Market ought to be made more effective by removing remaining obstacles to exchanges of goods and services, that capital markets should be more integrated, that there should be more mobility of persons and so on, but more so because it lacks common institutions and collective decision-making procedures to remedy its unintended negative effects. Efforts to set up common policies, or at least minimum standards, in such fields as minimum wages, workers social rights, fuel taxation and so on have so far been mostly unsuccessful and leave the way open to all kinds of non-cooperative national policies.

Notes

1. According to GDP measured in PPP dollars. IMF data.
2. A form of protectionism had appeared in European agricultural trade as early as 1969 with the creation of the so-called "monetary compensatory amounts". And protectionist temptations had surfaced on several occasions when currency devaluations had been regarded as "competitive". On the interplay between monetary arrangements and protectionism during the Great Depression, see Eichengreen and Irwin (2009). On the impact of exchange-rate variability on trade flows in the 1970s, see De Grauwe (1988).

3. "Pricing to market" is the strategy pursued by firms who set different prices for the same good in different markets, according particularly to demand elasticity. One of the first to use this phrase was Krugman (1986). For an empirical analysis of the degree of pricing to market in European automobile market prior to the completion of the Single Market, see Le Cacheux and Reichlin (1992).
4. Egan (2015) provides an interesting historical analysis of market integration, along with comparisons between the experience of the USA in the nineteenth century and that of today's European integration.
5. The Marrakesh Agreements that concluded the Uruguay Round GATT negotiations and instituted the World Trade Organization (WTO) were signed in April 1994.
6. On the trade strategy of Germany and the policies that were conducted to achieve this result, see Sinn (2006), Laurent and Le Cacheux (2010).
7. A definition and description of these services is available here: http://ec.europa.eu/social/main.jsp?catId=794.
8. According to WTO services trade database, the EU is the world leader in services exports to the rest of the world and intra-EU services trade flows represented about 55% of total services trade of EU countries in 2016.
9. The definition of "posted work" and the rules applying to these situations are described here: http://ec.europa.eu/social/main.jsp?catId=471&langId=en. In recent years, the 1996 directive on posted workers has been strongly opposed by a number of national governments, especially the French and German ones; an agreement on amending it has been reached in the European Council in December 2017 and the new directive is currently being discussed in the European Parliament, but the case of truck drivers has been set aside and has yet to be settled, in the framework of the "mobility package" prepared by the Commission in the Spring of 2018. See: https://www.iru.org/where-we-work/europe/europe-overview/european-commission-mobility-package.
10. The European Commission publishes country factsheets on posted workers. They can be found here: http://ec.europa.eu/social/keyDocuments.jsp?pager.offset=0&&langId=en&mode=advancedSubmit&advSearchKey=PostWork.
11. Not all these people are working, of course. There are significant numbers of inactive people, among whom retired people. And among those working in an EU country other their country of origin, some professions are more represented than others, such as health care and personal care. See European Commission (2018a).

12. In 2016, the UK hosted the largest population of "recent" EU movers: 1.8 million EU citizens residing in the UK had arrived over the previous ten years. This figure may shed light on one of the hotly debated issue during the "Brexit" referendum campaign.
13. A plan to create a "capital market union" (CMU) by 2019 has recently been put forward by the EU Commission. See: https://ec.europa.eu/info/business-economy-euro/banking-and-finance/financial-markets/capital-movements_en.
14. This is the well-known conclusion of Olson's (1965) theory of collective action. For an application to the EU case and an analysis of its implications for institutional reform, see Laurent and Le Cacheux (2006).
15. For a more detailed, theoretical and empirical, recent analysis of tax competition in the EU, along with references to the relevant literature, see Candau and Le Cacheux (2018).
16. The VAT directive adopted in 1991, on the eve of the completion of the Single Market, has instituted a "provisional" regime for VAT that has been much criticized, especially because it is highly prone to fraud, but is still ruling. Of course, switching from the destination to the origin principle, as promoted by the Commission at the time, would profoundly alter the nature of VAT, transforming it into a tax on production, which is quite orthogonal to its philosophy. According the Commission, the estimated amount of foregone tax revenue due to VAT fraud reached more than € 150 billion in 2015 for the EU28. See: https://ec.europa.eu/taxation_customs/business/tax-cooperation-control/vat-gap_en.
17. On "internal devaluations" and their effects and costs, see, for example De Grauwe (2013). It may be noted that Germany, not really a small country, has also resorted to this strategy in 2004–2005. A possible explanation of this German strategy is proposed by Laurent and Le Cacheux (2010).
18. The lowest VAT rates are also practiced by very small states: Luxembourg (17%) and Malta (18%). But other aspects of tax competition may explain these choices.
19. Note that international tax principles stipulate that individuals are taxed in the country of residence, whereas corporate incomes are taxed at source. These principles imply that tax fraud is mostly practiced by individuals not reporting their holdings abroad, whereas corporations tend to evade taxation, notably by resorting to "tax optimization" techniques, usually legal. The Commission uses the tools of competition policy,

namely the ban on state aids, to fight the most extreme, and clearly illegal, specific tax advantages granted by national governments to multinational corporations (see Candau and Le Cacheux 2018). On a much wider, global scale, the OECD has been waging a large effort in favor of automatic information exchange among national tax authorities, the *BEPS* (Base Erosion and Profit Shifting) initiative. See: http://www.oecd.org/tax/beps/.

20. Outside the EU, tax competition on corporate taxation has been reignited by the US tax reform, and may be fueled in the near future by the announced reduction of corporate tax rate in the UK after Brexit.
21. In much publicized cases, Margrethe Vestager, the EU Commissioner for competition, has inflicted large fines for illegal tax advantages to multinationals, the best known and largest one being the € 13 billion fine inflicted to Apple for privileged tax treatment in Ireland. See also Candau and Le Cacheux (2018).
22. In its recent proposal for the next Multiannual Financial Framework for the EU budgets over the period 2021–2027, the Commission has included a new resource in the form of 3% levy on corporate income tax revenue. More on the EU budget in Chap. 7.

References

Candau, Fabien, and Jacques Le Cacheux. 2018. Taming Tax Competition with a European Corporate Income Tax. *Revue d'économie politique.*

Cecchini, Paolo, et al. 1988, *Europe 1992. The Overall Challenge*. Report to the European Commission. http://aei.pitt.edu/3813/1/3813.pdf.

De Grauwe, Paul. 1988. Exchange Rate Variability and the Slowdown of Growth in International Trade. *IMF Staff Papers* 35 (1): 63–84.

———. 2013. Design Failures in the Eurozone: Can They Be Fixed?. *KU Leuven Euroforum*, April. https://lirias2repo.kuleuven.be/bitstream/handle/123456789/404628/De+Grauwe+-+Design+Failures+-+webversie.pdf;jsessionid=29B1FC3F143D8FB036243A3005C24BFF?sequence=1.

Egan, Michelle. 2015. *Single Markets. Economic Integration in Europe and the United States*. Oxford: Oxford University Press.

Eichengreen, Barry, and Douglas Irwin. 2009. The Protectionist Temptation: Lessons from the Great Depression for Today. *VoxEU.org*, March 27. https://voxeu.org/article/protectionist-temptation-lessons-great-depression-today.

Emerson, Michael, et al. 1992. *One Market, One Money. An Evaluation of the Potential Benefits and Costs of Forming an Economic and Monetary Union.* Oxford: Oxford University Press. Also published in *European Economy* 44 (1990). http://ec.europa.eu/economy_finance/publications/pages/publication7454_en.pdf.

European Commission. 2017. *Single Market Scoreboard.* http://ec.europa.eu/internal_market/scoreboard/_docs/2017/trade/2017-scoreboard-trade-goods-services_en.pdf.

———. 2018a. *2017 Annual Report on Intra EU Labour Mobility.* Brussels, January. https://publications.europa.eu/en/publication-detail/-/publication/2637906c-316a-11e8-b5fe-01aa75ed71a1/language-en

———. 2018b. *Social Agenda 51. Fair Mobility and Social Fairness.* Brussels, April. http://ec.europa.eu/social/main.jsp?catId=737&langId=en&pubId=8086&furtherPubs=yes.

Krugman, Paul R. 1986. *Pricing to Market When the Exchange Rate Changes*, NBER Working Paper n°1926, May. https://core.ac.uk/download/pdf/6586856.pdf.

Laurent, Éloi, and Jacques Le Cacheux. 2006. *Integrity and Efficiency in the EU: The Case Against the European Economic Constitution*, Harvard CES Working Papers 130. https://hal-sciencespo.archives-ouvertes.fr/file/index/docid/972707/filename/laurent-lecacheux.pdf.

———. 2010. The Irish Tiger and the German Frog. A Tale of Size and Growth in the Euro Area. In *Report on the State of the European Union* vol.3 *Crisis in the EU Economic Governance*, ed. Jean-Paul Fitoussi and Jacques Le Cacheux. London: Palgrave Macmillan.

Le Cacheux, Jacques, and Éloi Laurent. 2015. *Report on the State of the European Union. Is Europe Sustainable?* Vol. 4. London: Palgrave Macmillan.

Le Cacheux, Jacques, and Lucrezia Reichlin. 1992. Exchange Rates and Import Prices: Evidence of Pricing to Market in European Car Markets. In *International Trade Modeling*, ed. M.G. Dagenais and P.-A. Muet. London: Chapman & Hill.

Olson, Mancur. 1965. *The Logic of Collective Action*. Reprinted in 2009. Harvard University Press.

Sinn, Hans-Werner. 2006. *The Pathological Export Boom and the Bazaar Effect. How to Solve the German Puzzle*. CESIFO Working Papers 1708. https://www.econstor.eu/bitstream/10419/25753/1/516977253.PDF.

UNCTAD. 2018. *World Investment Report 2018*. United Nations Conference for Trade and Development. http://unctad.org/en/PublicationsLibrary/wir2018_overview_en.pdf.

5

Fiscal Policy: A Useful Tool After All?

Jérôme Creel and Francesco Saraceno

After presenting the genesis of the European fiscal rules that were put in place with the Maastricht and Amsterdam Treaties (see Chap. 3), the present chapter will deepen the analysis of the intellectual foundations of these rules and show how these foundations weigh on the different revisions of the fiscal rules before and after the global financial crisis. We will argue that recent empirical findings cast doubts on the effectiveness of the current institutional setup in managing the business cycle and in dampening the divergences that can occur following macroeconomic shocks. We will conclude the chapter by discussing a few possible paths for reform of the Eurozone fiscal governance.

J. Creel (✉)
OFCE, Sciences Po, Paris, France

ESCP Europe, Paris, France
e-mail: jerome.creel@sciencespo.fr

F. Saraceno
OFCE, Sciences Po, Paris, France

LUISS, Rome, Italy
e-mail: francesco.saraceno@sciencespo.fr

© The Author(s) 2018

J. Creel et al. (eds.), *Report on the State of the European Union*,
https://doi.org/10.1007/978-3-319-98364-6_5

The four criteria to be fulfilled by countries wishing to join the Euro as set by the Maastricht Treaty concern exchange rate stability, long-term interest rate convergence, inflation convergence and, last but not least, the stability of public finances (through constraints to public deficit and debt). These criteria are all *nominal*, that is they do not require convergence of real variables such as GDP in volume, unemployment, productivity and so on. This is not the product of Optimal Currency Area's (OCA's) literature, but the result of the very specific intellectual background against which the Maastricht Treaty was negotiated and eventually agreed upon.

1 The Rationale and Design for Rules Constraining Macroeconomic Policy

Introducing the foundations of fiscal rules in the European Union requires going into a few more details about the New Classical school of thought already mentioned in Chap. 2, that has its roots in the Neoclassical theory of the late nineteenth century (Saraceno 2018).

The so-called "New Consensus" that has dominated macroeconomics since the early 1980s is built around a dichotomy between nominal and real variables. The economy naturally fluctuates around a potential growth rate (which has its counterpart in a natural unemployment rate) which is only determined by supply side factors (the prevailing technology, the stock of physical and human capital, the quantity of labour). The natural rate is an attractor for the economy which following macroeconomic shocks tends to return to it thanks to the working of market adjustment. The presence of rigidities (real or nominal) may slow market convergence to the natural equilibrium,[1] and call for policy action to facilitate it, mostly through countercyclical monetary policy aimed at stabilizing inflation. But this is as far as macroeconomic policy needs to go. The main task of public policy is the removal of market frictions through structural reforms that reduce both natural unemployment and the length of business cycle fluctuations around it.

The task of macroeconomic policy, within the New Consensus, is therefore to provide a stable environment for rational agents whose capacity to coordinate on the natural equilibrium and to return to it may be hampered by erratic behaviour of fiscal and monetary authorities. This is the main rationale behind the call of the New Consensus for (monetary and fiscal) policy rules to be preferred to discretionary (and hence potentially erratic) government behaviour (Barro and Gordon 1983).

New Keynesian DSGE models are the main analytical (and forecasting) tool of the New Consensus and embed an error correction element: deviations from the steady state trigger an automatic nominal (price and wage) adjustment that eventually brings the system to the natural equilibrium. Policy can only, in the presence of market rigidities, speed an adjustment that will take place anyway.

It is no surprise, then, that against this intellectual background, the rules for European macroeconomic governance strongly limit policy intervention. The Maastricht Treaty criteria strengthened by the Stability and Growth Pact (SGP) in 1997 are meant to guarantee that fiscal policy curbs discretionary deficits, so as not to feed inflation and crowding out of private expenditure. Successful fiscal policy then will yield stable inflation (both present and expected, as embedded in the long-term interest rates criterion). The European Central Bank (ECB) statute, also contained in the Maastricht Treaty (Chap. 3) completes the framework by dictating an inflation-targeting mandate for a strongly independent ECB, that also contributes to price stability and policy predictability for supposedly efficient markets.

Consistently on the theoretical framework set by the New Consensus, the literature on fiscal policy since the 1980s has focused on the design, features and implementation of fiscal rules. This literature has received further impulse after the second largest economy of the world, the EMU, endowed itself of the SGP in 1997. Identifying the desirable features of a "good fiscal rule" is a crucial necessity. A seminal and still paradigmatic taxonomy of criteria to assess the goodness of fiscal rules is provided by (Kopits and Symansky 1998, pp. 18–19), who define eight criteria:

1. "a fiscal rule should be well-defined as to the indicator to be constrained, the institutional coverage, and specific escape clauses, in order to avoid ambiguities and ineffective enforcement";

2. "an essential characteristic of a durable fiscal rule is transparency in government operations, including accounting, forecasting, and institutional arrangements" in order to gain "popular support";
3. "rules should be characterized by simplicity to enhance their appeal to the legislature and to the public";
4. "rules must be flexible to accommodate exogenous shocks beyond the control of the authorities";
5. "fiscal rules should be adequate with respect to the specified proximate goal";
6. "a fiscal rule should be enforceable. (There is) a need for constitutional or legal statutes, possibly accompanied by penalties for non-compliance and authority for enforcement";
7. "a closely related criterion is for a set of fiscal rules to be consistent internally, as well as with other macroeconomic policies or policy rules";
8. "most rules cannot last for long unless they are supported by efficient policy actions. (…) From this perspective, (…) a fiscal rule may be viewed as a catalyst for fiscal reforms that would be necessary anyway to ensure sustainability".

These eight properties cover a mix of political and economic concepts. Properties 1–3 and 6 are more political than they are economic, whereas the reverse is true for properties 4, 5, 7 and 8. Kopits and Symansky in fact, to define the criteria, borrowed from the large literature on monetary rules. Thus, while some of these properties have no immediate economic interpretation, they have gained a large success in the monetary policymaking debate due to their supposedly inherent tendency to enhance credibility. In fact, taken together, the criteria require from rules that they are effective in enforcing fiscal discipline while minimizing discretion in their implementation and respecting the different political choices of governments (or, in the case of a monetary union, of different countries).

Kopits and Symansky acknowledged that no rule would exist that fulfilled the eight criteria at the same time: some "trade-offs" among them are inevitable. This is not to say that a fiscal rule should not aim to be as close as possible to the fulfilment of all the criteria. When a trade-off appears (e.g. between flexibility and transparency), the choice of which criterion should have higher priority depends on the institutional framework in which the rule is embedded, as well as of contingent factors such as the strength of the economy, the political preferences of the policy maker, or the need to preserve popular support for government action.

Thus, while they push for the adoption of fiscal rules because intrinsically superior to discretion, Kopits and Symansky are forced to acknowledge that the efficiency of rules, that is their capacity to ensure fiscal discipline together with high and stable growth, may differ in different situations. Implicit in this acknowledgment is, in other words, the recognition that rules could, and more importantly should, evolve as economic and political conditions change. This is an interesting point that in our opinion has not been underlined enough. European policy makers certainly forgot this. The initial choice to enshrine the European fiscal rules at the constitutional level (embedding them in Treaties), further reinforced during the sovereign debt crisis when signatories of the Fiscal Compact (see *infra*) were required to introduce in national constitutions the obligation of budget balance, de facto deprives the EU of the option of assessing, revising and improving its fiscal framework. And yet, as we will see next, the European fiscal rule is far from being efficient, both if assessed against Kopits and Symansky's criteria and against its performance during the first 20 years of existence of the euro (most notably during the sovereign debt crisis).

In Creel and Saraceno (2010a) we assessed the SGP against the criteria and concluded that it fares rather poorly. Contrary to others (e.g. Buti et al. 2003), who argued that the European fiscal framework only needed a few minor tweaks, we showed that the original SGP lacked enforceability, consistency and efficiency, while also not ensuring enough flexibility and transparency. We noticed in particular the focus on structural balance, an indicator that is appropriate in theory but in practice hard to compute without arbitrary (and questionable) assumptions.[2]

Following the numerous excessive deficit procedures (EDPs), particularly against Germany and France, a first reform of the SGP took place in 2005. It added new "flexibility clauses" to those already existing in the original pact (i.e. the existence of a serious recession) that allow exceeding the threshold of 3% without triggering the procedure for excessive deficit.

A country that can prove that its deficit is linked to the implementation of costly reforms in the short term (e.g. the transition from its pay-as-you-go system to a funded system or a public investment programme) will not be punished. In addition, the 2005 reform introduces the debt threshold, absent from the original version of the SGP, even though this criterion was neglected until the financial crisis.

It is precisely the crisis, interpreted in the euro area as a public debt crisis that caused the latest fiscal reform. The Treaty on Stability, Coordination and Governance in the Economic and Monetary Union (TSCG or Fiscal Compact), adopted in 2012 in an intergovernmental form that the UK and the Czech Republic did not ratify, reinforces the limits of the SGP and puts public debt at the centre of the agenda. The Fiscal Compact requires budget standards to be incorporated into constitutions of member states. These standards impose a limit on the structural deficit, to which is added the reduction of the public debt towards the 60% threshold. The cyclically adjusted deficit faces a limit at 0.5 percentage point of GDP of the EU member states.

The public debt reduction rule includes a 20-year horizon for the debt ratio to return to its threshold. For a member state whose public debt exceeds the threshold, the rule therefore stipulates that the public debt must decrease each year by one twentieth of the difference between the actual debt and the threshold.

The Fiscal Compact is also accompanied by the introduction of a European Semester. In the initial intentions, this was meant as a political procedure, between the member states and the Commission, for coordinating structural reforms, fiscal consolidation and reducing macroeconomic imbalances (see also Chap. 8). In the end, the macroeconomic imbalances component (which also appears to be the imbalance of current accounts) is neglected and the European Semester has become a right of preventive scrutiny by the Commission on the financial laws of the member states and a space for negotiation on the application (or not) of the flexibility clauses of the SGP.

In light of Kopits and Symansky's taxonomy, the Fiscal Compact and the subsequent interpretations of its application given by the European Commission were contradictory. On one side, by making sanctions automatic (unless the Council explicitly suspends them), the Fiscal Compact seemed to increase enforceability and transparency. On the other, faced with the negative impact of austerity on the economy of peripheral countries, the Commission was forced to engage in long negotiations on flexibility, on the consideration of exceptional circumstances, and so on, thus making the rule more flexible but at the price of arbitrariness and decreased transparency. Furthermore, the Fiscal Compact, like the SGP, still relies on sanctions in the case of breaches to the rules. The harshness of sanctions nevertheless makes it less likely that they are imposed (no country has been sanctioned so far) and therefore reduces enforceability. The conclusion reached in Creel and Saraceno (2010a) is therefore still valid, actually more so for the Fiscal Compact than for the original rule: the European fiscal framework is not even close to a good fiscal rule.

2 Fiscal Policy During the Crisis

The global financial crisis constitutes a textbook policy mix case. The initial reaction was left to monetary policy, consistently with the origin of the turmoil in the financial sector, but also with the New Consensus view that monetary policy was a quicker and more effective stabilization tool than fiscal policy. But the severity of the crisis and the deflationary pressures quickly pushed central banks of advanced and emerging economies alike towards the Zero Lower Bound. Monetary policy then lost traction, and fiscal policy had to take the witness. Most European countries put in place significant stimulus plans that took different forms (tax cuts, expenditure increases, financial institutions' bailouts, sectoral subsidies, etc.). While the fiscal stimulus in European countries was smaller in size than in the US or in Japan, it was nevertheless effective. The combination of accommodating monetary policy and generalized fiscal expansion is credited with shortening the length of the recession that in terms of intensity of the initial shock had been very similar to the Great Depression of 1929 (Eichengreen and O'Rourke 2009).

Figure 5.1 shows the fiscal impulse of a number of European countries, computed as the variation of the primary structural balance. Netting government balance of interest payments and of the cyclical component gives an acceptable measure of the government's fiscal stance.

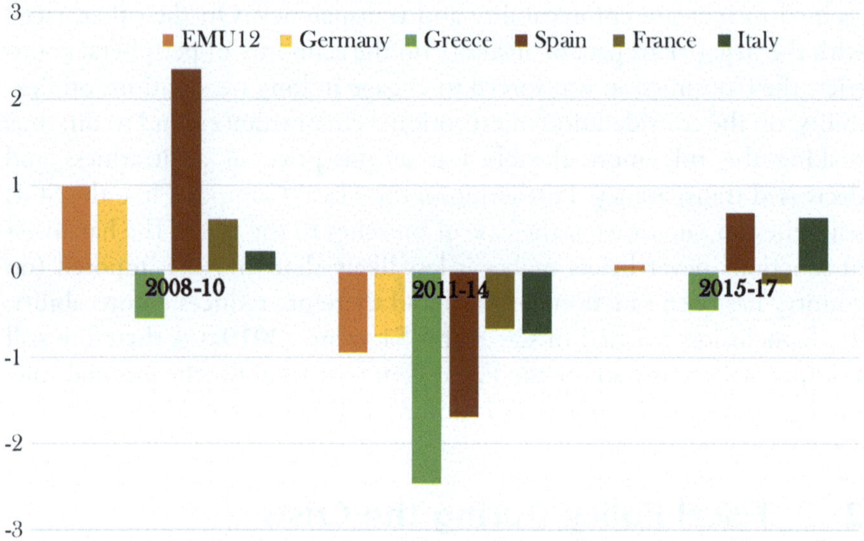

Fig. 5.1 Fiscal impulse—period averages. (Source: AMECO; Fiscal impulse is calculated as the variation of structural balance net of interest payments. A positive (resp. negative) figure shows an impulse (resp. contraction))

To isolate tendencies, we averaged over periods, with breaks at points that represent inflection points in policy. The figure shows that nearly all the countries considered had an expansionary stance (and the EMU12 as well), with the exception of Greece, where the massive consolidation plan(s) imposed in exchange for international assistance started already in 2010. Policy turned frankly contractionary starting from 2011 in all the countries considered, including those, like Germany, that had little need to rush into fiscal consolidation. It is now recognized that austerity in core countries was unnecessary; on the contrary, it made the consolidation of the periphery more painful through a contraction of foreign demand for these countries at a moment in which they were curbing domestic (public as well as private) expenditure; this is due to the initial interpretation of the sovereign debt crisis as caused by fiscal profligacy and not, as is now customary to believe at least in Anglo-Saxon countries, as the result of current account imbalances (Baldwin et al. 2015). The generalized austerity is the most likely explanation of the double dip recession experienced by the Eurozone in 2013.

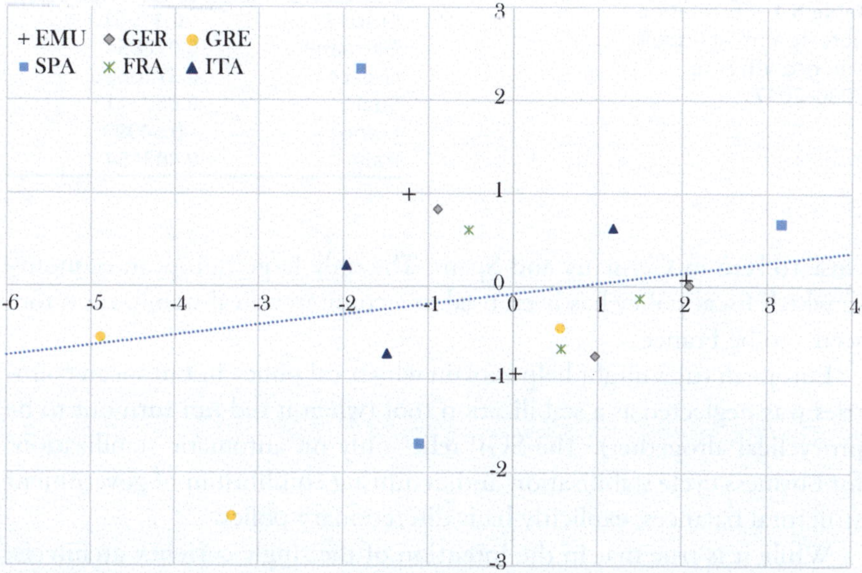

Fig. 5.2 GDP growth against fiscal impulse—period averages. (Source: Authors' calculations on AMECO data; the three periods are 2008–2010, 2011–2014, 2015–2017)

Figure 5.2 plots the fiscal stance against the growth rate for subperiods and for the same countries. Countercyclical policy should imply a negative relationship, that is a more contractionary stance when the economy grows less. The trend line shows that (albeit not significant) the slope of the relationship for EMU countries is positive (and is certainly not negative).

Thus, even if in the early stages of the crisis the Eurozone broadly behaved like the other countries, the overall stance of fiscal policy in the past decade has been procyclical and has contributed to the double dip recession before the slow recovery (EMU GDP only recovered pre-crisis levels in 2016, while in the US that happened in 2012).

Unfortunately, the poor record in managing the business cycle is not limited to the crisis. Table 5.1 shows the correlation between fiscal impulse and the growth rate since 2000. While for the Eurozone as a whole it is negative, it is strongly positive in Italy (and in Greece) and

Table 5.1 Correlation between fiscal impulse and growth rate: 2000–2017

EMU12	−0.17561
Germany	0.070854
Greece	0.371086
Spain	0.067311
France	−0.34093
Italy	0.403154

close to zero in Germany and Spain. The only large European economy in which fiscal policy has been used as a countercyclical stabilization tool seems to be France.

European rules might help explain why fiscal policy in European countries was neglected as a stabilization tool (when it did not turn out to be procyclical altogether). The SGP relies only on automatic stabilization[3] for business cycle stabilization and, requiring equilibrium of government structural balances, explicitly bans discretionary policy.

While it is true that in the intention of the single currency architects, discretionary policy should be limited if not avoided altogether, the story of the euro since 1999 is hardly a story of compliance with the fiscal rules. Not a single year passed in which at least one country was not placed under surveillance by the Commission and the Council through the EDP.[4] Thus, when the global financial crisis evolved into a Eurozone sovereign debt crisis in 2010, number of commentators blamed excessive deficits and laxness of the European fiscal framework.

But in fact, a deeper look at the behaviour of European governments shows that this is not an accurate description of developments in fiscal policies. Fitoussi and Saraceno (2008, 2011) argue that peer pressure and the fear of public reprobation played a major role in restraining fiscal activism of European countries, which de facto gave up fiscal (and monetary) policy. They show how on average the fiscal stance of each EMU country was different, but they all exhibited the same pattern, that is very limited variability if compared to the US, to Japan, or even the UK. Thus, while these latter governments did experience large swings in their structural (discretionary) balance, in EMU countries, the change was significantly lower. This pattern is also clearly visible in Fig. 5.3 from the evolution of the primary balance (expressed in percentage points of GDP) in the euro area, the US and the UK and Japan. The deficit period after the GFC was

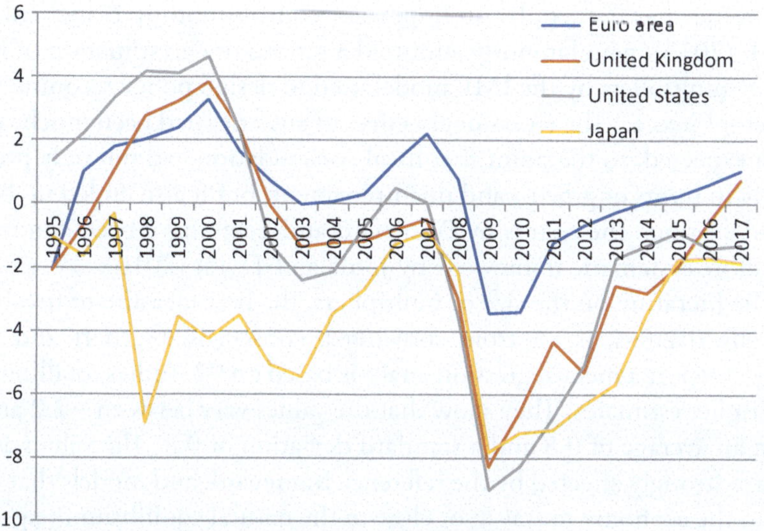

Fig. 5.3 Primary balance, % of GDP. (Source: Ameco)

quite short in the euro area, in sharp contrast with the US and Japan. There, deficits have been large and have persisted for at least for a decade.

To sum up, Eurozone countries deprived themselves of a tool for business cycle stabilization, while others used it. Thus, regardless of the actual imposing of sanctions, the European fiscal framework seems to have succeeded in entrusting to markets the task of taking care of fluctuations, as the Eurozone founding fathers had foreseen.

3 The Crisis: The Debate on the Size of Multipliers and the Reassessment of Fiscal Policy

The crisis has triggered a debate on the policy mix, and most notably on the role that fiscal policy should have in business cycles' stabilization. This large policy experiment challenged the previous consensus on fiscal policy, and the profession is now trying to reach a new consensus on the potential, and on the limits of government action. The debate was triggered, and somewhat framed, by an important contribution by Blanchard and Leigh (2013), who famously admitted a serious underestimation of fiscal policy multipliers by the IMF model used to design policy recommendation for Greece.[5] The recessionary effect of austerity had been much larger than expected, to the point that fiscal consolidation had not only proven costly in terms of growth and unemployment, but it also ended up being self-defeating. The results by Blanchard and Leigh have been confirmed is a more systematic framework by Jordà and Taylor (2016).

The literature on the size of multipliers, the best measure of fiscal policy effectiveness, is far from showing a consensus. Gechert and Will (2012) report a meta-regression analysis based on 92 studies totalling 743 multiplier estimates. They show that the values vary between −2.2 and 4, with an average of 0.8 and a standard deviation of 0.8. The values are of course strongly affected by the reference framework and models that constrain the economy to stay at or close to the natural equilibrium (e.g. Real Business Cycle models) tend to exhibit lower average values. However, it appears from this meta-analysis that negative fiscal multipliers are rare exceptions. It sheds light on the irrelevance of the so-called "expansionary fiscal contractions" and on the dogmatism with which some institutions like the European Commission have managed fiscal policies in the EU. Indeed, even within the RBC framework, the value of the multiplier is positive (the average is 0.5, close to the value used by the IMF and other international organizations before the crisis).

The large variability of the estimation is in fact not really surprising; a number of factors in fact help explain why multipliers (and hence the effectiveness of fiscal policy) may differ. *First*, if the economy is open, part of the increase in demand will go to foreign goods, thus reducing the value of the multiplier. This is why the G20 that met in April 2009 and announced the concerted fiscal stimulus plan to contrast the crisis insisted that this effort would be joint and coordinated, so as to maximize its effect.[6] *Second*, the financing of the fiscal expansion counts. When borrowing is the main source of financing, the risk of crowding out of private expenditure through higher interest rates is more important. The value of the multiplier will then be reduced. The risk of crowding out is larger when the savings is scarce, that is when the economy is close to full employment. Far from the natural equilibrium, when the economy exhibits an *ex ante* excess savings, the risk of crowding out is greatly reduced and the multiplier is larger. This leads us to the *third* reason for differences in the size of multiplier, the cyclical position of the economy. In a Keynesian as well as a classical framework, when the economy is close to full employment, an increase in public consumption can only take place if it forces a reduction of private expenditure. The multiplier cannot, therefore, be significantly different from zero. Creel et al. (2011) use a structural model of the French economy to show that the multiplier is significantly larger when the (negative) output gap is large. The same conclusion is reached by Glocker et al. (2017) as regards the UK, while for Germany, Berg (2015) finds the cyclical position to be less important than other factors (e.g. waves of optimism or pessimism) in explaining the variation in multipliers over time. Finally, a recent work by Ramey and Zubairy (2018) confirms that the multiplier is higher in bad times, but at the same time, find that its size is limited, and almost never larger than one. The only exception is when the economy is at the Zero Lower Bound and monetary policy is ineffective, which is the situation that the Eurozone encountered after 2011, although decision was taken to reduce, not raise, the deficit.

Thus, the literature on fiscal multipliers revived by the crisis allows us to reach one main conclusion: fiscal policy effectiveness is determined by a multitude of factors. The choice of whether to use or not the fiscal instrument cannot be a one-size-fits-all one. It needs to be weighed in the particular context in which it is taken.

This brings us back to the European fiscal rules that imposed a uniform behaviour to European countries even when individual conditions would have called for differentiated, and coordinated, efforts which would have been beneficial to all.

4 Conclusion: What Criteria for the Reform of Eurozone Fiscal Governance?

The discussion of all the reform proposals for European fiscal governance goes well beyond the scope of this chapter. Nevertheless, it is useful to take stock of the preceding discussion, and of the reassessment of fiscal policy triggered by the crisis, to try to sketch a few possible guidelines for the future discussion on fiscal rules.

The crisis changed the European fiscal rule in a contradictory way. On the one hand, it was made tighter (the Fiscal Compact introduces stricter constraints, most notably for high debt countries), and hence less adapted to challenges of policy in a world of Zero Lower Bounds and of increasing centrifugal forces. On the other hand, faced with pressure from the crisis, the Commission accepted to engage with negotiations with member countries to accord flexibility in the application of the norm, based on a very broad definition of exceptional circumstances (which could go from natural catastrophes to the refugee crisis, to the implementation of structural reforms). Thus, the criteria of transparency and consistency defined above seem to have been lost, as well as the one of enforceability (it is now customary for member countries to challenge the Commission's recommendations).

What is more important is that the current fiscal framework has led to a significant shortening of the time horizon of policy makers, which in a situation of uncertainty do not engage in long-term projects and instead navigate on a day-by-day basis. This is harmful for potential growth, and eventually for the very sustainability of public finances that the fiscal rule is supposed to enforce.

A renewed fiscal governance should therefore aim primarily at lengthening the decisional horizon of policy makers, and this would be obtained by enhancing transparency and simplicity (criteria 2 and 3 in Kopits and Symansky). Consistency (criterion 7) would also have to be enhanced.

Truger (2016) recently revived the arguments in favour of the adoption of a golden rule of public finances that would impose a structural balance net of public investment. Such a rule is based on the principle that public investment can be financed by debt because it bequeaths to future generations a stock of public capital, together with debt. Furthermore, debt would be stabilized, thus satisfying criterion 5 (adequate with respect to the objective that in this case would be sustainable public finances). Last, but not least, it would eliminate the bias against capital expenditure that characterizes all fiscal consolidation programmes. The rule has been implemented before (e.g. in the UK starting from the late 1990s) and has been associated with relatively large multiplier effects (see Creel et al. 2009). Its adoption would thus contribute to solve the "European investment crisis" (Revoltella 2014). Recovering a long-term perspective in policy making seems crucial to ensure stable and sustained growth. The new fiscal governance should be geared towards this objective.

Notes

1. Real rigidities may also cause a departure of the natural rate from the Walrasian first best equilibrium.
2. In the past few years, it became a somewhat depressing habit to see national governments and the Commission argue about the estimation of potential output, and therefore of the cyclical position and of the structural balance.
3. It is worth noticing that this created a further inconsistency: while automatic stabilization was given the task of stabilization, the long-term evolution of public finances yielded lower and lower capacity of the tax and expenditure system to act countercyclically. For details, see Creel and Saraceno (2010b).
4. The EDP is triggered by deficits above 3% (or, within the framework of the Fiscal Compact, by structural deficit that is not consistent with the debt reduction path). The EDP is a complex procedure that starts with an early warning, and eventually leads, after a few years of repeated misbehaviour, to a fine. No country was ever sanctioned so far.
5. It is worth recalling that Blanchard and Perotti (2002) revived the academic debate about the effectiveness of fiscal policy at a time only monetary policy was praised for its stabilization properties. Despite their conclusions in favour of the use of fiscal policy for macrostabilization, a gap remained between the academia and policy makers in the wake of the global financial crisis.
6. The communique can be found at https://www.imf.org/external/np/sec/pr/2009/pdf/g20_040209.pdf.

References

Baldwin, Richard, Thorsten Beck, Agnès Bénassy-Quéré, Olivier J. Blanchard, Giancarlo Corsetti, Paul De Grauwe, Wouter Den Haan, et al. 2015. Rebooting the Eurozone: Step 1 – Agreeing a Crisis Narrative Introduction and Summary. *CEPR Policy Insight* 85, November.

Barro, Robert J., and David B. Gordon. 1983. A Positive Theory of Monetary Policy in a Natural Rate Model. *Journal of Political Economy* 91 (4): 589–610. https://doi.org/10.1086/261167.

Berg, Tim Oliver. 2015. Time Varying Fiscal Multipliers in Germany. *Review of Economics* 66 (1). Lucius & Lucius: 13–46. https://doi.org/10.1515/ROE-2015-0103.

Blanchard, Olivier, and Roberto Perotti. 2002. An Empirical Characterization of the Dynamic Effects of Changes in Government Spending and Taxes on Output. *The Quarterly Journal of Economics* 117 (4): 1329–1368.

Blanchard, Olivier J., and Daniel Leigh. 2013. Growth Forecast Errors and Fiscal Multipliers. *American Economic Review* 103: 117–120. https://doi.org/10.1257/aer.103.3.117.

Buti, Marco, Sylvester Eijffinger, and Daniele Franco. 2003. Revisiting EMU's Stability Pact: A Pragmatic Way Forward. *Oxford Review of Economic Policy* 19 (1): 100–111.

Creel, Jérôme, and Francesco Saraceno. 2010a. European Fiscal Rules After the Crisis. *Journal of Innovation Economics* 6 (2): 95–112. https://doi.org/10.3917/jie.006.0095.

———. 2010b. The Crisis, Automatic Stabilisation, and the Stability Pact. *Revista de Economia Y Estadistica* XLVIII (1): 75–104.

Creel, Jérôme, Paola Monperrus-Veroni, and Francesco Saraceno. 2009. On the Long-Term Effects of Fiscal Policy in the United Kingdom: The Case for a Golden Rule. *Scottish Journal of Political Economy* 56 (5): 580–607. https://doi.org/10.1111/j.1467-9485.2009.00499.x.

Creel, Jérôme, Eric Heyer, and Mathieu Plane. 2011. Petit Précis de Politique Budgétaire Par Tous Les Temps: Les Multiplicateurs Budgétaires Au Cours Du Cycle. *Revue de l'OFCE* 116: 61–88.

Eichengreen, Barry, and Kevin O'Rourke. 2009. A Tale of Two Depressions. *VoxEU*. Last Update: 2010.

Fitoussi, Jean-Paul, and Francesco Saraceno. 2008. Fiscal Discipline as a Social Norm: The European Stability Pact. *Journal of Public Economic Theory* 10 (6). Blackwell Publishing Inc.: 1143–1168. https://doi.org/10.1111/j.1467-9779.2008.00400.x.

———. 2011. Inequality, the Crisis and After. *Rivista Di Politica Economica* 1: 9–28.

Gechert, Sebastian, and Henner Will. 2012. *Fiscal Multipliers: A Meta Regression Analysis*, vol. 97. IMK Working Paper. https://doi.org/10.1287/opre.1080.0628.

Glocker, Christian, Giulia Sestieri, and Pascal Towbin. 2017. *Time-Varying Fiscal Spending Multipliers in the UK*. Banque de France Working Paper 643, September.

Jordà, Òscar, and Alan M. Taylor. 2016. The Time for Austerity: Estimating the Average Treatment Effect of Fiscal Policy. *Economic Journal* 126 (590): 219–255. https://doi.org/10.1111/ecoj.12332.

Kopits, George, and Steven A. Symansky. 1998. *Fiscal Policy Rules*. IMF Occasional Papers, No. 162.

Ramey, Valerie A., and Sarah Zubairy. 2018. Government Spending Multipliers in Good Times and in Bad: Evidence from US Historical Data. *Journal of Political Economy* 126 (2): 850–901. https://doi.org/10.1086/696277.

Revoltella, Debora. 2014. The European Investment Crisis. *Intereconomics* 49 (4): 182–183. https://doi.org/10.1007/s10272-014-0499-6.

Saraceno, Francesco. 2018. *La Scienza Inutile. Tutto Quello Che Non Abbiamo Voluto Imparare Dall'economia*. Roma: Luiss University Press.

Truger, Achim. 2016. *The Golden Rule of Public Investment – A Necessary and Sufficient Reform of the EU Fiscal Framework?* IMK Working Papers 168–2016. IMK at the Hans Boeckler Foundation, Macroeconomic Policy Institute.

6

Reforming the European Central Bank

Christophe Blot, Paul Hubert, and Fabien Labondance

1 Introduction

In the early 1990s, the independence of central banks became a pillar of a new model of central banking oriented toward price stability. These changes have been part of a new paradigm stemming from theoretical literature on monetary policy of the mid-1980s (see Chap. 2). This literature has strongly influenced the setup of central banking in the European Monetary Union. The Bundesbank, because of its successes and influence, has established itself as the natural example in terms of credibility and functioning toward which the European Central Bank (ECB) was to

C. Blot (✉)
OFCE, Sciences Po, Paris, France

Université Paris Nanterre, Nanterre, France
e-mail: christophe.blot@sciencespo.fr

P. Hubert
OFCE, Sciences Po, Paris, France

F. Labondance
CRESE Université de Besançon, Besançon, France

© The Author(s) 2018
J. Creel et al. (eds.), *Report on the State of the European Union*,
https://doi.org/10.1007/978-3-319-98364-6_6

strive. All this has contributed to the Maastricht Treaty promoting this model and giving the ECB the main objective of price stability that has been included in the Treaty on the Functioning of the European Union (TFEU, see Chap. 3). Fiscal issues are certainly at the heart of recent thinking aimed at reforming and strengthening European governance; however, monetary policy and especially the role and tasks of the ECB cannot be completely overlooked.

Indeed, since the subprime and sovereign debt crises, the prerogatives and objectives of the ECB have been enlarged. Thus, the ECB has taken over the objective of financial stability and expanded the range of its instruments by purchasing massively public debt securities, which has increased the interdependencies between monetary and fiscal policies. The ECB is now responsible for the supervision of banks in the framework of the European Banking Union. All these actions have taken place without a change in the treaty. However, defining the objectives of the ECB is a central element of the treaty, which raises the question of potential reform. Similarly, the ECB has been pragmatic and has adapted its operational framework to deal with the crisis. It has thus taken decisions which had not been envisaged during the drafting of the treaty and whose legality was contested. Finally, since 1999, the euro area has grown from 11 to 19 members, which raises the question of the decision-making process. Though changes have already been implemented, there is still a need to make the decision-making process more efficient and transparent. This contribution looks back at these elements of the monetary governance of the euro area and suggests ways of reform that would improve the implementation of monetary policy. Thus, we discuss the issue of expanding the ECB's mandate to financial stability, the need to clarify the border between monetary policy and public finances and the reform of the decision-making process.

2 Broadening the Mandate of the ECB

Enhancing financial stability has been a major challenge in most industrialized countries since the outbreak of the Global financial crisis. Recent evidence over financial crises reminds that they are extremely costly in terms of economic performance (Creel et al. 2015a). It is therefore important that an economic authority tries to prevent instability. Historically, the creation of first central banks has often been motivated by the stabilization of the banking system. The regulatory role, particularly of the banking sector, has long been vested in central banks (Goodhart 2011) and the latter have recaptured it during the crisis.

Before the crises, the Jackson Hole consensus prevailed stating that central banks should primarily promote price stability and take into account financial imbalances only to the extent that they affect inflation expectations (Smets 2014). If the assumption of market efficiency had long been contested, the fact remains that the best contribution of central banks and monetary policy to financial stability should be to guarantee price stability. This idea—formulated by Schwartz (1995)—was based on the belief that price stability and financial stability were linked. A central bank that would ensure price stability would de facto achieve financial stability. But if this link is confirmed especially in times of hyperinflation, the Great Moderation, which corresponds to the period during which inflation remained stable and low in the 1990s and 2000s, and the Great Recession largely question this relationship. Blot et al. (2015) examine this relationship between price stability and financial stability in the United States and the euro area over the period of Great Moderation. They come to the conclusion that Schwartz's hypothesis is not confirmed for the periods analyzed. Since price stability is not a sufficient condition to guarantee financial stability, the question arises about the instruments that can be mobilized to achieve it and the actors in charge of their implementation.

The banking crisis and the sovereign debt crisis have exacerbated the pitfalls of the euro area governance and highlighted the imbalance between centralized monetary policy and decentralized regulatory and fiscal policies. Gradually, and following the jolts of the crisis, the financial supervision architecture of the euro area has been reformed. A first wave of reform has involved setting up new supervisory authorities. In September 2009, the European Commission proposed to modify the pre-existing system by introducing a European System of Financial Supervision. In January 2011, a European Systemic Risk Board (ESRB) and three European Supervisory Authorities (ESA) were established. The latter must coordinate the regulations of the national financial sectors within the European Union (EU). These authorities are the European Banking Authority (EBA), the European Securities and Markets Authority (ESMA) and the European Insurance and Occupational Pensions Authority (EIOPA). However, the principle of subsidiarity remains and regulatory powers remain national. It is only with the deepening of the sovereign debt crisis that member states of the euro zone, confronted with the question of the survival of the euro zone, have gone one step further and created the Banking Union which entered into function on November 4, 2014.

The Banking Union proposes a uniform regulation that applies to the main banking institutions in the EU (Antonin and Touzé 2014). In particular, these regulations lay down rules on own funds or the protection of depositors. The functioning of the Banking Union is based on two mechanisms. The first is a Single Supervisory Mechanism (SSM), which places significant banks (see ECB Regulation 468/2014) of the euro area countries under the supervision of the ECB. In the context of a second mechanism, and in the event of supervision being in default, the Banking Union also sets up a Single Resolution Mechanism (SRM) applicable in the event of a bank failure. Within this framework are created a single resolution fund and the terms of use of this fund and management of bank failures. In particular, the bail-in principle is preferred to external bailouts, particularly by the government (bail-out). Since January 2016, the single resolution fund has been funded by contributions mainly from credit institutions.

The crisis has also shown the need to go beyond micro-prudential supervision and promote a so-called macro-prudential tool dedicated to the analysis of aggregate trends and existing imbalances in the financial system that can create systemic risk. The objective of macro-prudential regulation is to ensure the viability of the economic and financial system as a whole. The macro-prudential tool aims to detect and prevent systemic risk by, for example, varying the capital requirements of banks in order to ensure their solvency when micro-prudential supervision is concerned with ensuring the safety of banks. The micro-prudential policy is now entrusted to the ECB while the ESRB, chaired by the President of the ECB, is in charge of macro-prudential policy. However, the ESRB does not define regulation but may issue warnings and recommendations for the European as a whole and for one or more member states. Concrete decisions are taken by national authorities.

Credit developments are critical to understanding potential occurrences of financial instability that can produce systemic risk (Creel et al. 2015b). Banking regulation, and particularly macro-prudential regulation, cannot be separated from monetary policy, as they both have influences on the supply and demand for credit. Therefore, it seems relevant that the central bank integrates prudential policy into its action (Beau et al. 2012), which was not the case at the origins of the euro zone, banking supervision being the responsibility of the competent national authorities.[1] The result of these various reforms is a complex financial regulatory architecture that intertwines national competences, euro area-specific competences and EU-wide competences. The jurisdiction of the banking regulatory authorities thus extends to the whole of the EU when the single banking supervisory mechanism is limited to the euro area a priori and relies on the competence of the ECB.

Finally, the crisis has also led to questions about the effect of monetary policy on financial stability, through the risk-taking channel emphasized by Borio and Zhu (2012). Consequently, all missions currently carried out by the ECB have an impact on financial stability, although the mandate of the ECB does not explicitly mention it.

One can now consider that, de facto, the ECB has three objectives: price stability, support for activity and financial stability (Blot et al. 2014). However, the articulation of this triple mandate deserves clarifications. Even without changes to existing treaties, it is important that ECB leaders be more explicit in the different objectives pursued and notably whether the stance of monetary policy will be adjusted for financial stability purposes. The priority over price stability no longer seems to correspond to the practice of monetary policy. Achieving maximum employment and financial stability seem as important. More transparency would make monetary policy more credible and certainly more effective at preventing another banking and financial crisis. Besides, it is not clear whether the complex architecture for dealing with financial stability will really help to achieve it. However, as macro-prudential inherently raises distributional issues, the responsibility of decisions may be assumed by elected bodies. Consequently, there is a trade-off between granting decisions regarding financial stability to central banks (to improve efficiency and internalize externalities between monetary policy and financial stability) and keeping financial supervisory and monetary authorities independent.

3 Clarifying the Border Between Monetary Policy and Public Finances

During the crisis, the ECB massively purchases sovereign bonds issued by euro area countries, first to contain the sovereign debt crisis and then to curtail the risk of deflation. The solution implemented by the ECB to the sovereign debt crisis was first to launch the SMP (Securities Market Program) in May 2010 and the OMT (Outright Monetary Transaction) announced in September 2012. However, this was disputed within and outside the ECB, since the case was brought to the Court of Justice of the European Union (CJEU, see also Chap. 3).

The objective of the SMP and OMT was to lower interest rates on sovereign debt through targeted purchases of securities.[2] Beyond a legitimate debate about the effectiveness and potential risks associated with these measures, their legality has been disputed. The SMP was debated within the ECB by Jürgen Stark, then a member of the Executive Board.[3] He considered that the SMP amounted to financing the debt of some member states, violating two provisions of the Treaty: the clause of non-bailout of states within the euro area and the ban on funding of budget deficits by the central bank. By resigning in September 2011, he expressed his deep disagreement with a policy that he felt was erasing the border between monetary policy and fiscal policy. The OMT, the second mechanism implemented by the ECB, was also strongly criticized by the Bundesbank and by German citizens considering that it might lead to a budgetary transfer between European countries. There is therefore implicitly a budget commitment of the German government without the prior consent of the Bundestag. The opinion of the CJEU, delivered in June 2015, validated the legality of the OMT, the Court considering not only that "the purchase of sovereign debt securities constitutes a measure of monetary policy" but also "that the acquisition of sovereign debt does not constitute monetary financing prohibited by the Article 123 of the TFEU". While the signal effect linked to the announcement of the program in 2012 has apparently helped to reduce the credit spreads that have emerged in the euro area (Altavilla et al. 2014), it has placed the ECB in a difficult position creating a legal uncertainty that has or could have limited the implementation of the program and thus its effectiveness.

In addition, if the ECB provides liquidity to banks in euro area countries as part of monetary policy operations, so-called Emergency Liquidity Assistance (ELA) operations continue to be implemented by national central banks with ECB agreement. Thus, despite the extension of the powers of the ECB in banking supervision, the role of lender of last resort remains under the responsibility of states and therefore of their central bank.[4] Whelan (2015) notes, however, that these transactions have so far been of a secret and discretionary nature. He criticizes the role played by the ECB during the Irish and Greek banking crises, which used these liquidity operations to exert political pressure on the states. In June 2015, the ECB refused to extend the ceiling of this liquidity a few days before the referendum organized by the government on a new agreement with European creditors, in a context marked by significant leakage of banking system deposits by fear of a Grexit. If the risk of exit from the euro area was real, the decision of the ECB strengthened it by precipitating the banking system in the crisis and taking the risk of leaving the Greek government no alternative to the issuance of a parallel currency. In the end, the ECB played a key role in lender-of-last-resort operations by allowing liquidity to be granted to Greek banks. But it also used this lever to exert political pressure on the Greek government. It should also be noted that the ECB is part of the troika, alongside the European Commission and the IMF, which is responsible for monitoring the implementation of refinancing agreements with creditors in countries under financial assistance. It entails influencing and monitoring national fiscal policies. This very political role is not part of the ECB's mandate. Central banks are non-elected bodies and cannot play a role for which they are not fully accountable.

What lessons can be drawn from these events? Firstly, it is contradictory that an independent institution which cannot request or accept instructions from another institution, government or other body of the Union is involved in a political process of monitoring budgetary policies of some member countries. In fact, the ECB is creditor of these states since it holds debt securities that they issued. But these securities were acquired as part of monetary policy operations and not as loans granted by the ECB to member states. Secondly, the decision of the CJEU on the OMT also validates the quantitative easing programs implemented by the ECB and thus confirms the independence of the ECB in its assessment of the means (the instruments) that it deploys to achieve its objectives and fulfill its mandate. Thirdly, it is necessary to clarify the role of the ECB as lender of last resort, a function that remains today entrusted to the national central banks. However, as part of the banking union, the ECB collects information that allows it to make a diagnosis on the solvency of banking institutions. From there, it can therefore fully judge the situation of banks and decide to grant liquidity when it considers that the institution is solvent or refer the issue of a possible restructuring or bankruptcy to the Single Resolution Board. This argument argues for this function to come back to the ECB (Goodhart and Schoenmaker 2014).

It should be reminded that the ECB derives its legitimacy from a treaty that aims to isolate its decisions from all political pressures on the pretext that they would have a mainly technical dimension (the setting of the short-term interest rate, terms of the refinancing operations, banking supervision), the objectives of monetary policy being set within a political framework defined by the TFEU ratified by all member states. During the crisis, the ECB played a key role in preserving, if not saving, the monetary union, making up for the shortcomings of fiscal and political governance. But these situations show that the decisions taken by central banks have a strong political dimension, especially in times of crisis. Securities purchase transactions have a direct impact on fiscal policy by their effect on the interest rate on sovereign debt. The decision to support a bank or not also has obviously a budgetary impact. The pressures exerted by the ECB on the governments of countries in crisis have been for political reasons rather than to achieve its objectives. These interactions justify a reflection on governance and the ECB's relations with political power.

We must consider recognizing the interactions by strengthening the debate and the democratic control of the ECB. Today, the only interactions of the ECB with democratic bodies are via the quarterly testimonies of the President of the ECB by the European Parliament. They are not sufficient to give democratic legitimacy to its action. The control cannot be solely that of the judge. It must be political so that the definition of objectives and the implementation of monetary policy can be regularly debated and defined within a representative political body.

The new instruments of monetary policy have significantly increased the interactions between monetary policy, fiscal policy and financial stability and increased interdependencies between those institutions in charge of these objectives. It thus requires greater coordination to avoid negative externalities, at least at the zero lower bound when public debt is partly monetized (Balls et al. 2016). The persistence of a deflationary risk (inflation risk, respectively) despite an expansionary monetary policy (respectively restrictive) calls for an expansionary (respectively restrictive) fiscal policy for the euro area as a whole. However, as long as national fiscal policies are fully decentralized, coordination will remain imperfect, if not impossible. This could be detrimental for growth in the euro area.

4 Reforming the Decision Process

The last issue on which the ECB could evolve concerns the decision-making process in the Governing Council, the main decision-making body of the ECB. Currently, it is composed of the six members of the Executive Board, and of the governors of the national central banks of the 19 countries of the euro zone. They usually meet twice a month to discuss issues related to the tasks and responsibilities of the ECB and the Eurosystem.[5] In order to ensure the separation between monetary policy missions and the other tasks of the ECB (banking supervision and prudential supervision), separate meetings of the Governing Council are organized. The Governing Council assesses economic and monetary developments and now takes its monetary policy decisions every six weeks.[6]

The President of the Council of the EU, the Eurogroup and a member of the European Commission can participate in the meetings, but they do not have the right to vote. Until the beginning of 2015, each member of the Board of Governors had one vote and, unless otherwise stated in the statutes, the decisions of the Board of Governors are taken by a simple majority. In the event of a tie vote, the President has the casting vote. Although the meetings are confidential, the Governing Council communicates the results of its deliberations, particularly those relating to the setting of key interest rates, through a press conference following the meetings on monetary policy decisions.

The accession of Lithuania to the euro area in 2015, bringing to 19 the number of its member states, led to a change in voting rights, as the Governing Council had envisaged in December 2002. The ECB has decided to implement a rotation system which rules the distribution of voting rights among the members of the Governing Council of the ECB. This rotation system is supposed to allow the Governing Council to retain its decision-making capacity despite the increase in the number of countries participating in the euro area. According to the EU Treaties, the rotation system had to be implemented as soon as the number of governors exceeded 18.

In this rotation system, the countries of the euro area are divided into several groups according to the size of their economy and their financial sector. A ranking is established to determine which group each national central bank governor belongs to. The governors of countries ranked from 1 to 5 (currently Germany, France, Italy, Spain and the Netherlands) share four voting rights. The other 14 countries have 11 voting rights. Governors vote in turn on a monthly rotation. At each meeting, 21 votes are cast, the members of the Executive Board of the ECB having a permanent right to vote.

By way of comparison, the Monetary Policy Committee of the Federal Open Market Committee (FOMC) uses a system similar to that of the ECB. The FOMC has 12 voting members, seven are members of the Board of Governors with permanent voting rights. The president of the Federal Reserve Bank of New York votes systematically, the presidents of the Banks of Chicago and Cleveland every other year and the nine presidents of the other regional reserve banks vote one year out of three. Rotation in the United States occurs annually, whereas it is done monthly for the ECB.

A first criticism of the ECB's decision-making process concerns the "national" mode of representation of the Governing Council. Whether before January 1, 2015 with the principle of "one member, one vote", or with the rotation system that has come into force since, 19 of the 25 members are appointed in relation to their national responsibility and ultimately their nationality. Since the ECB's monetary policy is conducted for the euro area as a whole, this characteristic of the composition of the Governing Council raises the question of the relevance of this criterion for determining its composition. If the objective of the ECB is to maintain the stability of the euro area consumer price index, the nationality of the members of the committee should be of little importance.[7] The fear that national concerns may bias votes of national governors—and even of members of the Executive Board—explains why the ECB has been reluctant up to now to release the votes as is done by the Bank of England and the Federal Reserve. Like Buiter (2014), we argue that making all votes public would make the members of the Governing Council more responsible and accountable of their decisions. This composition, regardless of its relevance, raises a second question. The principle of "one central bank, one vote" tends to overweight the weight given to small countries: the governor of the Banque de France who represents more than 65 million people has the same weight as the governor of Malta who represents 400,000. The choice of a national composition thus generates a representativity bias.

The forced resignation of Lorenzo Bini Smaghi, a member of the ECB Executive Board from June 2005 to November 2011, is symptomatic of the importance of the issue of nationality in the Governing Council. He had to resign when Mario Draghi was appointed President of the ECB because three Italians (with the Governor of the Bank of Italy) would have been present on the Board of Governors.

The rotation system does not answer either of the two questions. Small countries are always overrepresented and the composition still depends on nationality. It also raises another remark. With this system, there are now three categories of members on the Board of Governors: the members of the Executive Board who vote at all meetings, the governors of the five major countries that vote at 80% of meetings and those of the 14 small countries that vote in 78% of meetings. This system disadvantages small countries in favor of members of the Executive Board. It is therefore subject to criticism from small countries committed to the principle of equality between the countries of the euro zone and critics of the major countries which, at a meeting out of five, no longer have the right to vote.

A first way to respond to these criticisms is to fix the voting rights in proportion to the capital held by each central bank to the capital of the ECB or in proportion to the population (or GDP) of each country in relation to the population (or GDP) of the euro area. This would answer the question of representativeness. Such a measure, however, would only accentuate criticism of the national composition of the Governing Council. A second track therefore concerns the number of members of this council. There is no obvious reason, if the monetary policy of the ECB is conducted for the euro area as a whole, to have a number of members equal to the number of countries making up the euro area. Thus, the FOMC in the United States does not include 50 members as the number of states, while the Bank of England's monetary policy committee is made up of nine members, regardless of the number of regions in the United Kingdom. This number of members could be set in relation to other criteria (see Sah and Stiglitz (1988) on the optimal size of committees) and regardless of the number of countries in the euro area.

5 Conclusion

This chapter deals with central banking and monetary policy issues in the euro area. We first observe that the powers of the ECB have been enlarged during the crisis. It is now strongly involved in financial stability. These new functions have been devoted to the ECB without any change in the treaty. It remains that it has raised the complexity of the institutional setup for dealing with financial instability. Besides, the ECB should also make clearer by an appropriate communication whether monetary policy will also account for financial stability. The crisis has also made necessary the use of additional for monetary policy, increasing the interactions between monetary and fiscal policy. Consequently, it requires closer coordination between the ECB and institutions in charge of fiscal policy. Finally, there is room to make the decision-making process of the ECB on monetary policy more efficient and transparent. We point to the risk of national bias in the votes of the member of the Governing Council and to the over-representativeness of small countries. A proposition might be to reduce the number of personalities sitting in the decision-making body and to avoid appointing them upon nationality criteria.

Notes

1. See paragraph 6 of Article 127 of the TFEU.
2. In fact, the maximum outstanding amount of Greek, Portuguese, Irish, Spanish and Italian sovereign securities acquired under the SMP reached 219 billion in March 2012. As for the OMT, it has never been mobilized.
3. We should also remember that before Jürgen Stark, Axel Weber, the President of the Bundesbank who opposed the measures adopted in May 2010, also resigned.
4. In concrete terms, this implies that the risks and potential losses on ELA loans are borne by the national central banks, which is not the case for standard liquidity and losses are shared between EU member states.
5. The Eurosystem defines and implements the monetary policy of the euro area. It is composed of the ECB and the national central banks of the countries that have adopted the euro.
6. Prior to 2015, meetings on monetary policy guidance were monthly and from 1999 to November 2001, Governing Council could decide to change the stance of monetary policy twice a month. However, only the first meeting was followed by a press conference. Yet, in practice, most, if not all, changes in monetary policy were made during the first meeting.
7. Hayo and Méon (2013) illustrate the ambiguities of this process and suggest that the governors of national central banks take their decision according to national objectives.

References

Altavilla, Carlo, Domenico Giannone, and Michele Lenza. 2014. *The Financial and Macroeconomic Effects of OMT Announcements*. Centre for Economic Policy Research (CEPR).

Antonin, Céline, and Vincent Touzé. 2014. *Europea bancaire:l'Union fait-elle la force ?* Note OFCE, No. 46.

Balls, Ed, James Howat, and Anna Stansbury. 2016. *Central Bank Independence Revisited: After the Financial Crisis, What Should a Model Central Bank Look Like*. M-RCBG Associate Working Paper Series 67.

Beau, Denis, Laurent Clerc, and Benoit Mojon. 2012. *Macro-prudential Policy and the Conduct of Monetary Policy*. Banque de France Working Paper, No. 390.

Blot, Christophe, Jérôme Creel, Paul Hubert, and Fabien Labondance. 2014. Dealing with the ECB's Triple Mandate? *Revue de l'OFCE-Debates and Policies* 134: 163–173.

Blot, Christophe, Jérôme Creel, Paul Hubert, Fabien Labondance, and Saraceno Francesco. 2015. Assessing the Link Between Price and Financial Stability. *Journal of Financial Stability* 16: 71–88.

Borio, Claudio, and Haibin Zhu. 2012. Capital Regulation, Risk-Taking and Monetary Policy: A Missing Link in the Transmission Mechanism? *Journal of Financial Stability* 8 (4): 236–251.

Buiter, Willem. 2014. Central Banks: Powerful, Political and Unaccountable? *Journal of the British Academy* 2: 269–303.

Creel, Jérôme, Paul Hubert, and Fabien Labondance. 2015a. Financial Stability and Economic Performance. *Economic Modelling* 48: 25–40.

Creel, Jérôme, Paul Hubert, and Fabien Labondance. 2015b. *The Intertwining of Financialisation and Financial Instability*. OFCE Working Paper, No. 14.

Goodhart, Charles A. 2011. The Changing Role of Central Banks. *Financial History Review* 18 (2): 135–154.

Goodhart, Charles, and Dirk Schoenmaker. 2014. *The ECB as Lender of Last Resort?* VOX CEPR's Policy Portal.

Hayo, Bernd, and Pierre-Guillaume Méon. 2013. Behind Closed Doors: Revealing the ECB's Decision Rule. *Journal of International Money and Finance* 37: 135–160.

Sah, Raaj Kumar, and Joseph E. Stiglitz. 1988. Committees, Hierarchies and Polyarchies. *The Economic Journal* 98 (391): 451–470.

Schwartz, Anna J. 1995. Why Financial Stability Despends on Price Stability. *Economic Affairs* 15 (4): 21–25.

Smets, Frank. 2014. Financial Stability and Monetary Policy: How Closely Interlinked? *International Journal of Central Banking* 10 (2): 263–300.

Whelan, Karl. 2015. *The ECB and Financial Assistance Programs: Has ECB Acted Beyond Its Mandate?* Monetary Dialogue, October.

7

Real Divergence: How to Fix It?

Jacques Le Cacheux

Within the European Union (EU), the gap in economic performance between rich and poor, countries and regions alike, seems to have widened since the 2009 Great Recession and the subsequent sovereign debt crisis: the "Northern bloc" of member states of the Euro Area (EA) (Germany, Austria, Belgium, the Netherlands and Finland) have recovered relatively rapidly and soon surpassed their pre-crisis income levels, whereas the "Southern bloc" (Greece, Italy, Portugal and Spain) suffered a severe "double-dip" recession, in large part engineered by the austerity measures implemented shortly after the sovereign debt crisis in order to consolidate public finances and restore competitiveness; France, as usual, lies in the middle (Le Cacheux and Ross 2014). While prosperous Germany is often cited as a model, Greece has suffered a 25% drop in per capita income and strains to recover from a decade of

J. Le Cacheux (✉)
Université de Pau et des Pays de l'Adour, Pau, France

Ecole Nationale des Ponts et Chaussées, Marne-la-Vallée, France

Sciences Po, Paris, France
e-mail: jacques.lecacheux@sciencespo.fr

© The Author(s) 2018
J. Creel et al. (eds.), *Report on the State of the European Union*,
https://doi.org/10.1007/978-3-319-98364-6_7

recession. The gap between German and Greek per capita GDP was almost € 13,000 in 2000, and reached € 21,000 in 2016; less dramatic but quite significant, the gap between German and French per capita GDP was about € 1500 in 2000, and had widened to almost € 4500 by 2016. Taking snapshots of an income indicator, the picture of gaps is similar: in 2001, per capita gross national incomes (GNIs) in Germany, France and Italy were practically equal (around € 28,000), and in Greece it was € 7000 less; in 2016, the German per capita GNI was reaching almost € 50,000, the French one being € 8000 lower, the Italian one € 12,000 lower, and the Greek one € 24,000 lower (OECD *National Accounts*)![1]

Economic and social cohesion has, from the very preamble of the Rome Treaty (1957), been placed high on the agenda of European integration. It ought to be regarded as an overarching objective of the EU and, given the large gaps existing in initial conditions and economic development levels among member states and regions, it certainly implies some form of upward convergence, the economic catching-up of those countries/regions that are better off by those that are lagging behind, that is a reduction of territorial inequalities. At first sight, it does not seem to have been the case in recent years: all sorts of anecdotal evidence rather point to the contrary: national and regional economies seem to be diverging, with economic activity, dynamism and riches agglomerating in a handful of large metropolitan areas and rich regions, and the remainder of the EU territory suffering a persistent economic decline.

But is it so? Are EU economies drifting apart, and if so what are the causes and consequences? The first section of this chapter purports to put together evidence concerning economic convergence/divergence among EU countries and regions. In the second section, some of the causes of the poor economic performance observed in Southern European EA member states are documented and analyzed. The third section questions the policies imposed on these countries to foster macroeconomic adjustment and fiscal consolidation after the sovereign debt crisis of 2010–2012. The fourth section asks whether the European Fund for Strategic Investment (EFSI) created in application of the Juncker Plan in 2015 is the appropriate response to economic divergence. Finally, the fifth section is dedicated to discussion of the past efficacy and future orientations of the EU structural and cohesion policies, and more generally of the EU budget.

1 Symptoms of Real Divergence Among Nations and Regions

How economically divergent are countries and regions in the EU? There exists a vast empirical economic literature trying to assess convergence/divergence and, when applied to the European context, also attempting to estimate the effects of EU budget structural funds on regional growth/convergence. And the evidence is rather inconclusive: depending on the period, the spatial level, the sample, the variable considered, and the method used, convergence is or is not found to operate, comforting the first sight impression that some countries/regions do seem to be catching up with the best-performing ones, whereas others seem to be falling behind.[2]

The simplest way of assessing whether convergence is operating over time is to look at dispersion. Focusing first on the most widespread economic performance indicator, per capita Gross National Product (GDP), the most straightforward descriptive statistics is standard deviation: when taking the full sample of 28 member states over the last two decades, there does appear to have been convergence, at the level of national economies: standard deviation almost steadily declines from 1999 till 2014, with a slight increase over the last two years for which data are available (2015 and 2016); the 2009 Great Recession and the sovereign debt crisis do not seem to have disturbed the convergence process, but recent developments may be signaling an inversion.[3]

When restricting the sample to the member states of the EA, the picture is very much the same. However, when the sample is restricted to those countries that have been in the EA since the beginning (the 11 initial members plus Greece, who joined in 2002), the time pattern of standard deviation is different: it decreases from 1999 till 2007, then increases. Thus, confirming other recent studies (e.g. Alcidi et al. 2018), and as also apparent on Chart 7.1a and b, while there has clearly been a convergence of new member states from Central and Europe, there is evidence of real divergence within the group of initial EA members, and it has more specifically negatively affected Southern European states: Greece, Portugal, Spain and Italy, whereas Germany and Austria have been moving in the opposite direction.

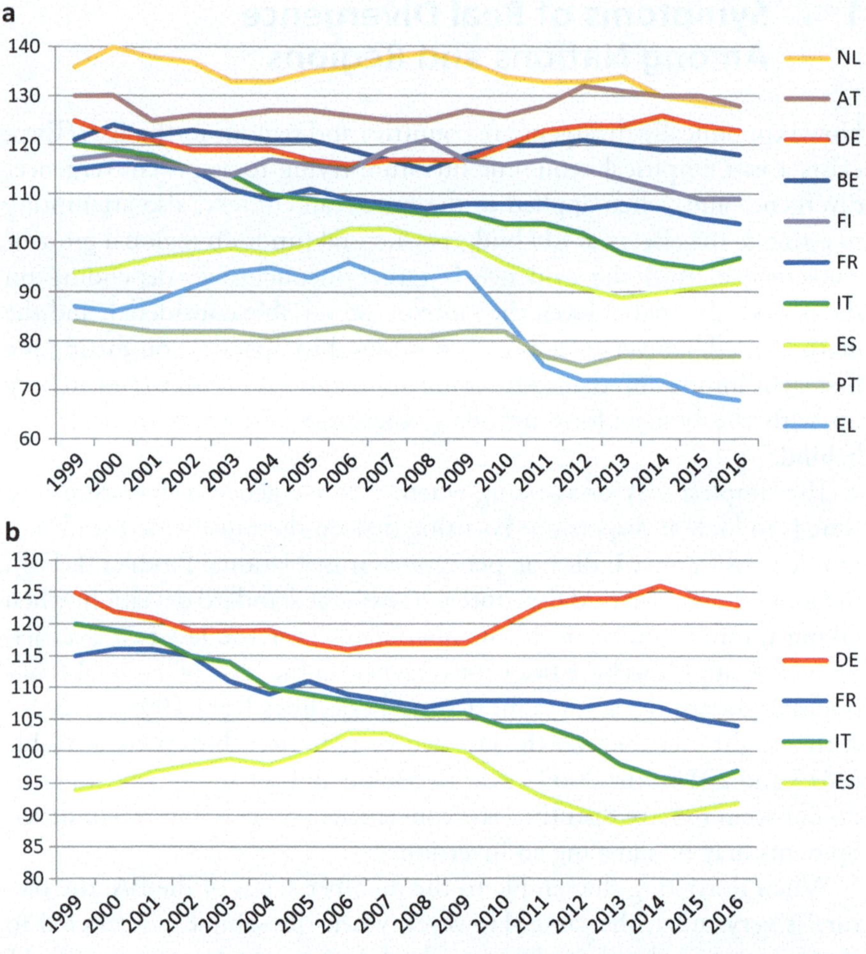

Chart 7.1 Per capita GPD of EA countries, 1999–2016 (EU28 = 100). **(a)** Initial member states, excluding Ireland and Luxembourg. **(b)** The four large EA members. (Note: Ireland and Luxembourg have been excluded because their GDP is artificially inflated by multinational corporations and financial firms declared economic activity, making this indicator rather meaningless; Source: Eurostat)

Looking at a finer spatial scale, the picture is more clearly one of real divergence. Using the same simple measure (standard deviation), this time on regional per capita GDP, the time pattern (Chart 7.2) is similar to the one found among initial members of the EA: a marked reduction

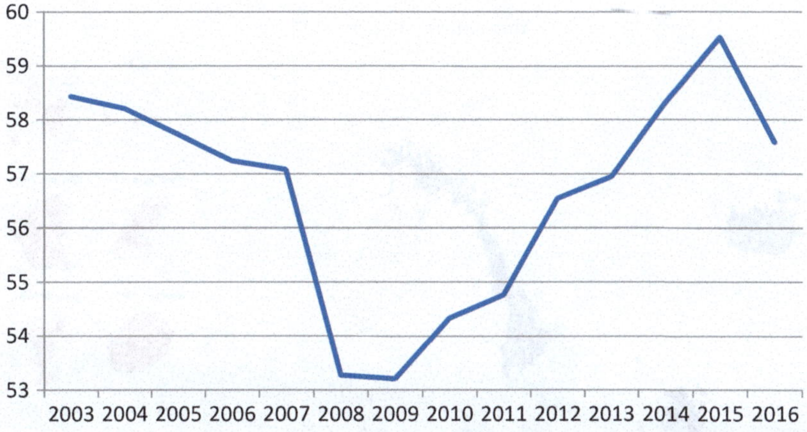

Chart 7.2 Standard deviation of regional per capita GDP of EU28 regions, 2003–2016. (Note: Regional per capita GDP are expressed as index, with EU28 = 100; Source: Eurostat, author's calculation)

in dispersion over the first period (2003–2008), followed, after the Great Recession, by a sharp increase in dispersion, only slightly reduced over the last two years of the sample, confirming the impression of real divergence among EU regions, inside and outside the EA alike, and suggesting that even in countries, such as those of Central and Eastern Europe, that have enjoyed real convergence by catching up, some regions have been left behind.[4]

The regional distribution of unemployment in the EU comforts this conclusion of a specific poor economic performance of peripheral regions, especially in Southern Europe (Chart 7.3): almost ten years after the 2008 financial crisis, unemployment rates are persistently higher in the periphery than in the core of the EU.[5]

2 Underlying Causes of Economic Divergence

Divergent paths of economic development among EA historical member states, and among regions, may be attributed to a variety of causes (see e.g. European Central Bank 2015). Lack of competitiveness and/or

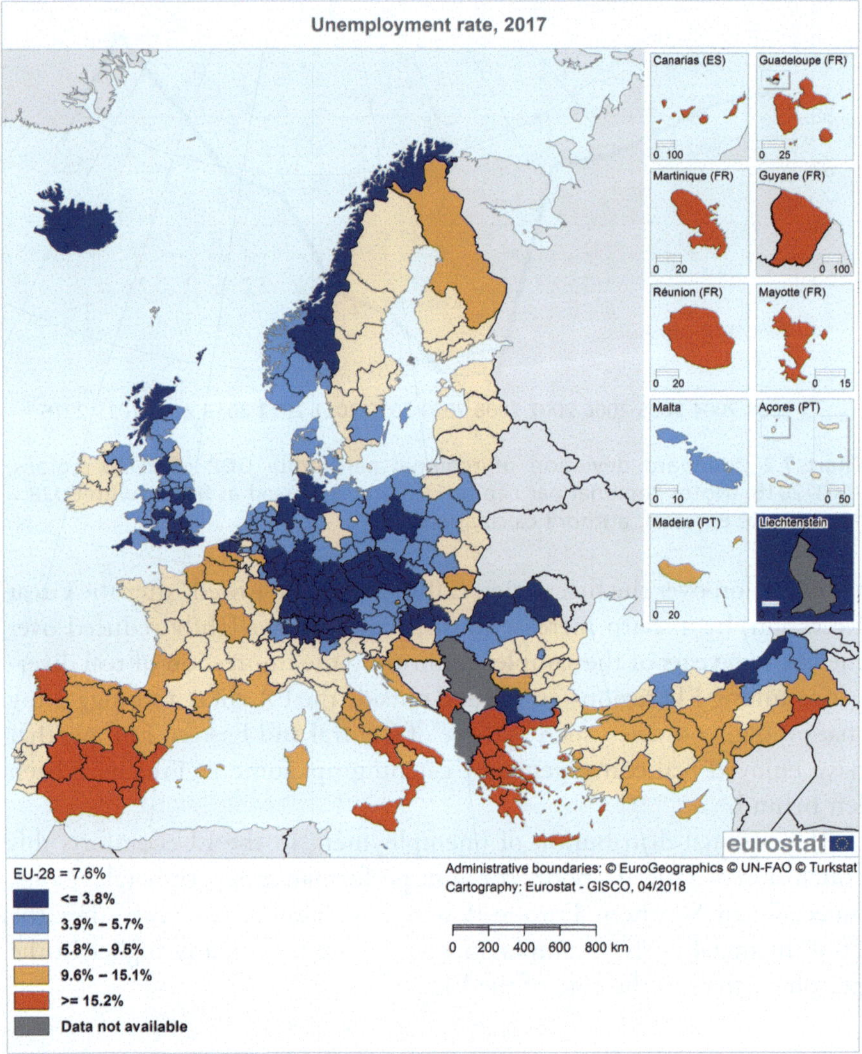

Chart 7.3 Regional unemployment rates in the EU, 2017. (Source: Eurostat, EU Commission)

attractiveness is often pointed out. Indeed, even though the symptoms of the sovereign debt crisis that hit a number of Southern European member states of the EA in 2010–2012 were high public debt ratios, the underlying causes of their difficult economic situation was usually attributed to poor competitiveness, materializing among other things in persistent current account deficits (Le Cacheux 2009).

Competitiveness is usually appraised by an indicator of production costs, in general labor costs.[6] As appears on Chart 7.4, nominal unit labor costs have been following quite divergent paths in EA countries since its creation in 1999. In a number of countries, such as Greece, Ireland and Spain, they have tended to increase very fast over the decade preceding the 2008 crisis, whereas unit labor cost increases have been especially moderate in Germany over the same period; they even declined between 2005 and 2008. After the Great Recession and the sovereign debt crisis, unit labor costs declined in those countries that had been most severely hit, while they tended to accelerate in the countries that had experienced wage moderation before.

Unit labor costs are simply defined as labor costs divided by labor productivity, so that their evolution results from divergences between these two variables. Labor productivity is particularly important in that respect.

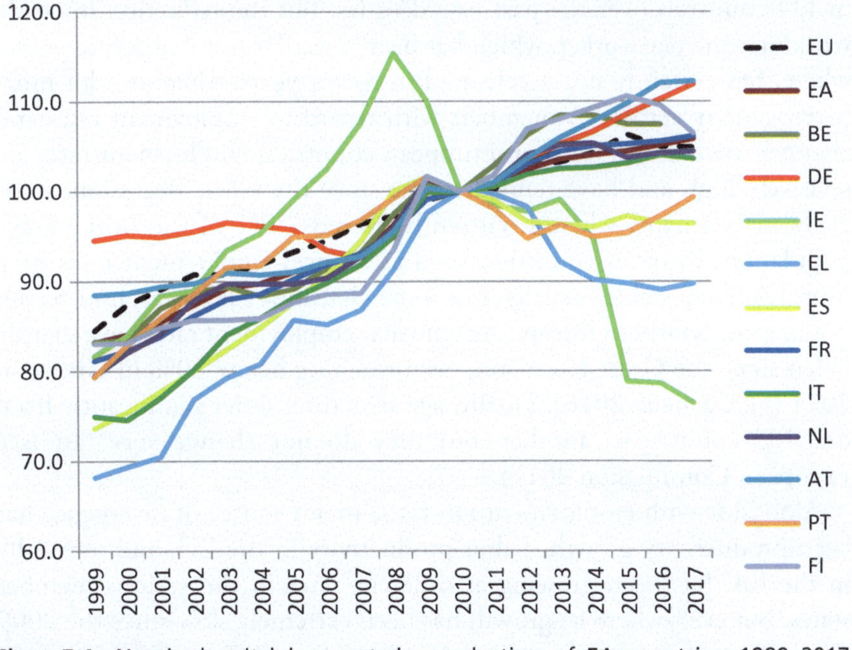

Chart 7.4 Nominal unit labor costs in a selection of EA countries, 1999–2017 (2010 = 100). (Source: Eurostat)

In order to better grasp the relative importance of often quoted factors, it may be helpful to start with a simple identity. Consider the following decomposition of per capita GDP:

$$(\textit{Per capita GDP}) = (\textit{GDP / Number of hours worked}).$$
$$(\textit{Number of hours / worker}).\begin{pmatrix}\textit{Number of workers employed /} \\ \textit{Working age population}\end{pmatrix}.$$
$$(\textit{Working age population / Total population})$$

The first term is real hourly productivity of labor; the second is average working time (per year); the third is the employment rate; and the fourth is a kind of total dependency ratio, which is mostly influenced by demographics, but also by the conventional definition of working age, notably by retirement legislation.

A lot of adjustments and variations in working time have taken place in EU countries over the past two decades; but the reduction in yearly working time per worker, which has been a secular trend observed everywhere, has certainly not accelerated in recent years. There is a lot more heterogeneity across EA members with regard to employment rates and changes thereof: in Northern European countries, employment rates are relatively high and have tended to rise since the Great Recession, especially in Germany, where it currently exceeds 70% of the working age population; in other countries, such as France, employment rates have been relatively stable, usually at a somewhat lower level (around 65%); but in most Southern European countries, employment rates have sharply fallen since the Great Recession, even reaching below 50% in Greece in 2014 (Le Cacheux 2016). Finally, age structures differ significantly from one EU country to another, but they do not change very fast (see European Commission 2017).

Alongside with employment rates, the major source of divergence has been productivity growth. Labor productivity in the EU, and especially in the EA, has been growing at different rates in the various member states, but everywhere its growth has been extremely slow since the 2009 Great Recession: even the "champions", Spain and Germany, have registered a mere 7% increase in the past seven years. Some countries stand out, with especially poor productivity performances: Greece, which has suffered a continuous and very large (10%) reduction in labor productivity since 2007; and Italy, which has had almost flat labor productivity since 2000 (Chart 7.5).

Slow growth of labor productivity, though with differences across EA member states, is clearly a common feature at least since the Great Recession. This phenomenon is not limited to the EU, and has fueled fears of a "secular stagnation"; but the slowdown is particularly marked in EA countries. What are the causes behind this productivity standstill? There are many candidates, among which is the oft-denounced "labor market rigidities" (see e.g. European Central Bank 2015). But one obvious factor is low investment: in all EU countries, the ratio of productive investment to GDP has shrunk by 2 points between 2008 and 2015, with only a small increase since then; in Southern European EA member states, the contraction of investment volume has been considerable (−25% in Italy between 2007 and 2016, more than −30% in Portugal

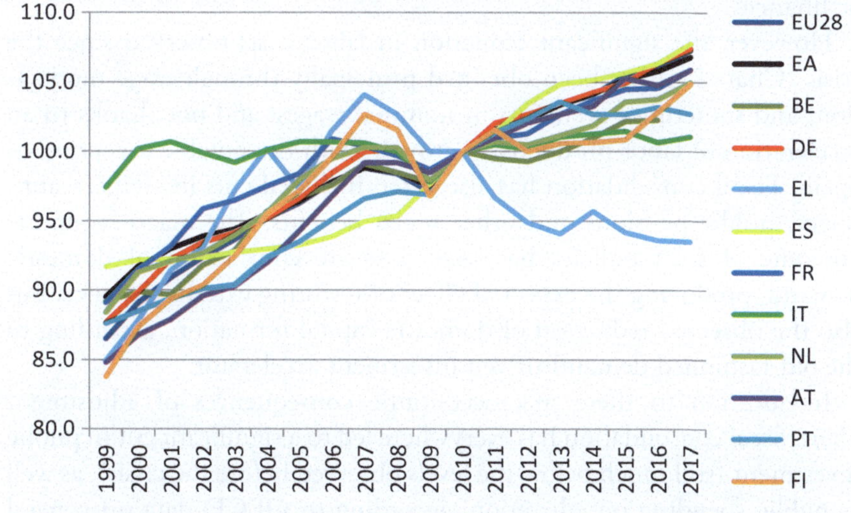

Chart 7.5 Real productivity per hour worked in selected EA member states, 1999–2017 (2010 = 100). (Note: Ireland and Luxembourg have been excluded for reasons of significance of GDP; the most recent members of the EA are not represented either; Source: Eurostat)

and Spain, and divided by a factor 2.6 in Greece!) and lasting, so that the stock of productive capital is probably well below its pre-crisis level, and likely technologically obsolete.[7]

3 Fiscal Consolidation and Structural Reforms: Curing Evil with Evil?

With the Great Recession, productive investment has declined everywhere in the EU; but in Southern European EA members, it has been literally slashed to extremely low levels, from which it has been very slowly recovering over the past two years. Such a large and protracted contraction of productive capital formation is itself the result of the several years of austerity policies enacted after the sovereign debt crisis. Indeed, three out of these four countries (Greece, Portugal and Spain) have had to resort to EU financial assistance and have submitted been to policies that were meant to restore competitiveness and consolidate public finances.

However, the significant reduction in labor costs observed since the crisis (Chart 7.4) has been obtained principally through wage moderation, and sometimes even cuts in nominal wages, and not thanks to an acceleration of labor productivity growth, with the notable exception of Spain. Fiscal consolidation has also often included cuts in civil servants' wages, public pensions and other social benefits. The macroeconomic outcome of such policies has been a severe contraction of domestic demand, producing the expected effect of restoring external balance, but also the observed reduction of domestic capital formation, according to the old-fashioned demand-driven investment accelerator.

In addition to these macroeconomic consequences of adjustment plans, fiscal consolidation has everywhere led to a significant cut in public investment (still much below the levels observed before the crisis), as well as public spending on education: according to OECD data on general government spending, three out of these four countries (Greece, Italy and Spain) are now at the very bottom of the OECD ranking on this item, with public education spending around 4% of GDP (Portugal spends

5% of its GDP on education, but it dedicated as much as 7% of GDP to it in 2010). Thus, two essential ingredients of long-term competitiveness, good infrastructure and a well-trained labor force, have been sacrificed in the process of fiscal consolidation.

4 The European Investment Plan: Benefitting the Rich?

That fiscal consolidation and wage moderation policies would generate sluggish productivity growth and low productive investment almost everywhere in the EU had been diagnosed by many economists early on the adjustment process.[8] It did eventually lead to a policy reaction at the EU level: the EU Investment Plan ("Juncker Plan") launched in 2014, with the creation of the EFSI in 2015.[9] Supposed to mobilize as much as € 500 billion over the following five years by using about € 21 billion EU public funds endowment as leverage to secure private financing, this fund may help in boosting productive investment, in particular in the most advanced technologies and in sustainable development projects.

However, at least in the initial phase of EFSI existence, most of the investment projects selected to benefit from EFSI support have been located in the wealthier EU member states (Núñez Ferrer et al. 2016). In the most recent years though, an effort has been made to elicit viable investment projects, notably in the fields of transport and energy transition and redirect EFSI funding to peripheral EA countries, and especially to Southern European EA member states.

5 The EU Budget, Cohesion and Structural Funds: Past and Future

Could the EU budget be used to fix real divergence? The question is all the more legitimate as the four countries identified above as "laggards" are precisely those, with exception of Italy, that, along with Ireland, had been identified as the "cohesion countries" in the 1990s and early 2000s, that is, countries benefitting from the cohesion funds of the EU budget, in principle aiming at fostering economic catching-up.

If based on the superficial evidence of budgetary "net balances",[10] the four Southern EA member states did benefit from net financial flows from the EU budget over the two Multiannual Financial Framework (MFF) periods following the Maastricht Treaty (1993–1999 and 2000–2006) (Laurent and Le Cacheux 2015); but the distribution of EU budgetary "net balances" drastically changed with the wave of EU enlargement in 2004–2007: in the previous (2007–2013) and even more so in the current (2014–2020) MFFs, the main recipient of budgetary net financial transfers have been the new member states from Central and Eastern Europe, especially Poland and Hungary, whereas the "net balances" of former "cohesion countries" have shrunk or even reversed sign (in the case of Ireland). As a share of GNI, the leading beneficiaries of the "net balances" in 2015 were Bulgaria (more than 5% of GNI), Hungary (almost 4.5%) and Slovakia (4%); among cohesion countries, only Greece still had a positive "net balance" exceeding 2% of its GNI.

As is well known, the major expenditure items in the EU budget are Common Agricultural Policy (CAP) and structural/regional policies. Although declining as a share of total, these two expenditure items have together been representing more than two thirds of the total EU budget over the past two decades.[11] And while a large fraction of structural funds is explicitly targeted at poorer regions, a small part of CAP expenditures aims at promoting rural development, which should also benefit poorer regions.

This spatially redistributive functioning of the EU budget is often criticized and induces reluctance by the national governments of "net contributors" to increase the overall size of the budget (Laurent and Le Cacheux 2015). First, when looking at the underlying theory, some analysts have questioned the premise that the EU should promote catching-up by poorer regions: the best-known example of this strand of thinking is the Sapir Report (2003) that in substance argues that economic agglomeration forces should be left free to play in economically integrated union. Structural and other regional policies aiming at supporting catching-up in poorer, most often peripheral, regions are to be avoided, precisely because they impede spontaneous agglomeration of economic activity in the most productive regions/metropolitan regions. Because agglomeration is expected to generate efficiency gains, it should result in a higher total EU output: in a pure Paretian tradition, the report concludes that agglomeration is Pareto improving, and that some purely redistributive policy may then compensate those who are lost in the process.

But a prior question concerns the effectiveness of such instruments: Have these policies aiming at promoting economic catching-up been effective? There is a large body of empirical literature trying to estimate their effects, with rather contrasted results: in most of the published studies, EU structural and cohesion policies are found to have had little or even no effect on the catching-up by poorer regions, though a number of studies do identify positive effects on the poorest regions and sometimes on the richer regions in relatively poorer countries.[12]

Will the future EU budget be more effectively promoting real convergence and the economic catching-up of poorer regions? The Commission has recently published its proposal for the next MFF covering the period 2021–2027. In an effort to conciliate the demands of the national governments of both “net contributors”, who are asking for a small budget, and “net beneficiaries”, who would like a larger budget, and in the face of a significant revenue shortfall resulting from Brexit (a net annual loss estimated to be between € 10 and €15 billion, the UK having been a “net contributor” to the EU budget in spite of its “rebate”), the Commission has essentially carried forward existing policies, with only minor changes and a few small innovations (see European Commission 2018). The overall size of the budget is almost constant: as a share of EU GNI, it should hover slightly above 1%, in line with recent trends, in spite of new objectives, accompanied by some financing, in such pressing policy areas as migrations and border control, defense and so on. While CAP expenditures for direct income support of farmers are to be frozen in nominal terms, implying their relative importance will shrink over time, as has been the case in the current MFF, funding for cohesion and structural policies are projected to initially fall and return to their current real level, which also corresponds to a relative reduction. Funding for rural development is also essentially kept constant.

Some innovations and specification changes in the proposed future EU budget may however work in favor of more economic convergence of poorer countries/regions.[13] But the amounts are smaller than what may be thought at first sight, since a number of extra-budgetary items, such as the EU funding of EFSI, will now be integrated in the EU budget. It is therefore unlikely that the future EU budget after 2020 will be more effective at fighting real economic divergence than it has been in the recent past.

One last question remains open: insofar as real divergence has been shown to affect essentially Southern European EA members in recent years, would a stabilization budget for the EA work more effective to reduce divergence? Of course, it would not be a substitute for structural funds or for national policies geared at improving labor productivity, but given the linkages that have been emphasized above between macroeconomic consequences of adjustment policies and poor performance in investment and labor productivity, it may be the case an EA budget designed to cushion asymmetric shocks would at least mitigate real divergence.

Notes

1. Economic performance indicators are many, and the various sources of data often display significant differences in figures, that may be due to different statistical methodologies or differences in the precise definition of economic aggregates. Thus, Eurostat and OECD National Accounts data do give different figures for the same aggregate. Gross domestic product (GDP) is the most widely used indicator of economic performance; but it measures production on the territory considered, not income. Gross national income (GNI) is a better measure of income accruing to the residents of this territory, and may be significantly different from GDP in the case of a small, open economy, such as Luxembourg, Ireland or regions in the EU. As is well known, these indicators are not good measures of well-being. See Stiglitz-Sen-Fitoussi Commission (2009) and Chap. 12.
2. Recent empirical studies of economic convergence in the EU include Alcidi et al. (2018) and Diaz del Hoyo et al. (2017). Both offer additional references.

3. Although when Ireland and Luxembourg are eliminated from the sample, the inversion of the last two years disappears.
4. This corroborates results obtained in other studies using different, more sophisticated methods to assess the degree of real convergence, in particular Alcidi et al. (2018) and Esposti and Bussoletti (2008). Once again though, it should be kept in mind that regional GDP data are extremely fragile, as the methods by which they are obtained are to a large extend conventional.
5. Two points of caution though: officially reported unemployment rates are influenced by labor market institutions, which may explain part of country-specific patterns; and the map uses the administrative definition of regions in EU, implying a high degree of heterogeneity in size, economic diversity and so on.
6. However, it should be noted that labor costs represent only a fraction of total production costs, and a small one in most modern economic activities.
7. Adding to this prolonged productive investment slump, there has probably been a significant amount of capital scrapping during and after the Great Recession. Unfortunately, data on the productive capital stock are not reliable due to the conventions used in building the figures.
8. See, in particular, the various installments of iAGS reports: https://www.iags-project.org/.
9. EFSI is hosted by the European Investment Bank. For more information on EFSI, its functioning and achievements so far: http://www.eib.org/efsi/#.
10. Of course, "net balances" are not an appropriate measure of the economic effects of the EU budget on individual member states, for reasons that have presented in Le Cacheux (2005) and in a number of more recent studies and are summarized in Núñez Ferrer et al. (2016).
11. The most recent annual EU budget data are for 2017: out of a total of € 158 billion, 37% went to "natural resources" (mostly CAP) and 34% to cohesion policies. See https://europa.eu/european-union/about-eu/money/expenditure_en.
12. A representative sample of this literature includes Puga (1999) and more recently Becker et al. (2010). As argued above, the fragile nature of regional GDP data used in these studies makes their results difficult to interpret, and possibly misleading.
13. Among the innovative measures contained in the Commission's proposal for the next MFF are a number of small additions to the main source of revenue. Current financing of the EU budget essentially relies on national

contributions, and mostly on the GNI-based national contribution. In the future, additional, more genuinely own resources would come from the receipts of the EU Emission Trading System, a tax on plastic bags, and a small fraction of the revenue from corporate income taxation after the adoption of the Common Consolidated Corporate Tax Base (CCCTB, see Chap. 4). Obviously, these changes are quite modest, compared to what had been proposed in the HLGOR report (Monti et al. 2017), and some national governments may well block them in the Council, where budget decisions require unanimity. In any case, they would not alter the overall effect of the EU budget on divergence.

References

Alcidi, Cinzia, et al. 2018. *Income Convergence in the EU: A Tale of Two Speeds.* CEPS Commentary, January 9. https://www.ceps.eu/publications/income-convergence-eu-tale-two-speeds.

Becker, Sascha O., Peter H. Egger, and Maximilian Von Ehrlich. 2010. Going NUTS: The Effect of EU Structural Funds on Regional Performance. *Journal of Public Economics* 94 (9–10): 578–590. https://www.econstor.eu/bitstream/10419/26540/1/592000451.PDF.

Diaz del Hoyo, Juan Luis, et al. 2017. Real Convergence in the Euro Area: A Long Term Perspective. *ECB Occasional Papers* (203), December. https://www.ecb.europa.eu/pub/pdf/scpops/ecb.op203.en.pdf?8ff80dd3a3b58f231105f3e4835b2928.

Esposti, Roberto, and Stefania Bussoletti. 2008. Impact of Objective 1 Funds on Regional Growth Convergence in the European Union: A Panel-Data Approach. *Regional Studies* 42 (2): 159–173.

European Central Bank. 2015. Real Convergence in the Euro Area: Evidence, Theory and Policy Implications. *ECB Economic Bulletin* (5). https://www.ecb.europa.eu/pub/pdf/other/eb201505_article01.en.pdf.

European Commission. 2017. *The 2018 Aging Report.* Directorate for Economic and Financial Affairs, November. https://ec.europa.eu/info/publications/economy-finance/2018-ageing-report-underlying-assumptions-and-projection-methodologies_en.

———. 2018. *A Modern Budget for a Union that Protects, Empowers and Defends. The Multiannual Financial Framework for 2021–2027.* Com (2018) 321 final. https://eur-lex.europa.eu/resource.html?uri=cellar:c2bc7dbd-4fc3-11e8-be1d-01aa75ed71a1.0023.02/DOC_1&format=PDF.

Juncker Plan. https://ec.europa.eu/commission/priorities/jobs-growth-and-investment/investment-plan-europe-juncker-plan_en.

Laurent, Éloi, and Jacques Le Cacheux. 2015. *Report on the State of the European Union*. Vol. 4, *Is Europe Sustainable?* Basingstoke: Palgrave Macmillan.

Le Cacheux, Jacques. 2005. European Budget: The Poisonous Budget Rebate Debate. *Note de Notre Europe/Delors Institute* (47), June. http://institutdelors.eu/publications/european-budget-the-poisonous-budget-rebate-debate/.

———. 2009. The Challenges and Trappings of Convergence. *L'Europe en formation/Journal of Studies on European Integration and Federalism* 50 (351): 35–47.

———. 2016. Für eine Cooperative Strategie in der Eurozone. Zentrifugale Kräfte bekämpfen. *DGAPanalyse* 12, December 22. https://dgap.org/de/think-tank/publikationen/dgapanalyse/fuer-eine-kooperative-strategie-der-eurozone.

Le Cacheux, Jacques, and George Ross. 2014. France in the Middle. In *European Social Models, From Crisis to Crisis: Employment and Inequality in the Era of Monetary Integration*, ed. Jon Erik Dølvik and Andrew Martin, 105–143. Oxford: Oxford University Press.

Monti, Mario, et al. 2017. *Future Financing of the EU*. Final Report of the High Level Group on Own Resources. Brussels, January. http://ec.europa.eu/budget/mff/hlgor/final-report/index_en.cfm.

Núñez Ferrer, Jorge, et al. 2016. *Study on the Potential and Limitations of Reforming the Financing of the EU Budget*. Study for the High Level Group on Own Resources, chaired by Mario Monti. Brussels, June. http://ec.europa.eu/budget/mff/hlgor/library/highlights/hlgor-studies-external-studyonfinancingofeu-budget-june-2016_en.pdf.

Puga, David. 1999. The Rise and Fall of Regional Inequalities. *European Economic Review* 43 (2): 303–334.

Sapir, André, *et al.* 2003. *An Agenda for a Growing Europe: Making the EU Economic System Deliver*. Report of an Independent High-Level Study Group Established on the Initiative of the President of the European Commission, Brussels. http://citeseerx.ist.psu.edu/viewdoc/download?doi=10.1.1.620.4948&rep=rep1&type=pdf.

Stiglitz-Sen-Fitoussi Commission. 2009. *Report of the Commission on the Measurement of Economic Performance and Social Progress*. Paris. http://ec.europa.eu/eurostat/documents/118025/118123/Fitoussi+Commission+report.

8

The Future of the Euro Area: The Possible Reforms

Jérôme Creel and Francesco Saraceno

1 Introduction

The previous chapters have analysed the euro area economic governance and showed its several shortcomings. Reforming its design remains an important issue. Two fundamental principles oppose when reforms are concerned: solidarity and market discipline. They both cope with the EU original project, but they also have some perverse effects. Solidarity may induce some moral hazard, that is larger risk-taking, whereas market discipline may induce excessive limitations on deficits and debts. The road

J. Creel (✉)
OFCE, Sciences Po, Paris, France

ESCP Europe, Paris, France
e-mail: jerome.creel@sciencespo.fr

F. Saraceno
OFCE, Sciences Po, Paris, France

LUISS, Rome, Italy
e-mail: francesco.saraceno@sciencespo.fr

© The Author(s) 2018

J. Creel et al. (eds.), *Report on the State of the European Union*,
https://doi.org/10.1007/978-3-319-98364-6_8

to economic governance reforms is thus paved with these two principles but bordered by their perverse effects.

Many proposals to improve economic governance have emerged. They can be grouped into two views. The first, usually attributed to German officials, focuses on better compliance with agreed rules and faith in market discipline. The second view is embodied by E. Macron, since his Sorbonne speech in September 2017 highlights risk-sharing and coordination between the EU Member States.[1]

These two views imply different tools. The first view requires debt-restructuring mechanisms (without transfers) for Member States to resolve legacy issues and build some fiscal space before a next economic crisis occurs, whereas the second one focuses on the creation of a Eurozone budget, funding for common European public goods (refugees' policies, defence, investment in technology) and social and tax harmonization. These two paths of reform could be insufficient though to address the vulnerabilities of the euro area like diverging competitiveness or boom–bust cycles.

2 Compliance with the Original Fiscal Framework and Market Discipline

2.1 The Fundamental View

The first path of reform has been clearly delivered by the former German Minister of Finance, M. Schaüble, in his legacy paper.[2] While his position cannot be mixed up with the official position of Germany (they are exposed at the end of the chapter), it is evocative of a legal-prone position about the EU fiscal framework. Yet, it is based upon two principles. The first one is the fulfilment of current fiscal rules. To ease their implementation, simplification of rules is required: the public deficit at 3% of gross domestic product (GDP) and the convergence rule towards the debt threshold at 60% of GDP (or 1/20th debt rule) should be the cornerstone of fiscal surveillance, and other rules (on the cyclically adjusted deficit or on public spending) should be removed. The fiscal framework would allow some margins for manoeuvre around the deficit threshold conditional on the actual decline of the debt to GDP ratio at the expected pace. Moreover, fiscal surveillance could be ultimately handled by a non-political body, for example the EMS, at the expense of the Council which continues to keep the final word. This change would remove the political interferences about the respect of fiscal rules. The legal dimension of fiscal policymaking would weigh on the economic and political dimensions so that, in the end, the fiscal framework would apply rigorously.

The second principle relates to market discipline as the natural device to reduce economic and financial risks jeopardizing cohesion between euro area Member States. In this respect, a government unable to pay interests or repay its debt claims should suffer an increase in its liquidity or default premium, that is an increase in the interest rate on its debts. This market mechanism would be expected to urge a shift in fiscal policy by the government, namely to implement a fiscal consolidation. The supporters of market discipline argue that currently there are two obstacles to its proper functioning in the euro area. First, the Assets Purchase Programme (APP) of the ECB dampens liquidity and default risks and blurs the consequences of fiscal profligacy on interest rates. The APP should then stop and the bail-out principle should be reasserted. Second, prudential regulation assumes that public bonds are risk-free. This creates a sovereign-bank loop: banks have an incentive to hold public debts to fulfil their regulatory constraint while governments easily match their supply of bonds with demand at a (relatively) low yield. This loop also intensifies the fragmentation of the banking and financial markets in the euro area: banks usually hold domestic public debts, hence raising the issue that a default on public debt might produce bankruptcy in the domestic banking sector. To break this loop, sovereign risks should differ across the euro area Member States: it would oblige banks holding riskier debts either to raise their capital or to sell debt instruments. After a change in the regulatory treatment of domestic public debts, the subsequent interest costs would not be equally distributed across banks and countries though. Indeed, where banks hold large shares of risky public debt, interest rates might increase via either higher demand for loanable funds or lower demand for public bonds. Liquidity and default crises may follow and destabilize the whole euro area.

To avoid these bad outcomes, reforming the ESM would also be on the agenda. The ESM has been a permanent "international financial institution" resulting from an intergovernmental treaty among the euro area Member States since 2012 and a successor to the European Financial Stability Facility born in 2010. The ESM can provide financial assistance to Member States experiencing or threatened by severe financing problems. The ESM can grant loans conditional on macroeconomic adjustment programmes; it can also help recapitalize banks. The total loan capacity is € 500 billion out of a capital of € 700 billion. While the ESM seems close to the International Monetary Fund (IMF) in its functioning, it does not share the preventive arm of the IMF: it has no capacity to monitor economies to prevent liquidity or default crises via, for example automatic liquidity support. The transformation of the ESM into a European Monetary Fund (EMF) would require a credible application of the no bail-out principle to limit moral hazard (Wyplosz 2017). It could be obtained via the creation of a debt-restructuring mechanism in the EMF toolkit. This would permit the orderly default of a non-complying Member State without jeopardizing the whole euro area. Finally, the EMF would monitor country risks and the implementation of the Stability and Growth Pact (SGP).

2.2 Discussion

There are a few shortcomings with this reform path. First, advocating more market discipline assumes market efficiency. This assumption is at odds with the lessons drawn from the GFC: markets were unable to prevent the crisis; worse they fuel it via systematic under-estimation of risks during upturns. Increasing the sensitivity of the European governance framework to market perceptions and market volatility seems ill-designed, unless financial stability prevails. The latter also rests on a strong assumption. Second, reliance of conditionality on the implementation of structural reforms and on former compliance with the fiscal framework is contradictory. Indeed, there are many issues with structural reforms (Manassé and Katsikas 2018): they take time to design and implement before they may be effective; they may modify the behaviours of firms and households only slowly; they are often painful in the short run and therefore prevent political consensus on the necessity for reforms. There are also many issues with the EU fiscal framework (see Chap. 4). Third, extended market discipline without a risk-free European public bond will definitely transform the domestic bonds of a Member State into the benchmark. This is already the case with German Bunds and it feeds financial divergence between a so-called risk-free issuer and the other Member States which incur a spread vis-à-vis Germany. Additionally, the introduction of risk on sovereign debt may have substantial implications for the domestic banking sectors. In light of European Banking Authority's guidelines involving the imposition of risk-weights on public debt holdings, banks capital ratios could decline unevenly across Eurozone member states, generating higher rather than lower banking risk.

To avoid having a national benchmark in a monetary union, some departures from the fundamental view are required. Supporting the creation of a European safe asset is one possibility. There have been some proposals in this respect which introduce some risk-sharing between the euro area Member States. Delpla and von Weizsäcker (2010) propose to pool the public debts that are in compliance with the 60% debt to GDP requirement in the TFEU. In the case of a sovereign default, a State would treat "blue debt" preferentially, whereas "red debt", which is the debt issued above 60%, would be junior debt. Brunnermeier et al. (2016) propose two pooled assets, next to regular bonds, that would be put into a tranched CDO. The CDO would pool the underlying debt contracts, including the safest debt in the senior tranche, called European Safe Bonds (ESBies) and the riskiest in the junior tranche, called European Junior Bonds (EJBies). Similar to Delpla and Weizsäcker, the overall pool should only contain a limited amount of government debt, so that the rest would be treated as "red bonds". The proposition of junior bonds was revived by Bénassy-Quéré et al. (2018).

There are also needs for some forms of immediate reductions in debt payments. Corsetti et al. (2015) propose that in addition to a safe bond, the ESM should be augmented with a "Stability Fund". This fund would buy back European debts above 95% of GDP of a country and swap the debt with zero yielding perpetuities. Pâris and Wyplosz (2014) argue that their Politically Acceptable Debt Restructuring Fund for the Eurozone (PADRE) regime would require that the ECB buys and swaps Member

States bonds into zero-interest perpetuities. The ECB would purchase domestic debts in proportion to the ECB capital key. To limit free riding from Member States, they add strict enforcement rules. Should a country start to accumulate debt again, the ECB could opt to swap the perpetuities back to normal yields, and countries would face market discipline. Corsetti et al. (2017) promote a "Eurozone Fund" which would be able to issue non-defaultable debt by issuing bonds which would be convertible at par into currency once they mature. In all these proposals, the fund would be financed by collecting taxes, usually part of VAT, and seigniorage incomes.[3]

3 Options for Deepening Euro Area Governance

The second path of reform departs from market discipline to highlight the necessity of shock absorbers and coordination between the Member States.

The EU framework has been built on the belief that market flexibility and nominal targets (inflation, deficit, etc.) would be sufficient to ensure real convergence in the euro area both in times of growth and in times of crisis. This was an illusion, given the evidence available since the early 1990s that even in the United States transfers from the federal budget help to absorb a substantial amount of asymmetric shocks.

Euro area countries therefore need mechanisms with which they can offset asymmetric shocks. They also need mechanisms to cope with inbuilt tendencies within EMU for countries to diverge due to the difference in real interest rates generated by a single nominal interest rate and differential inflation rates. Dealing with the asymmetry of shocks also requires some coordination. Thus, a central coordinating institution would be invaluable in maximizing real convergence and EMU-wide growth.

The Five Presidents Report of June 22, 2015 made a first attempt in setting out the principles to be followed to provide the euro area with an absorption capacity. The report highlights that a federal budget should provide for a stabilization of asymmetric shocks in normal times, be neutral from the budgetary point of view over the medium term, and not in charge of stabilization in the event of a major crisis. Moreover, the euro area budget should not hinder the functioning of the fiscal rules which discipline the Member States (irrespective of effectiveness of the rules themselves).

Since the publication of the report, the discussion has evolved and focused on the management of economic crises. The French President E. Macron, in September 2017 at La Sorbonne, defended the adoption of a Eurozone budget to provide investment, emergency financial assistance and crisis absorption capacity, to be placed under the responsibility of a European minister of economy and finance under parliamentary control. Achieving such a budget would require new funding resources, like a European tax on digital companies or ecological taxes. E. Macron also promotes social convergence via converging corporate tax rates (more precisely, a "corridor" for corporation tax rates) and the adoption of a European norm on minimum wage: "in social affairs, we need to guarantee a minimum wage for all, adapted to the economic realities of each country, and regulate social contribution competition".

A Eurozone budget may help provide transnational public investments, which could avoid the complicated construction of the Juncker Plan, and it may also help fund migration and refugees policies at European level, whose management and costs currently fall on a few countries' shoulders. A streamlined and centralized supply of these European public goods would be very important to boost growth and increase productivity; especially if one thinks of the important investment, and economies of scale, related to the environmental transition. In other areas, such as border security, the benefits are more of a political nature, resolving a collective action problem to the ultimate benefit of all countries. Thus, the coordination and management at European level of such efforts offers potentially significant improvements over the present situation. In itself this part of the European budget could not help the cyclical stabilization and the absorption of asymmetric shocks, because it is linked to structural needs. However, nothing would prevent the European minister from using it also for stabilization purposes. Directly, even if the horizon of needs remains "structural" and multi-year, the minister would have some flexibility in the management of the budget in the short term. There would be nothing to prevent or delay spending allocated to a certain region/country according to the cycle, while ensuring long-term coherence at the aggregate level. More indirectly, by centralizing part of the investment expenditure at the global level, the Eurozone budget would free up resources for member countries, which could be used for social protection and the cyclical stabilization of each country. A similar idea was put forward by Martin Sandbu (2018) regarding the use of the European Union budget, which by its very nature aims to promote the development of certain sectors and the long-term convergence of European economies. Sandbu notes that contributions and payments to the European budget could be indexed to the cyclical conditions of the economy, with a substantial stabilizing effect.

The proposal of adopting an investment strategy to dampen economic shocks contrasts with the proposal of a European unemployment insurance (EUI) scheme as pioneered in the Marjolin's Report (1975) and later relaunched by Dullien (2007). If this scheme had complemented existing domestic unemployment insurance systems during the crisis, the stabilizing effect on GDP and income would have been non-negligible (see e.g. Apparisi de Lannoy and Ragot 2017). However, the studies reviewed by Beer et al. (2014) suggest that EUI would lead to permanent transfers. If EUI had been in place since 1999, the core countries would have been net contributors and peripheral countries net beneficiaries. This result does not only depend on the fact that structural unemployment is higher in the peripheral countries, but also on the differentiated short-term (cyclical) reaction of unemployment to shocks. To remain budget neutral, EUI needs clawbacks (*ex post* additional contributions) or experience ratings (*ex ante* modifications in contributions), hence periodic re-parameterization of the EUI which greatly complicates its operations and may reduce the extent of stabilization.

4 The European Commission's Proposals

On December 6, 2017, the Commission set out its proposals of reform. They highlight a balanced focus on market discipline, with support to structural reforms, and budget integration, with a euro area stabilization function. It must be stressed that the latter element does not modify risk-sharing between the euro area Member States.

The Commission proposes a new instrument to improve the functioning of the euro area. A "reform delivery tool" should financially support Member States in committing to the implementation of structural reforms. The area of reforms is broad, from product and labour markets to public administration reforms. A complementary tool would consist in technical support. According to the Commission's communication of May 2, 2018, the Reform Support Programme would have a budget of €25 billion over the next Multiannual Financial Framework (MFF).

The Commission requires the integration of the fiscal rule on the cyclically adjusted deficit (stemming from the Fiscal Compact of 2012) into EU legal framework. This initiative would unfetter the Commission from the intergovernmental dimension of the Fiscal Compact and permit it to resume control over all the budgetary rules. It also shows its willingness to improve commitment to the rules and their stricter application, although it does not demonstrate that these rules have been effective so far (see Chap. 5).

The Commission is also proposing the transformation of the ESM into a European Monetary Fund (EMF), no doubt also to avoid an intergovernmental mechanism—the ESM—which reduces its power of initiative and control (see e.g. Creel 2018a). The EMF would make adopting a preventive component of budget crises possible. In the future, the establishment of a stabilization function could be attributed to the EMF. This function would be triggered in the case of "large asymmetric shocks". The proposal of the Commission departs from Schaüble's in two respects: first, according to the latter, the EMF would remain inter-governmental (at least in the short run); second, he claims that a European stabilization function is not necessary.

The adoption of a stabilization function at European level that the Commission proposes "would provide the possibility to activate resources rapidly to deal with shocks that cannot be managed at the national level alone". In the Commission's communication of May 2, 2018, this stabilization function is labelled the "European Investment Stabilisation Function" (EISF). While distinct from other existing fiscal instruments, national or European, it retains the usual properties of budget instruments: it must be neutral in the medium-term; and it must not lead to permanent transfers between the euro area Member States. Moreover, it is conditional on former compliance with the EU surveillance framework. Its net payments would be capped at around 1% of euro area GDP.

This proposal raises several remarks. First, the creation of the EISF would help improve resilience of euro area Member States to macroeconomic shocks. Second, it opens discussion on the identification of shocks, like "a large temporary negative deviation from the unemployment or investment trend". However, it does not propose—at this stage—a systematic method to identify these shocks and distinguish between demand and supply shocks (see e.g. Creel 2018b). Third, necessary compliance with the EU surveillance framework is contradictory with the inability of this framework at successfully achieving the EU objectives and at enforcing fiscal rules so far. Moreover, under its current form, the EU budget is balanced and therefore irreconcilable with macroeconomic stabilization of large shocks (which it was not responsible for until then). To be effective, the stabilization function should be associated with a debt capacity over the long run which has not been mentioned so far. The size of the stabilization function is also limited: According to its communication of May 2, 2018, the Commission announced "back-to-back loans under the EU budget of up to €30 billion" for the EISF for the next MFF (2021–2027). Per year, this extra financial support represents less than 0.05% of euro area gross national income. Finally, the preferred way of envisaging the stabilization function by the Commission is via a public investment support rather than a European Unemployment Reinsurance Scheme. The rationale can be traced back to the decline in public investment that follows a negative shock. The stabilization function would then remove the risk of sacrificing public investment on the altar of austerity. Nevertheless, if negative shocks on demand are clearly identified, austerity measures will no longer appear as a panacea after a shock and the slack on public investment will disappear. Moreover, as a stabilization function, automatic stabilizers are certainly more timely than public investment policy to dampen a "large asymmetric shock".

5 What About Macroeconomic Imbalances?

The causal relationship between real divergence across euro area Member States and the European sequel to the global financial crisis (see e.g. Sinn 2014) raised EU initiatives in 2011 with the adoption of the "6-pack" and the establishment of the European Semester to improve policy coordination in the EU beyond fiscal questions.

The "6-pack" adds to the preventive and corrective arms of the SGP, a Macroeconomic Imbalance Procedure (MIP) drawing on indicators related to current account positions, competitiveness and financial stability. The purpose is "to provide an early-warning signalling of potentially harmful macroeconomic imbalances in Member States". The MIP scoreboard resorts to pinpointing the position of countries regarding thresholds, an approach close to the one already used for identifying excessive deficits in the SGP.

Most indicators in the scoreboard are asymmetric. For instance, the current account threshold is set between a surplus of 6% of GDP and a deficit of 4% of GDP. There is no economic rationale for these specific thresholds; and there is no economic rationale as well for introducing an asymmetry in the current account threshold. What makes a deficit above 4% more dangerous to the stability of the euro area than a surplus above 4% (but below 6%)? Yet, a large current account deficit in Portugal might lead to default on its external debt, but a large current account surplus in Finland can mirror a lack of investment opportunities and weak internal demand. Under the current asymmetric thresholds, the risk of default on private debt in Portugal outweighs the risk of deflationary forces in Finland and it takes for granted that the spillovers of the former on the euro area are greater than the latter. This is a disputable statement.

This is certainly even more disputable if differences in the size of countries add to the asymmetry in the thresholds. Change Portugal into Greece and Finland into Germany in the above example. Can one be sure that the spillovers on the euro area of a default on private debt in Greece outweighs deflationary forces in Germany after keeping in mind that a current account deficit of 4% of GDP in Greece amounts to € 7 billion, whereas a current account surplus in Germany of 6% of GDP amounts to € 160 billion?

Other indicators in the scoreboard relating to competitiveness and market shares are even more asymmetric: the burden of responsibility is exclusively borne by deficit/debtor countries. This is notably the case for the net international investment position, which is by construction the accumulation of past current account balances. Because of this bias in signalling only a certain type of imbalances, it is possible to miss the fact that a market share loss by a given euro area country may have as counterpart a market share gain by another one. Therefore, there is a risk of gearing recommendations towards deficit countries and urging them to adjust wage costs downward or to implement restrictive policies. Conversely, it will fail to signal that surplus countries have run competitive disinflation policies. The differences in the size of countries will amplify the asymmetry in the management of macro imbalances. As stressed by De Grauwe (2012), the current governance of macroeconomic imbalances in the euro area enhances the "tyranny" of creditor countries, among which Germany, by far the largest country in the euro area. The result is that the euro area goes on implementing a global disinflationary policy. By only signalling competitiveness losses, the MIP actually misses to signal a coordination problem among euro area countries.

The same remarks hold for indicators of internal imbalances. By considering only the increases in private sector credit flows, the scoreboard only signals Member States facing overheating although weaknesses in internal demand may also be a source of disequilibrium. Macrosurveillance in accordance with the objectives of the EU should not only point out the risks of an excess development in credit and asset prices. For instance, a slowdown in credit flows may signal a situation of credit crunch or weakness in internal demand. It would then be useful to consider a lower limit to the credit flows to the private sector.

Moreover, policy coordination draws on indicators on which Member States do not have full control. While it is conceivable that governments can change at least part of their budget to abide by the SGP, it is just unconceivable that they can change even a part of the current account imbalance in the short term in order to abide by the recommendations following the MIP.

It is certainly very revealing about the current reform agendas of EU countries or institutions that no reform proposal pertains to the MIP.

Reform proposals so far do not address the vulnerabilities of the euro area like diverging competitiveness or boom–bust cycles. On the latter point, Creel (2018b) argues that the threshold on private debt included in the MIP (at 133% of GDP) should be transformed into an *operational* target and complemented with the adoption of a policy tool. This tool could take the form of a specific tax on banks to help limit the risk of a boom in a domestic credit market.

6 Conclusion

The TEU clearly states that the Union's overall "aim is to promote [...] the well-being of its people" (Article 3 (1)) and goes on to specify in paragraph 3 that it shall work, amongst other things, for sustainable development, social progress and improving the quality of the environment. Reforming EMU economic governance should therefore take such primary economic objectives as a point of departure. However, since the 2008 economic and financial crisis, reforms of economic governance in the EU have been decided in an ongoing state of emergency, guided by the principle "whatever it takes to preserve the euro", formulated later on by ECB president Mario Draghi in 2012. Proposals have emphasized crisis prevention and resilience to economic shocks.

Especially now that the immediate pressure for crisis management has eased in parallel to economic recovery, policy makers should pay more attention to the longer-term overall economic objectives while reforming EMU economic governance to foster sustainable well-being and upward convergence.

In the previous sections, we have set out and analysed some of the many proposals to reform the EMU. On the one hand, proposals emphasize economic stability created by disciplining "unsound" policies at the national level, either through markets or intergovernmental institutions; on the other hand, proposals stressing the need for more risk-sharing, solidarity, and policy coordination to foster upward convergence.

The current agenda of reforms in the Eurozone may have a limited impact, for at least four reasons. First, it is not comprehensive enough. Steps to manage macroimbalances symmetrically are absent from mainstream reform agendas. Second, the outcome of these projects is not for tomorrow as the horizon to reach an agreement on the various aspects of reforms (Eurozone budget, EMF, domestic fiscal rules) could extend to 2025. Unfortunately, for the euro area, the status quo could last and macroimbalances and economic fluctuations could remain. This may lead policymakers to continue keeping an eye on the short term rather than on the long term. Third, the margins for manoeuvre embedded in a Eurozone budget (if it were adopted) would remain limited in size to produce a sharp and positive public impetus for investment that would extract the euro area from a stagnation trap. Fourth, the achievement of a more equal Eurozone requires more than the multiplicity of "productivity boards" without clear cooperation tools and a vision of structural reforms that continues to aim for flexibility and competition, even though both have already reached high levels in Europe. To promote growth that cares for the future, the EU should turn away from the recipes of the past (an accounting approach of fiscal policy and market-oriented structural reforms), which have not been helpful for fixing the European crisis. In contrast, EU governments should invest in the future and incentivize innovations via tax and fiscal policies. Last, the contradictions arising in the German government in Spring 2018 will not help choose a path of reform: both in press interviews, the German Chancellor made a step in the direction of the Commission, whereas her Minister of Finance made a step aside. Mrs. Merkel advocated the transformation of the ESM into an EMF (though in her view it should retain its intergovernmental approach), the creation of a new financial incentive for countries to adopt structural reforms and an investment budget as new cohesion funds (with "low double digits billions"). In contrast, Mr. Scholz argued for an EU Unemployment Reinsurance Scheme. If even the German government struggles to reach a consensus, the odds for a comprehensive and effective reform of European governance are slim at best.

Notes

1. Maybe it was best expressed in his speech in Aachen in May 2018: "Europe (…) can no longer function on successive hegemonies. It can only be built on constant solidarity".

2. See W. Schäuble's Non-paper for paving the way towards a Stability Union, available at http://media2.corriere.it/corriere/pdf/2017/non-paper.pdf.
3. Seigniorage income reflects the interests that the central bank earns on the money it lends to banks or the return it receives on the assets it purchases.

References

Aparisi de Lannoy, L., and X. Ragot. 2017. *Une (ré) assurance chômage européenne*. OFCE Policy Brief 28, November 30.

Beer, C., W. Köhler-Töglhofer, and A. Stiglbauer. 2014. A Common European Unemployment Insurance – A Much Debated Route Toward European Fiscal Union. *Monetary Policy & the Economy* 4: 35–52.

Bénassy-Quéré, A., M. Brunnermeier, H. Enderlein, E. Farhi, M. Fratzscher, C. Fuest, P.-O. Gourinchas, P. Martin, J. Pisani-Ferry, H. Rey, I. Schnabel, N. Véron, B. Weder di Mauro, and J. Zettelmeyer. 2018. *Reconciling Risk Sharing with Market Discipline: A Constructive Approach to Euro Area Reform*. CEPR Policy Insight No. 91.

Brunnermeier, M.K., L. Garicano, P.R. Lane, M. Pagano, R. Reis, T. Santos, and D. Vayanos. 2016. The Sovereign-Bank Diabolic Loop and ESBies. *American Economic Review* 106 (5): 508–512.

Corsetti, G., L. Feld, P.R. Lane, L. Reichlin, D. Vayanos, H. Rey, and B. Weder di Mauro. 2015. *A New Start for the Eurozone: Dealing with Debt*. London: CEPR Press.

Corsetti, G., L. Dedola, M. Jarociński, B. Mackowiak, C. Allard, J. Bluedorn, and B. Weder di Mauro. 2017. Business Cycle Stabilisation in the Eurozone: Ways Forward. *VoxEU*, November 15.

Creel, J. 2018a. Le Fonds Monétaire Européen: un instrument plus politique qu'économique. *Revue de l'euro* 52.

———. 2018b. Convergence in EMU: What and How? *In-Depth Analysis*, ECON, European Parliament, May.

De Grauwe, P. 2012. The Governance of a Fragile Eurozone. *Australian Economic Review* 45 (3): 255–268.

Delpla, J., and J. von Weizsäcker. 2010. Bruegel Policy Brief No. 2010/03, Brussels.

Dullien, S. 2007. *Improving Economic Stability: What the Euro Area Can Learn from the United States' Unemployment Insurance*. Working Paper Stiftung Wissenschaft and Politik FG 1, 2007/11.

Manassé, P., and D. Katsikas. 2018. *Economic Crisis and Structural Reforms in Southern Europe*. Routledge Studies in the European Economy. London: Routledge.

Marjolin, R., F. Bobba, H. Bosman, G. Brouwers, L. Camu, B. Clappier, I. Foighel, F. Forte, H. Giersch, P. Lynch, D. MacDougall, H. Markmann, F. Peeters, A. Shonfield, and N. Thysegen. 1975. *Report of the Study Group 'Economic and Monetary Union 1980'*. Brussels: European Commission.

Pâris, P., and C. Wyplosz. 2014. *PADRE: Politically Acceptable Debt Restructuring in the Eurozone*. Geneva Reports on the World Economy, Geneva/London.

Sandbu, M. 2018. Make Do and Mend in the EU. *Financial Times* – Free Lunch, February 5.

Sinn, H.-W. 2014. Austerity, Growth and Inflation: Remarks on the Eurozone's Unresolved Competitiveness Problem. *World Economics* 37 (1): 1–13.

Wyplosz, C. 2017. *A European Monetary Fund?* Paper requested by the European Parliament, PE 602.076, IPOL, EGOV.

Part III

Beyond the Euro: The Futures of Europe

9

Mitigating the Inequality Crisis

Guillaume Allègre

The low growth performance in the European Union (EU) in the last decade has increased concerns regarding income inequality. Since the early 1980s, inequality has been on the rise in most countries and world regions. According to the World Wealth and Income Database, the top 10% pre-tax income share has grown in China from 27.2% in 1980 to 41.4% in 2016, in India from 31.5% to 55.5%, in Northern America from 34.2% to 46.7%, and in Europe from 32.6% to 37.1% (WID. world 2017). Inequality is therefore lower in Europe and has grown less rapidly than in other world regions. Most European countries have also seen a rise in inequality: in Germany, the top 10% pre-tax income share has grown from 31.9% in 1980 to 38.9% in 2011; in France from 31.3% to 35% (2014); in the United Kingdom from 36.9% (1990) to 40% (2014); in Poland from 21.8% (1983) to 39.5% (2015); and in Sweden from 22.8% to 30.6% (2013). The increase in inequality in each of these countries has different explanations. Obviously, Poland went from a planned/socialist economy to a market economy. Sweden, which

G. Allègre (✉)
OFCE, Sciences Po, Paris, France
e-mail: guillaume.allegre@sciencespo.fr

© The Author(s) 2018
J. Creel et al. (eds.), *Report on the State of the European Union*,
https://doi.org/10.1007/978-3-319-98364-6_9

experienced one of the biggest increase in inequality amongst OECD countries, reformed its social-democratic model (through deregulation, privatization and tax cuts on capital and top marginal rates) after a deep economic crisis in the early 1990s; it is however still one of the most equal country in the world. In the United Kingdom, inequality increased greatly in the 1980s following Thatcher's social and economic policies (cut in income tax, deregulation, privatization, reduction of the power of trade unions). In Germany, the increase in inequality has been linked to Hartz reforms: earnings inequality increased following the creation of "mini jobs" in 2003 (Hartz II reforms); unemployment insurance is less generous since Hartz IV in 2005. France is one of the developed countries where the increase in inequality has been the lowest. The differences in the levels and trends in inequality amongst developed countries show that confronted with the same economic environment, different countries have taken different paths.

In the first section, we will discuss the social and economic cost of inequality. The second section concerns the factors explaining the rise of income inequality. In the third section, we show that there is large differences in inequality across EU countries and discuss the different factors explaining this heterogeneity. In the last section, we show that tax competition within the EU could reduce the progressivity of the tax system. In the conclusion, we discuss ways to maintain inequality low in the EU.

1 The Social and Economic Cost of Inequality

If economists rediscover the question of inequality today, it is because they had largely lost interest in it during the last half-century. With the long period of growth following the Second World War, material conditions quickly improved for all. Even with 2% per capita growth per year, 36 years is enough to double the average income of the population. In these conditions, it is not difficult to ensure that everyone has better material conditions than those of his parents, so that the question of inequality becomes less important. Today, most developed economies are experiencing both relatively low growth and growing inequality. As a result, in many countries, middle-class income stagnates or falls. The trickle-down theory, according to which the enrichment of the better off is ultimately beneficial for the less well-off, becomes much less convincing. Conversely, as growth slows and inequality grows, arguments that inequality may even be harmful to growth tend to be more convincing.

For a long time, economists tended to believe in an equity-efficiency trade-off concerning inequality. This line of reasoning was developed by Okun in his 1975 book, *Equality and Efficiency: The Big Tradeoff*. The main argument concerned incentives: inequality increases incentives to work, to invest and to take risks, and thereby increases growth. There is however a growing literature that questions the impact of inequality on growth. There are different channels by which inequality can have a negative impact on growth. The political economy channel has been proposed by Meltzer and Richards (1981): according to the authors, with growing inequalities, voters (in a democratic context) will want more redistribution, and redistribution is supposed to decrease national income. However, empirical analysis tends to reject this channel (Perotti 1996). According to a second channel, inequality produces political instability that threatens property rights (Alesina and Perotti 1996). This threat reduces investment and growth. Also, unequal societies have more difficulties in implementing pro-growth reforms (Rodrick 1999). According to Putnam (2000), inequality reduces social cohesion and therefore reduces the financing of public goods. Anderson et al. (2008) show that it is not inequality per se that reduces the financing of public goods but perceived injustice. Another theoretical channel linking inequality and growth is underinvestment related to imperfections in the capital market. In the presence of imperfect capital markets, the poor invest less when inequalities increase, especially in their education and entrepreneurship but also in their health and that of their children (Galor and Zeira 1993). The fact that the poorest households cannot make profitable investments reduce growth and makes it even more inegalitarian. A last channel goes through savings and investment. Traditionally, it was thought that the better off saved more of their income, therefore higher inequality meant higher savings and higher investment (Kaldor 1957). However, in case of a savings glut, higher inequality could have a negative effect on growth. According to Summers (2014), the increase in inequality increases the risk of secular stagnation. Secular stagnation is defined by the fact that monetary policy is not able to attain the full-employment equilibria: the natural interest rate, at which the desire for savings and the desire for investment are equal at a level with full capacity of the factors of production (full employment, full use of equipment), is negative. Under these conditions, the real interest rate is higher than the natural rate and the consumption is too low to allow the full use of the factors of production. Growth is therefore weaker than its potential. In case of secular stagnation, there is excess savings and a decrease in inequality, if it results in a reduction of savings, then it has a positive impact on growth. Weak aggregate demand resulting from inequality has also been linked to the credit bubble and the financial crisis of 2008. In the United States, the reduction of income of the poorest households due to increasing inequality was offset by unsustainable private borrowing (Stiglitz 2012; Saraceno 2014).

Apart from its impact on growth, recent studies have found other adverse effects of inequality. Corak (2013) shows that countries with more inequality also experience less earnings mobility across generations. The curve showing the relationship between income inequality and intergenerational earnings elasticity in developed countries has been called *The Great Gatsby Curve*. It shows that mobility across generations is highest in Nordic countries (Finland, Norway, Denmark and to a lesser extent Sweden) where income inequality is low and lowest in Anglo-Saxon countries (United Kingdom, United States) where income inequality is relatively high. Fajnzylber et al. (2002) show that crime rates and inequality are positively correlated within and between countries and that the correlation reflects causation from inequality to crime rates, even after controlling for other crime determinants. In *The Price of Inequality*, Stiglitz (2012) devotes a chapter on how inequality harms the democratic process. There is of course an American bias: the impact of inequality surely depends on how political parties and elections are financed (publicly or privately). However, some of the conclusions might hold for Europe: Schäfer (2013) shows that in Europe, people are less satisfied with the way democracy works in countries with greater income inequality and that citizens in these countries trust politicians and parliaments less.

2 Why Did Income Inequality Rise in Developed Countries?

As we have seen in the introduction, rising inequality can be due to different factors depending on the country. However, it is not a coincidence if inequality rose in most developed countries: countries might have reacted differently policy wise—and hence inequality did not rise at the same rate in different countries—but they were confronted to the same forces. Two forces have been highlighted: technological change and globalization.

The impact of technological change is the more consensual: economic theory and empirical studies in the mid-decade of the 2000s have shown that technological change is skilled-biased (it favours skilled over unskilled labour) and thus increases inequality (everything else being equal). However, everything else is not equal: Goldin and Katz (2008) have shown that there is a race between education and technology: Education can raise the skill level of the workforce and therefore the supply of skilled labour. If the supply of skilled labour increases as fast as the demand, the skill premium does not increase. In the United States, until the 1980s, the supply of college graduates rose rapidly, but this rise stopped in the 1980s. Whereas the United States had an educational leadership over other developed economies (including Western European countries) until the 1980s, it has lost this leadership since then: the number of college graduates rose more rapidly in the rest of the developed countries, which might explain why inequalities rose more rapidly in the United States than in Western Europe. More recent empirical studies have shown that skilled-biased technological change has been replaced by routine-biased technological change: the tasks replaced by automation are the routine tasks that are currently performed by medium skill workers. This has led to wage and employment polarization: the share of intermediate jobs is declining sharply in favour of an increase in both low-skilled and high-skilled jobs. This polarization concerns European countries as well as the United States. The policy implications of polarization are not as straightforward as for skilled-biased technological change (for which the obvious implication was to increase the skill of the workforce): should we qualify the low-skilled if medium-skilled jobs are getting scarcer?

Does globalization increase wage inequality in developed countries? Theoretically, developed countries are supposed to specialize in skill-intensive goods and services and import goods and services produced by low-skilled workers, which should increase wage inequality. For a long time, economists have minimized the impact of trade on wage inequality in developed countries. In the 1990s, the consensus was that the impact of trade was modest. This is the conclusion of a 1995 Krugman article. The reason was that trade was mostly intra-trade where similar countries export and import similar products: in 1992, 64% of British imports and exports were with other European nations. In the United States, the effect of trade with developing countries on skilled-unskilled wage ratio was estimated at 3 percentage points. However, in 2007, Krugman reconsidered his position on the impact of trade. The US imports of manufactures from developing countries surpassed imports from developed countries, consequently, the average hourly wage of US trading partners dropped from 81% of US average in 1990 to 65% in 2005. The entry of China in the World Trade Organization had a big impact on the composition of trade. A more recent paper by Autor et al. (2013) analyses the effect of rising Chinese import on US labour market. It concludes that Chinese import competition alone explains 33% of the US manufacturing employment reduced US manufacturing employment by 548,000 workers between 1990 and 2000 and 982,000 workers between 2000 and 2007. It therefore explains 16% of the US manufacturing employment decline between 1990 and 2000 and 26% of the decline between 2000 and 2007. A similar study has been conducted in France. The estimation is that 13% of manufacturing employment decline in France from 2001 to 2007 is due to Chinese imports (Malgouyres 2018): over this period, 90,000 manufacturing jobs and 190,000 jobs in total have been destroyed by Chinese import competition.

Other factors have been put forward to explain the rise of inequality in advanced economies, notably the decline of trade union membership and the weakening of employment protection. The OECD (2011) calculated the contribution of globalization, technological advancement and changes in polices and institutions (trade union density, employment protection, tax wedge and unemployment benefits) to the overall rise in inequality between the early 1980s and the late 2000s. During this period, the D9/D1 ratio of wage dispersion grew on average by 0.47% annually. According to OECD estimations, technology's contribution was 0.32%, institutions 0.42, education 0.50 (according to this study, education has therefore won the race against technology) and the impact of trade globalization was not significant (like the IMF, the OECD still minimizes the role of globalization). However, such decomposition has many limits, notably it does not take into account the fact that the different factors are interrelated. Globalization and technology have negatively impacted the employment in the manufacturing sector which explains partly why trade union membership has declined. Likewise, institutions might have reacted to the trade and technology environment.

3 Unequal Inequalities in the EU

3.1 Within-Country Inequality in the EU

Figure 9.1 shows within-countries inequality as measured by the Gini of equivalent disposable income (after-transfers) and the Gini of equivalent before social transfers income (mostly household wage and pensions). Social transfers include unemployment benefits, family allowances, housing allowances and social exclusion benefits. An equivalence scale is used to take into account economies of scale in the household and lesser needs of children.[1]

The figure shows that three Central European countries (Slovakia, Slovenia and Czech Republic) have very low income inequality. What is striking is that other former communist countries have very high income inequality, notably Bulgaria and Romania. The difference does not come from transfers but from before transfers income: in Slovakia and the Czech Republic, wage inequality has been kept relatively low (although obviously higher than during communism), while wage inequality is high in Bulgaria and Romania. The divergence in wage inequality of Eastern European countries is not well explained by the literature. In a cross-country

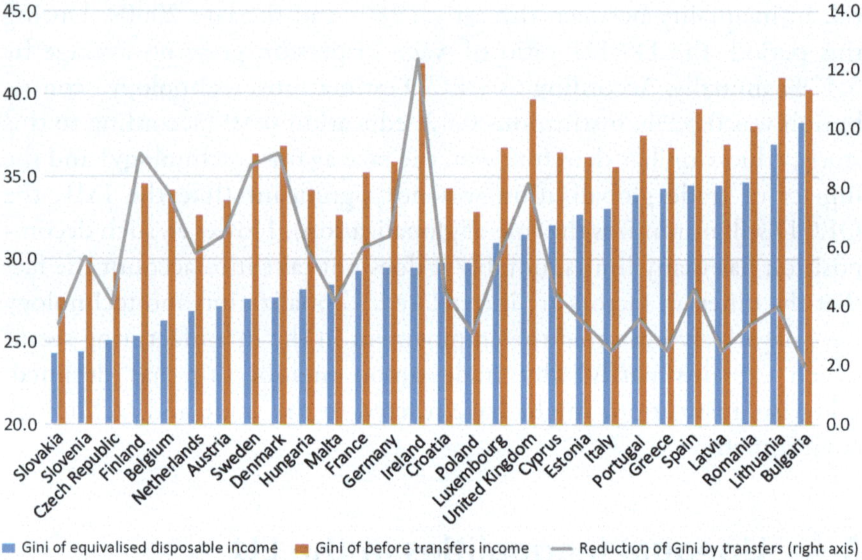

Fig. 9.1 Gini of disposable income and of before transfers income, 2016. (Source: Eurostat)

perspective, Milanovic and Ersado (2012) show that large-scale privatization and infrastructure reforms were significantly pro-inequality, whereas small-scale privatization and democracy are pro-poor.

Following the liberal welfare regime (Esping-Andersen 1990), Anglo-Saxon countries (United Kingdom, Ireland) have very high wages inequality but reduce inequality by targeted transfers. Ireland is the European country that has the largest before social-transfers income inequality, but it is also the country that reduces inequality with social transfers the most.

Nordic social-democratic countries (Finland, Sweden and Denmark) also enjoy low levels of inequality. This is due in large part to high levels of redistribution: as the figure shows, transfers reduce inequality by a large amount in these three countries.

In Southern countries (Italy, Portugal, Greece and Spain), before transfers inequality is not much higher than in Nordic countries, but the reduction of inequality by social transfers is very weak. Consequently, disposable income inequality is relatively high.

Continental countries (Belgium, Netherlands, France and Germany) have low to moderate levels of inequality: in these countries, wages inequality tends to be lower than average and transfers tend to reduce inequality more than average.

How can we explain differences in before-transfer inequality? Jaumotte and Buitron (2015) investigate the link between inequality and labour market institutions in advanced economies. In line with prior literature (e.g. Card et al. 2004), the authors find that the weakening of unions contributed to the rise of inequality. They also find a strong cross-country link among OECD countries between union density and top earners' income shares. Financial deregulation and the growth of the financial sector is also found to be a contributor to the rise of inequality, also in line with prior literature (Philippon and Reshef 2013). The authors also find that reductions in the minimum wage relative to the median wage are related to significant increases in inequality. This point is more controversial, since minimum wages theoretically have an ambiguous effect on inequality: on one hand, minimum wages compress wages at the bottom of the distribution; but on the other hand, a higher minimum wage might raise unemployment. Dreger et al. (2015) review the link between wage dispersion and labour market institutions in a cross-country perspective in the EU. They also find that higher levels of inequality are present in countries with less unionization and lower minimum wages relative to median wages. Moreover, government intervention in wage bargaining and coordination of wage setting are linked to lower inequalities. A number of studies have indeed found that the distribution of wages is more compressed in countries with more centralized wage-bargaining systems (Blau and Kahn 1996; OECD 1997). Centralization seems to facilitate the reduction of interfirm and intersectoral wage differentials, since more firms are included in the process (Rueda and Pontusson 2000).

Table 9.1 shows the calculation of a "full-time equivalent non-employment rate". This indicator was proposed by Duval (2017) as an alternative to unemployment rates. The indicator is a better representation of the inclusiveness of the labour market. Unlike the unemployment rate, it takes into account inactivity (and especially women's inactivity), part-time employment (and especially women's part-time employment)

Table 9.1 Full-time equivalent non-employment rate, 25–59-year-olds

	Non-employment (A)	*Female non-employment*	Part-time (% employment) (B)	*Female Part-time*	Length of part-time / full-time* (C)	Full-time equivalent non-employment (D**)
Czech Republic	15%	*22%*	5%	*9%*	50%	17%
Lithuania	18%	*18%*	6%	*8%*	52%	21%
Hungary	19%	*25%*	4%	*6%*	54%	21%
Estonia	19%	*23%*	8%	*11%*	51%	22%
Slovenia	20%	*23%*	7%	*10%*	50%	23%
Slovakia	21%	*27%*	5%	*7%*	46%	23%
Sweden	14%	*17%*	20%	*31%*	58%	24%
Denmark	18%	*22%*	18%	*28%*	46%	24%
Poland	22%	*28%*	5%	*8%*	51%	25%
Latvia	22%	*23%*	7%	*10%*	51%	25%
Finland	21%	*23%*	11%	*15%*	47%	25%
Portugal	22%	*25%*	8%	*11%*	41%	25%
Bulgaria	25%	*28%*	2%	*2%*	48%	25%
United Kingdom	18%	*24%*	22%	*39%*	45%	27%
Germany	17%	*21%*	26%	*48%*	46%	27%
Romania	25%	*34%*	6%	*6%*	58%	28%
Luxembourg	21%	*27%*	18%	*35%*	54%	28%
Malta	24%	*40%*	12%	*26%*	54%	29%
France	22%	*26%*	17%	*29%*	56%	29%
Cyprus	25%	*30%*	12%	*14%*	45%	29%
European Union	**23%**	***29%***	**18%**	***31%***	**49%**	**29%**
Austria	19%	*22%*	28%	*49%*	48%	30%
Euro area	**24%**	***30%***	**20%**	***35%***	**49%**	**31%**
Ireland	26%	*32%*	19%	*30%*	48%	33%
Croatia	31%	*36%*	5%	*6%*	48%	33%
Belgium	23%	*28%*	24%	*42%*	58%	34%
Spain	30%	*36%*	14%	*23%*	46%	35%
Netherlands	19%	*24%*	44%	*74%*	49%	36%
Italy	32%	*43%*	18%	*33%*	53%	39%
Greece	37%	*47%*	9%	*13%*	46%	39%

Source: Eurostat
*All ages
**D = A + (1 – A)* B* (1 – C)

and the length of part-time employment. The indicator is calculated on the 25–59-year-olds because youth and senior non-employment can be due to respectively longer education and earlier retirement. Table 9.1 shows that Eastern European and Nordic countries tend to have low levels of full-time equivalent non-employment rates due to high level of female employment and low levels of female part-time employment. On the other hand, southern European countries (Spain, Italy and Greece) have high levels of non-employment. This indicator is correlated (also not perfectly) to the Gini of before transfers disposable income: high inclusiveness on the labour market tends to reduce inequality of before transfers (household) income.

3.2 Between-Country Inequality in the European Union: Convergence Limited to the Lowest-Income Countries

We have discussed so far within-country inequality. However, inequality between countries is also relevant. Figure 9.2 shows the growth of real GDP per capita between 2001 and 2017 according to initial GDP per capita (2001) across EU members. The figure shows that real convergence has taken place among the 28 EU members: countries with low initial GDP have grown more rapidly than countries with higher initial GDP. Lithuania, Latvia, Romania and Bulgaria have recorded the highest degree of convergence. In fact, convergence is mainly limited to Eastern European countries with the lowest GDP per capita in 2001. For high-income countries (above 15,000 euros of per capita GDP), there is no convergence: on the contrary, there is even a form of divergence. Portugal and Greece, for example have had lower growth than higher income economies like Germany or the Netherlands. Consequently, no convergence has taken place for the 12 countries that had adopted the euro in 2001. This

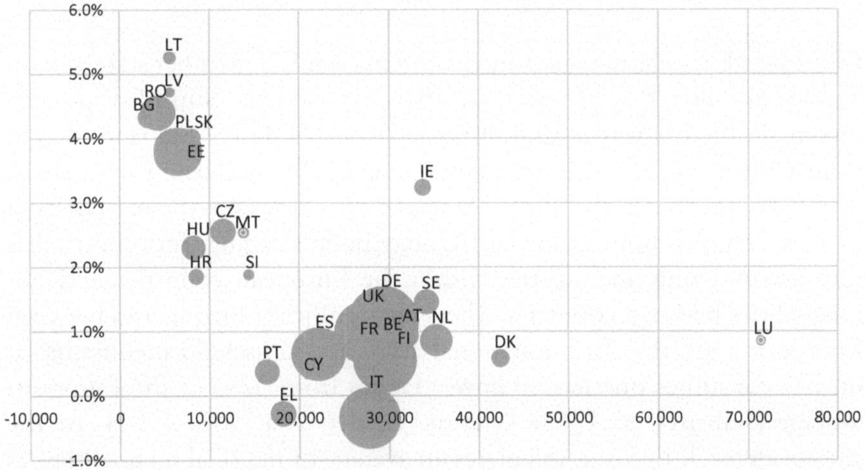

Fig. 9.2 Growth of GDP (2001–2017) according to initial GDP (2001) in the EU. (Source: Eurostat)

is contrary to the expectation that deeper monetary and financial integration would trigger faster real convergence. Diaz del Hoyo et al. (2017) explain that several countries in the euro area (including Spain, Portugal and Greece) experienced temporary GDP convergence until the global economic crisis in 2008 when accumulated external and domestic imbalances led to a painful economic adjustment. This was the case according to the authors because the large capital inflows prior to the crisis did not set in motion a process of sustainable convergence: capital inflows consisted mainly of investment in debt instrument (including government debt), which, contrary to foreign direct investment, was not conducive to supporting productivity growth but contributed to a credit-driven domestic demand boom. This led to an overestimation of growth potential and pro-cyclical fiscal policy. Also, unit labour costs increased relatively to the core Euro countries which led to large current account deficits. With the economic crisis of 2008, fiscal revenues dropped, which led to an increase of public debt and later a public debt crisis. Competitiveness was to be restored through deflation which caused a double-dip recession.

3.3 Global Inequality in the EU

Every year Eurostat measures inequality in each EU member state and on average amongst the 28 states. In 2016, the average Gini of disposable income in the EU was at 30.8. It ranged from 24.3 in Slovakia to 38.3 in Bulgaria (see Fig. 9.1). Measured on average, it lies well below the Gini of disposable income in the United States (39.0). However, the presentation of an average Gini index in the EU may be misleading. Indeed, it takes into account only inequalities within the European countries and not inequalities between countries. There are significant inequalities between European countries. In the national accounts, household income based on EU consumer purchasing power ranges from 37% of the European average (Bulgaria) to 138% (Germany), that is a ratio of 1–4. At the European level, Eurostat calculates an average of national inequalities, as well as the international inequalities. On the other hand, Eurostat does not calculate inequalities between European citizens: what would inequality be if national barriers were eliminated and European inequality was calculated at the European level in the same way that one calculates inequality within each nation? It might seem legitimate to calculate inequality between European citizens like this insofar as the EU constitutes a political community with its own institutions (Parliament, executive, etc.). In the preamble to the treaty establishing the European Economic Community, the Heads of State and Government declare that they are "resolved to ensure the economic and social progress of their countries by common action to eliminate the barriers which divide Europe". Calculating inequality amongst European citizens is a way to eliminate these barriers.

The EU-SILC database, which provides the equivalent disposable income (in purchasing power parity) of a representative sample of households in each European country makes such a calculation possible. The result is that the overall level of inequality in 2014 in the EU is the same as that in the United States (39.0). What conclusion should be drawn? If we look at the glass as half-empty, we could emphasize that European inequality is at the same level as in the world's most unequal developed country. If we look at the glass as half-full, we could emphasize that the EU does not constitute a nation with social and fiscal transfers, that it has recently expanded to include much poorer countries and that, nevertheless, inequality is no greater than in the United States.

4 The Future of Inequality in the EU: Towards Less Progressive Taxation?

As we have seen in Fig. 9.1, the tax-benefit system contributes to reducing within-country inequality in the EU. However, there is a trend towards less progressivity in taxation. Figure 9.3 shows the average standard VAT rate, and average, minimum and maximum corporate income tax (CIT) statutory rates and personal income tax (PIT) top marginal rate in the EU. There is a clear trend of decreasing tax rates for both the corporate and the PIT, while the standard VAT rate is increasing. Mobile tax bases (corporate income and top personal income) are therefore taxed less while immobile tax bases are taxed more.

Several studies have shown that part of the tax base of the CIT is mobile: multinationals have several income-shifting strategies in order to

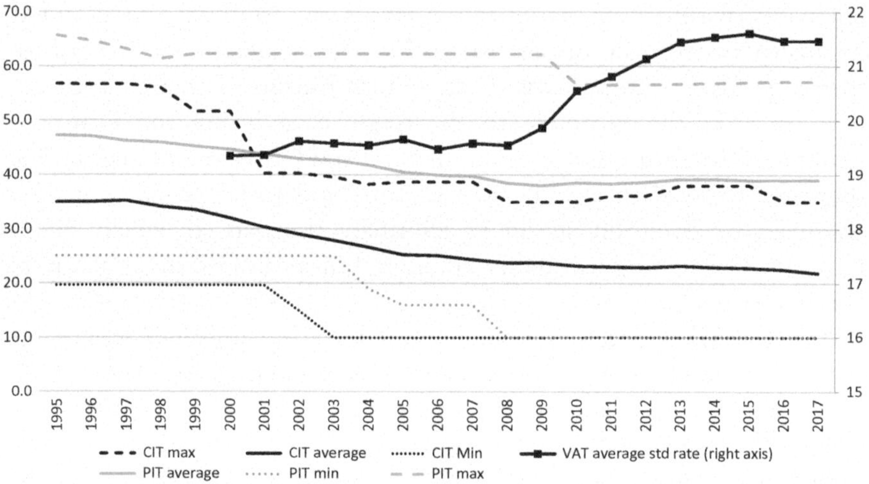

Fig. 9.3 VAT average standard rate, CIT statutory rate and PIT average, minimum and top marginal rate in EU (28 members as of 2017), 1995–2017. (Source: European Commission)

decrease the tax base of their subsidiary in high-tax-rate countries and increase the tax base in low-tax-rate countries. They can use transfer pricing, leverage, mismatches in tax jurisdiction in bi-lateral treaties in order to attain double non-taxation. However, the decrease in statutory rates has not translated into a decrease in corporate income taxation in percentage of GDP. According to Piotrowska and Vanborren (2008), the driving factor for these diverging trends is corporatization: as CIT rates declined, the size of the corporate sector increased. There has been a shifting in income from the non-corporate form to the corporate form, and therefore from personal to CIT, due to the decrease in CIT rates. This should decrease the progressivity of the tax system.

The decrease in the PIT top marginal rate is not as pronounced as the decrease in the CIT rate. The decrease happened in the pre-crisis period: since 2008, average rates slightly increased. Tax competition is less fierce over the PIT, since individuals are less mobile than corporate income.

In response to the debt crisis, many countries have raised their standard VAT rates: while the average standard rate across the EU was 19.5% in 2008, it increased to 21.5% in 2017.

Overall, these trends lead to less progressive taxation. If the EU wants to keep its level of inequality low, it therefore needs to respond to this development. Tax sovereignty should not lead to a situation where nation-states are led to tax only the immobile tax bases.

5 Conclusion: Keeping Inequalities Low in the EU

The EU is the region in the world with the lowest economic inequalities, despite some heterogeneity. Member countries with the lowest inequalities achieve it with different strategies: high tax and benefit redistribution or low wage inequality through high minimum wages, collective bargaining and/or investment in education.

If inequalities are to be kept low in the EU, through redistribution and investment in education, countries need to be able to raise taxes. Therefore, there needs to be some form of tax harmonization on the most mobile bases, notably corporate tax. Through its current common corporate tax base proposal, the European Commission is proposing a set of common rules for determining the tax base of companies. However, this is insufficient, as it would not stop tax competition within the EU: a minimum rate must be put in place in order to stop the race to the bottom.

Competition within the EU is not limited to taxation: some countries are pursuing uncooperative low wage growth strategies, either by choice, or in order to reduce macroimbalances. This leads to increased inequality (and deflation pressures in the euro area). This can be answered through a coordination of national wage policies or a generalization of minimum wages in all countries (e.g. at 50% of median wage).

Note

1. The equivalised household size is defined as HS = 1 + 0.5* (HM14plus − 1) + 0.3* HM013 where HM14plus is the number of household members aged 14 and over and HM013 is the number of members aged 13 or less. Total disposable income is divided by the equivalised household size to compute equivalent disposable income.

References

Alesina, Alberto, and Roberto Perotti. 1996. Income Distribution, Political Instability, and Investment. *European Economic Review* 40 (6): 1203–1228.

Anderson, Lisa, Jennifer Mellor, and Jeffrey Milyo. 2008. Inequality and Public Good Provision: An Experimental Analysis. *The Journal of Socio-Economics* 37 (3): 1010–1028.

Autor, David, David Dorn, and Gordon Hanson. 2013. The China Syndrome: Local Labor Market Effects of Import Competition in the United States. *American Economic Review* 103 (6): 2121–2168.

Blau, Francine, and Lawrence Kahn. 1996. International Difference in Male Wage Inequality. *Journal of Political Economy* 104 (4): 791–837.

Card, David, Thomas Lemieux, and Craig Riddell. 2004. Unions and Wage Inequality. *Journal of Labor Research* 25 (4): 519–559.

Corak, Miles. 2013. Income Inequality, Equality of Opportunity, and Intergenerational Mobility. *Journal of Economic Perspectives* 27 (3): 79–102.

Diaz del Hoyo, Juan-Luis, Ettore Dorrucci, Frigyes Ferdinand Heinz, and Sona Muzikarova. 2017. *Real Convergence in the Euro Area: A Long-Term Perspective*. European Central Bank Occasional Paper Series, No. 203.

Dreger, Christian., Enrique López-Bazo, Raul Ramos, Vicente Royuela, Jordi Suriñach. 2015. Wage and Income Inequality in the European Union. Policy Department Working Paper 282015.

Duval, Guillaume. 2017. Alternatives Economiques lance son contre-indicateur du chômage. *Alternatives économiques*, Septembre.

Esping-Andersen, Gosta. 1990. *The Three Worlds of Welfare Capitalism*. Princeton: Princeton University Press.

Fajnzylber, Pablo, Daniel Lederman, and Norman Loayza. 2002. What Causes Violent Crime? *European Economic Review* 46: 1323–1357.

Galor, Oded, and Joseph Zeira. 1993. Income Distribution and Macroeconomics. *Review of Economic Studies* 60 (1): 35–52.

Goldin, Claudia, and Lawrence F. Katz. 2008. *The Race Between Education and Technology*. Cambridge, MA: Harvard University Press.

Jaumotte, Florence, and Carolina Osorio Buitron. 2015. *Inequality and Labor Market Institutions*. IMF Staff Discussion Note 15/14. Washington, DC: IMF.

Kaldor, Nicholas. 1957. A Model of Economic Growth. *The Economic Journal* 67 (268): 591.

Malgouyres, Clément. 2018. The Impact of Chinese Import Competition on the Local Structure of Employment and Wages in France. *Rue de la Banque* 57. Paris: Banque de France.

Meltzer, Allan H., and Scott F. Richard. 1981. A Rational Theory of the Size of Government. *Journal of Political Economy* 89 (5): 914–927.

Milanovic, Branko, and Lire Ersado. 2012. Reform and Inequality During the Transition: An Analysis Using Panel Household Survey Data, 1990–2005. In *Economies in Transition, The Long-Run View*, ed. Gerard Roland, Studies in Development Economics and Policy. Basingstoke: Palgrave Macmillan.

OECD. 1997. Economic Performance and the Structure of Collective Bargaining. *Employment Outlook*, July. Paris: OECD Publishing.

———. 2011. *Divided We Stand: Why Inequality Keeps Rising*. Paris: OECD Publishing.

Okun, Arthur. 1975. *Equality and Efficiency: The Big Tradeoff*. Washington, DC: Brookings Institution Press.

Perotti, Roberto. 1996. Growth, Income Distribution, and Democracy: What the Data Say. *Journal of Economic Growth* 1 (2): 149–187.

Philippon, Thomas, and Ariell Reshef. 2013. An International Look at the Growth of Modern Finance. *The Journal of Economic Perspectives* 27 (2): 73–96.

Piotrowska, Joanna, and Werner Vanborren. 2008. The Corporate Income Tax Rate-Revenue Paradox: Evidence in the EU. *Taxation Papers*, Working Paper No. 12, European Commission.

Putnam, Robert. 2000. *Bowling Alone: The Collapse and Renewal of American Community*. New York: Simon and Schuster.

Rodrick, Dani. 1999. Where Did All the Growth Go? External Shocks, Social Conflict, and Growth Collapses. *Journal of Economic Growth* 4: 385–412.

Rueda, David, and Jonas Pontusson. 2000. Wage Inequality and Varieties of Capitalism. *World Politics* 52: 350–383.

Saraceno, Francesco. 2014. L'impact économique des fortes inégalités : problèmes et solutions. *Revue de l'OFCE* 134: 187–200.

Schäfer, Armin. 2013. Affluence, Inequality and Satisfaction with Democracy. In *Society and Democracy in Europe*, ed. Silke I. Keil and Oscar W. Gabriel. London: Routledge.

Stiglitz, Joseph E. 2012. *The Price of Inequality: How Today's Divided Society Endangers Our Future*. New York: W. W. Norton & Company.

Summers, Larry. 2014. U.S. Economic Prospects: Secular Stagnation, Hysteresis, and the Zero Lower Bound. *Business Economics* 49 (2): 65–73.

WID.world. 2017. *World Inequality Database*. http://wid.world/.

10

A Dynamic Towards Gender Equality? Participation and Employment in European Labour Markets

Hélène Périvier and Grégory Verdugo

In most European countries, female participation in the labour force increased dramatically over the last decades. Nevertheless, even if it varies across countries, the gender gap in participation remains large. Beside these trends, the most recent business cycles affected differently female and male employment and the gendered impact of the great recession is now well documented in the literature (Eydoux et al. 2014; Karamessini and Rubery 2013). In this chapter, we describe the evolution of the European labour markets with a gender perspective, studying 11 core Eurozone countries plus the United Kingdom and Sweden.[1] We analyse the trends in two major indicators, participation and employment rate,

H. Périvier (✉)
OFCE, Sciences Po, Paris, France

PRESAGE, Sciences Po, Paris, France
e-mail: helene.perivier@sciencespo.fr

G. Verdugo
OFCE, Sciences Po, Paris, France

Université d'Evry, Évry, France

© The Author(s) 2018

J. Creel et al. (eds.), *Report on the State of the European Union*,
https://doi.org/10.1007/978-3-319-98364-6_10

considering the type of gender regime that characterized each country. For each indicator, we distinguish the structural evolutions from the cyclical dynamic explained by the crisis.

In the first section, we analyse the participation of women and men and document the evolution of labour supply by gender. The increase in female participation in European countries is a long-term process driven by many factors. In addition to the willingness of women to be economically emancipated, public policies that improve the work life balance contributed significantly to these evolutions. The increase in the access of women to education, in particular, higher education, is also an important explanation for the narrowing gender gap in participation rate. In the recent decade, Europe has been characterized by a large increase in graduations rates from university and college, notably in South Europe, and particularly so for women. Since educated women are more likely to participate in the labour force, the expansion of higher education has contributed to the rise in the labour force participation rate (LFPR) in Europe. Beside these structural changes, the business cycle can explain part of the evolution of gender gap in LFPR and employment, as it is not gender neutral (Rubery 1988). Focusing on the 2007 great recession, we shed light on the mechanism that can explain gender difference in terms of participation.

In the second section, we focus on the evolution of employment rates. We present the role of the European Union's (EU's) gender equality framework and discuss how it affected the employment policies implemented in European countries. Even though gender gap in employment rate has been narrowed in most of countries that we consider, female part-time employment plays a key role in explaining the persistence of gender inequalities, especially regarding the gender wage gap. We analyse the evolution of employment during the crisis and the austerity phase and show that the consequences are different for men and women. We discuss how the EU attempted to monitor the increase in female involvement on the labour market and the decrease in the gender gap. By focusing on employment rate without considering part-time employment, the European Employment Strategy (EES) has limited the achievement in terms of gender equality, especially for countries with a high share of women working part-time. The H2020 framework contains no gender targets. Overall, the momentum in the European Commission behind regular gender analysis of core employment trends has declined (Fagan and Rubery 2018).

1 Gender Gap in the Participation and Gender Regime

1.1 The Long-Term Trends in Participation: The Role of Women's Education

The specific interrelation between the type of welfare state and the sexual division of labour defines the type of "gender regime" (Lewis 1992, 2002). The female participation in the labour market and the gender gap in participation are two indicators to describe the type of gender regime each country can be associated to. Analysing the evolution of these indicators is a first step to characterize the change in gender regime. Graph 10.1 gives the long-term evolution of the gender gap in participation rate for persons aged from 15 to 64 years. In Sweden and Finland, the

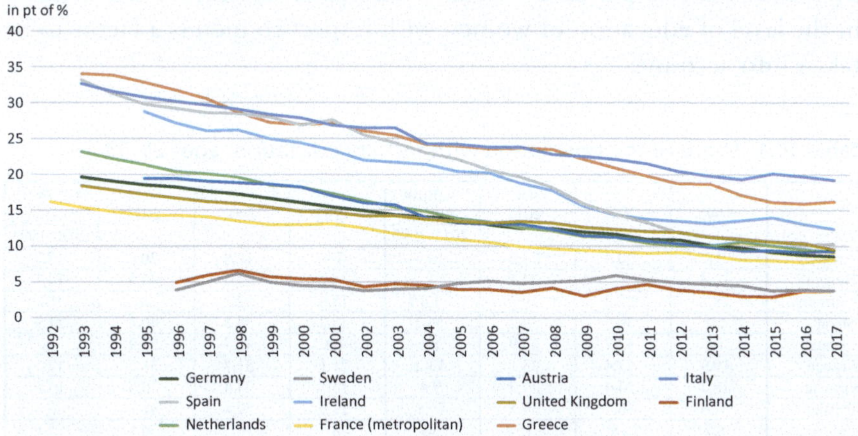

Graph 10.1 Evolution of the gender gap in participation rates in a panel of European countries (15–64 years). (Source: Eurostat, Employment and activity by sex and age—annual data [lfsi_emp_a])

gap is low and stabilized below 5 points of percentage. The group of countries that includes France, Germany, the United Kingdom, the Netherlands and Austria are characterized by a gender gap between 8 and 10 points of percentage at the end of the period. Italy and Greece have the highest gender gap of 19 and 16 percentage points in 2017, respectively. Spain and Ireland have both experienced a dramatic decrease in the gender gap during the 2000 decades: in Spain (respectively in Ireland) the gap went from around 15 points (25 points) at the end of the 1990s to 8 points (12 points) in 2017. The evolution of these gender regimes has been driven both by societal changes and by the economic growth those countries have experienced before the Great Recession. These trends indicate that in most countries under review, female labour force participation has risen and women can no longer be considered secondary earners, at least in terms of labour market participation. The implementation of public policies to work life balance and the development of childcare and the subsidies to cover the cost of childcare for parents have plaid a key role to strengthen the position of women on the labour market (Akgunduz and Plantenga 2015; Brilli et al. 2016; Vuri 2016). Even though women are still performing a large part of family and domestic tasks, part of the care work is externalized outside the family. Beside the role played by the institutional environment, the increase in the level of education of women with respect to men is a factor to be taken into account.

Table 10.1 Share of the population with tertiary education, ages 25–54

	1995	2007	2013	% point change 2013-1995	1995	2007	2013	% point change 2013-1995
Austria	9,8	20,6	23,2	13,4	7,9	16,4	20,6	12,7
Belgium	26,4	32	34,4	8	28,2	37,7	42,5	14,3
Germany	28,8	27,2	30,2	1,4	18,6	22,2	28	9,4
Spain	20	30,5	34,2	14,2	18,2	34,3	40,1	21,9
Finland	na	32,2	35,9	na	na	46,3	51,9	na
France	19,9	27,4	33,1	13,2	21,1	31,7	38,6	17,5
Greece	18,7	24,4	27,9	9,2	15,1	24,4	30,6	15,5
Ireland	22,4	30,7	39,5	17,1	21,3	37,8	48,1	26,8
Italy	8,7	13	15	6,3	8	16,5	20,1	12,1
Netherlands	na	32,7	34,8	na	na	31,1	35,6	na
Portugal	10,9	11,8	16,7	5,8	14,6	18,6	26,3	11,7
UK	25	32,9	39,4	14,4	21,8	33,8	43	21,2

Sources: EU-LFS and CPS for the United States. Authors' computations

We explore the specific role played by the increase in women's education in the dynamic of their participation in the labour market. The levels of education in the last decades have increased rapidly in Europe, in particular for women. The consequences of this education expansion on the wage structure have been analysed for Spain (Carrasco et al. 2015) and France (Verdugo 2014). Table 10.1 illustrates the increase in the level of education is more marked for women than for men: the share of women with tertiary education has grown more than the share of men between 1995 and 2013. As the LFPR of women depends strongly on the education level, this dramatic increase in education could explain part of the increase in female participation rate in Europe.

To assess the role of education, we report in Table 10.2 the results of regressions of the LFPR in 1995, in 2005, and 2013 for people aged 25–54. In column 1, we regress the LFPR on a constant and a dummy variable for 2005 for the 1995–2005 period and respectively a dummy variable for 2013 for the 2005–2013 period. By definition, the dummy captures how the LFPR changed respectively between 1995 and 2005 and between 2005 with respect to 2013. To assess how controlling for education affects this change, we add three education dummies to the regression in column (2) which implies that changes captured by the time dummy in this specification are net of the effect of education.[2] In column (1)–(2), we report the difference between the two parameters that indicates how the growth in education contributed to the increase in the LFPR for the two periods under review. The 1995–2005 period illustrates the general trend in LFPR and the role of education, whereas the 2005–2013 period describe the trend during the crises.

The results show that the contribution of education to the evolution of the LFPR for men is negligible during the two periods under review (less than 2 percentage point in most countries except in Sweden between 1995 and 2005). In contrast, the increase in education explains more than 5 percentage points of the dynamic of LFPR of female between 1995 and 2005 in Spain, Ireland and Italy. The contribution of the growth of female education to their LFPR is of 3.6 percentage points in Greece, Sweden and the UK. During the following period the (2005–2013), the contribution is lower (except in Ireland). The increase in the level of education is not the only factor explaining the trend in participa-

Table 10.2 Contribution of education to the evolution of the labour force participation rate between 1995 and 2005, and between 2005 and for prime age workers, by sex

	Women						Men					
	1995–2005			2005–2013			1995–2005			2005–2013		
	Observed (1)	Adjusted (2)	Contribution of education to the evolution of the LFPR (1)–(2)	Observed (1)	Adjusted (2)	Contribution of education to the evolution of the LFPR (1)–(2)	Observed (1)	Adjusted (2)	Contribution of education to the evolution of the LFPR (1)–(2)	Observed (1)	Adjusted (2)	Contribution of education to the evolution of the LFPR (1)–(2)
Austria	7.8	5.1	2.7	6	5.3	0.7	−0.2	−1	0.8	−0.3	−0.6	0.3
Belgium	8.3	4.3	4	3.1	0.7	2.4	0.1	−0.8	0.9	−1.3	−1.9	0.6
Germany	5.5	4.5	1	3.1	2.2	0.9	0.5	0.4	0.1	−0.7	−0.8	0.1
Spain	12.3	6.1	6.2	12.9	10.1	2.8	−0.4	−1	0.6	−0.4	−0.6	0.2
Finland	3	0.8	2.2	−0.6	−1.6	1	2.4	1.3	1.1	0.9	0.2	0.7
France	3.2	1.6	1.6	2.9	1.1	1.8	−1.2	−1.4	0.2	−1	−1	0
Greece	12.9	9.3	3.6	6.3	4.1	2.2	0.1	−0.1	0.2	−1.3	−1.4	0.1
Ireland	15.1	9.1	6	3.9	−1.3	5.2	1.7	−0.2	1.9	−2.6	−4	1.4
Italy	8.7	3.7	5	3.6	1.1	2.5	0.7	0.5	0.2	−2.4	−2.7	0.3
Portugal	7	6	1	4.7	1.9	2.8	−0.9	−0.9	0	−2	−2.3	0.3
Sweden	−0.5	−4.1	3.6	0.7	0.5	0.2	0	−2.4	2.4	−0.3	−0.4	0.1
United Kingdom	3.5	−0.1	3.6	1.6	−1.2	2.8	−1.6	−2.9	1.3	0.5	0	0.5

Source: EU-LFS. Authors' computations

tion as the business cycle among others factors, affect also the participation in the labour market. However, the growth in the share of university graduates observed is likely to reflect in large part secular factors.

1.2 Gender Gap in Participation and the Great Recession

The gender impact of the Great Recession that hit European countries in 2009 is well documented in the literature (Allègre and Verdugo 2017; Eydoux et al. 2014; Karamessini and Rubery 2013; Périvier 2014). The sex segregation of employment by gender (across occupations or sectors) and the potential dualization of the labour market imply that men and women face different labour market situations in terms of level of unemployment and type of job they can access to. The sectoral dimension of the recession therefore strengthens the impact of the recession on labour supply of men and women. The gendered impact on the workforce of the different phases of the crisis highlights the structural character of the gender division of labour and the inequalities between men and women in labour markets and more generally in societies. The impact was felt differently in each country for reasons related to the configuration of the labour market, the type of welfare regime and the prevailing gender norms. Then, although the public and economic policies (either stimulus or austerity) aimed at tackling the crisis were implemented in gender-blind fashion, they were not gender neutral because of these structural gender inequalities. As suggested by Villa and Smith (2013), the impact of business cycles from the gender perspective must be analysed in the light of long-term trends, such as gender regime, family model and institutional environment, all of which change over time (Bettio et al. 2013).

During a recession, the dramatic increase in unemployment modifies the behaviour of workers in term of participation. Two effects can be distinguished: the discouraged worker effect and the added worker effect.

The discouraged worker effect arises when job seekers have little prospect of finding suitable work and consequently withdraw from the labour market or are not included in statistics related exclusively to the job-seeking activities of unemployed persons. As shown in Périvier (2018), in Spain and Greece (and to a lesser extent in the United Kingdom, Denmark and Italy), the participation effect for men was clearly negative. This is consistent with the fact that job destruction for the most part concerned part-time male workers. In the United Kingdom, the positive demographic effect partially compensated for the negative participation effect for men, whereas in Greece, the negative demographic effect reinforced the negative participation effect observed for men, so that the male labour force contracted, offsetting the rise in the male unemployment rate (Karamessini and Koutentakis 2014). In Italy, the discouraged worker effect seems to have been in the same range for both men and women in 2009, a trend explained by the increase in unemployment during this period for both sexes. After 2010, however, the participation rate has increased, indicating the emergence of a potential opposite effect attributable to intra-family decisions.

The added worker effect is based on the hypothesis that couples "share risk": if the primary earner becomes unemployed, the secondary earner may seek an additional job to compensate for the loss of income. This causes the labour force to expand but can potentially increase unemployment if the demand is not dynamic enough. It can appear at the extensive margin if it implies a transition from inactivity to participation in the labour market, or at the intensive margin if it implies an increase in working time (from part-time to full-time employment). The added worker effect obviously has a gendered dimension, since it relies on the sexual division of labour within couples and on the fact that women may still be considered secondary earners in some countries. The change in arrangement it involves may be transitory or may have long-term implications for the couple's division of labour and household tasks. The literature on that effect is unclear: some previous studies have found significant but small responses in female labour supply when the spouse is unemployed (Lundberg 1985; Mincer 1962), while others have found no evidence at all (Heckman and Macurdy 1980). A severe recession that is especially harsh for male employment, as it was the case during the Great Recession, might induce a strong added worker effect.

In Sweden, France, Germany, the United Kingdom and Denmark, the added worker effect is expected to be small or at the intensive margin in these countries. The high level of social protection and the existence of unemployment insurance limits the potential added worker effect.

Furthermore, in the United Kingdom, married women are discouraged from entering the labour market if their partner becomes unemployed because unemployment insurance is means-tested (Bredtmann et al. 2014); the magnitude of the recession has nonetheless limited this specific effect, as people became particularly cautious about their jobs (Bryan and Longhi 2013). What is more, Gush et al. (2015) have shown using a qualitative approach that additional spousal labour is only one of the alternatives open to couples facing serious financial hardship (Gush et al. 2015). There is no sign of a strong positive participation effect for women in these countries (Périvier 2018).

Southern countries where the participation of women remained low have experienced a stronger added worker effect during the recession. A positive participation effect in Italy, Spain and Greece is observed. In Spain, this must be interpreted in line with the long-term trend towards female participation, which has destabilized the male breadwinner model. During the crisis, poorly educated women showed signs of household compensating strategies, that can be interpreted as an added worker effect (Addabbo et al. 2015). In Italy, female participation rates are structurally low, but regional differences exist because the gender regime has not evolved homogeneously throughout the country: the female employment rate is above the European average in the North, but far below it in the South (Karamessini and Rubery 2013). Nevertheless, part of the increase in female participation during the crisis is due to the added worker effect, according to the literature (Bredtmann et al. 2014; Verashchagina and Capparucci 2014). A similar trend is observed in Greece: inactive women joined the labour market, which can be interpreted as a supply-side response, or added worker effect. In both countries, the increase in female participation raised the female unemployment rate because of the sharp deterioration in the labour market (Bredtmann et al. 2014; Karamessini and Koutentakis 2014; Verashchagina and Capparucci 2014).

For countries in which an added worker effect has been observed during the Great Recession, the question of its persistence is crucial. The labour supply of both men and women is embedded in the economic and social regime: the fact that married women might increase their participation in the labour market when their partners lose their jobs does not guarantee that, conversely, the partners are going to increase their participation in domestic and family work. The "substitutability" of female and male labour when it comes to paid work is not necessarily compensated by substitutability in unpaid work. In Italy, for instance, greater female labour participation was not associated with a transformation in the role of men inside the household; rather, it was sustained by an inflow of migrant women performing domestic and care labour, thereby enabling educated women to work (Verashchagina and Capparucci 2014). Similarly, during the decade preceding the recession, the dramatic increase in Spanish women's employment was not associated with greater participation by men in childcare and housework (Gonzalez Cago and Segales Kirzner 2014). As suggested by Rubery (2015), path dependency has to be taken into account, as changes in family organization and social norms related to the gender division of labour are not readily reversible.

2 Employment, Part-Time Job and Gender Wage Gap

2.1 The European Employment Strategy: A Decreasing Interest for Gender?

Gender equality is a "funding value" of EU: equal pay for equal work was included in article 119 of the Treaty of Roma.[3] The motives of such inclusion in the international treaty are discussed among scholars, showing that the fair competition among workers predominated the objective of justice (Ellina 2003; Hoskyns 1996; Rossilli 1997). Nevertheless, since then, the EU has played a key role in encouraging member states to narrow the gender gap in different dimensions by using different frames. At the end of 1990, thanks to the coordination of different types of stakeholders, the launch of the EES gave visibility to gender issues concerning labour market (Bettio et al. 2013). Equal opportunity was stated as one of the four pillars of the EES. The 2000 Lisbon Council paid specific attention to the contribution of women to European labour markets. The agreement on quantitative targets was reached with the distinction of female and male objectives with a target of 60% for women and 70% overall to be fulfilled by 2010. The strategy involved promoting the contribution of women's employment, through quantitative targets in terms of female employment and in terms of childcare system,[4] but the ultimate goal was to increase the overall employment level. As shown by Stratigaki, the gender equality objectives became part of the political agenda of the EU only after their meaning has been transformed to satisfy economic priorities, such as the increase in the labour force (Stratigaki 2004). Indeed, the 2000 Lisbon Council sheds light on the contribution of women in European labour markets. In 2010, these key targets were due, and most countries achieved the assigned objective and quantitative progress had occurred in all European countries.

Progressively, gender equality measures and gender mainstreaming have declined in the frame of the EES: the reformulation of the strategy in 2003 led to "a greater focus on the 'more' rather than the 'better' jobs stressed in earlier formulations of the Strategy". The gender perspective has been marginalized or ignored in national and EU policy responses to the recession and austerity policies implemented in the aftermath of the crisis were gender blind but not gender neutral (Périvier 2018).

The 2010 revision of the EES under the 2020 banner reinforced this tendency of gender blindness: in the frame of the H2020 Strategy, the targets to be reached is 75% (aged 20–64) by 2020[5] without regards for gender gap (Fagan and Rubery 2018). The employment target is no more gendered explicitly, even though women represent the most important reserve force, as female employment rate is lower than male's in most European countries.

In 2016, 8 out of 28 countries fulfil this objective. The Graph 10.2 gives the respective contribution of men and women to the overall employment rate; the green bar in the graph gives the increase in employment rate if the number of employed women reaches the level of the men's.

The fact that the H2020 target is gender blind implies that incentives to increase female employment are effective for countries in which the flexibility to reach the overall target (75% for both sexes) is to reduce the gender gap: this is the case in countries where the gender gap is high (Italy, Greece and Spain).

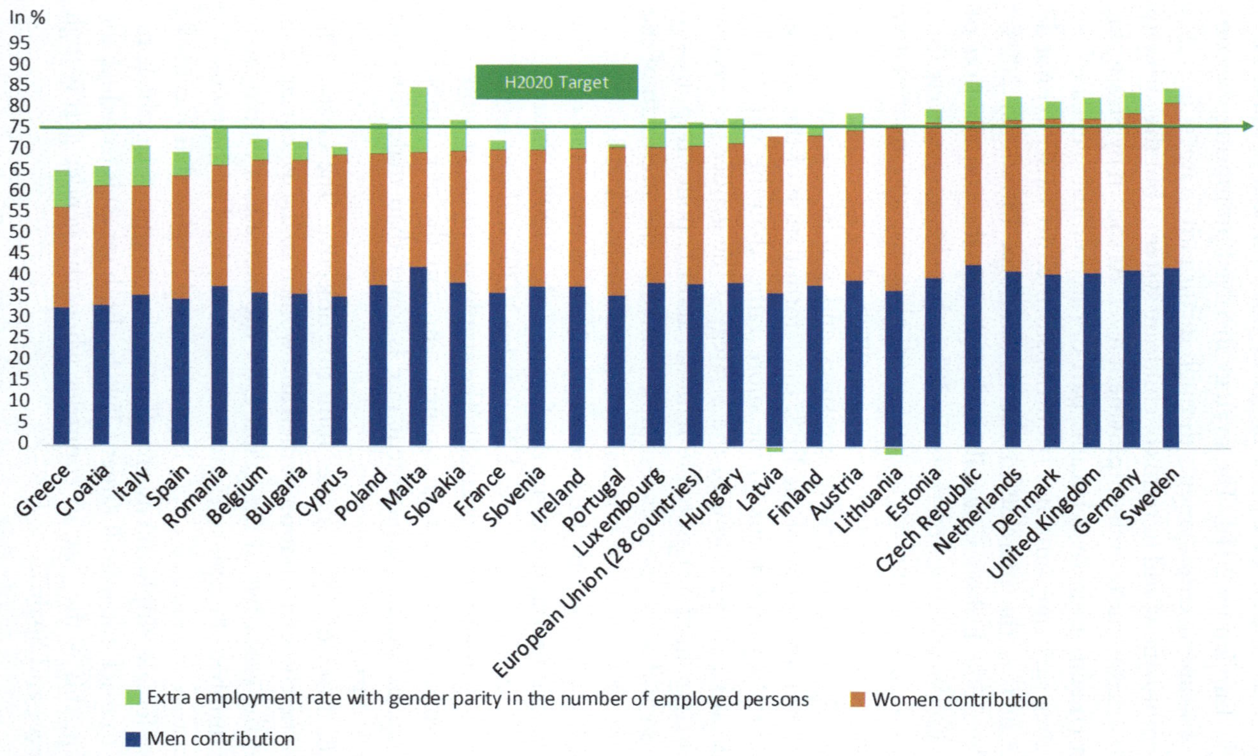

Graph 10.2 Contribution of men and women to the total employment rate in Europe (aged 20–64) in 2016. (Source: Eurostat, [lfsi_emp_a])

In countries for which the employment rate is above the recommended threshold, some improvement can be done in terms of gender equality in employment, as the contribution of women to this rate is lower than the men's (Germany, Austria, the Netherlands, the United Kingdom and Denmark). But they have no incentives coming from the European strategy to do so. At the same time, some countries do not reach the target even though the contribution of men and women to employment rate is equal, as it the case in Portugal. In some countries for which the overall employment rate is far below 75%, the extra contribution of women to the labour market would not be sufficient to fulfil this target (Greece, Italy or Spain). For those cases, the increase in employment rate presupposed to increase female employment rate.

The European commitments in terms of gender equality are now set outside the overall strategy, H2020 and this increases the risk of a decrease in the attention for gender equality issue at the national level.

As far as the business cycle is concerned, the gendered effect of the crisis is well known (see amongst others Karamessini and Rubery 2014; Eydoux et al. 2014). In general, the recession stage has affected more deeply male employment than female one due to sex sectorial segregation. This so-called "He-Cession" phenomenon should be looked at with care: in some countries, like in the United Kingdom, the share of women per sector has changed in the sense that they been more affected relatively (Périvier 2018). The austerity phase is not gender neutral: fiscal consolidation policies have jeopardized or stop the dynamic of narrowing the gender inequalities through different channels (Périvier 2014). The austerity measures induce a modification of the structure of European welfare states and gender regimes through a decrease in the degree of defamilialization and in the degree of decommodification of welfare states. Gender equality has been relegated to the background (Smith and Villa 2014).

2.2 Part-Time Employment and Gender Wage Gap

Beyond the quantitative target of employment, the type of jobs held by women is still different than the ones held by men, in particular regarding working time. In some countries, the reduction of unemployment goes through an increase in female part-time jobs. Countries in which the level of female participation in the labour market is high and in which female unemployment rate is low are also those in which female part-time employment rate is the highest. It is the case in the Netherlands, where more than 76% of working women are part-time and female unemployment rate is about 6.5%; in Germany, where the female part-time employment rate is 46.5% and the female unemployment rate is 3.8%; and the United-Kingdom, with more than four working women out of ten working part-time and with a female unemployment rate of 4.8%. In contrast, countries with similar level of female participation in the labour market face a higher female unemployment rate and a lower part-time rate: Finland (respectively in Sweden), the female part-time rate is around 20% (35.6%) and the female unemployment rate is 8.7% (6.7%). In France, where the overall level of unemployment is high, part-time rate for women is below 30% and the female unemployment rate is close to 10%.

The strategy of promoting female part-time jobs helps to boost female employment but at the same time, as the gender gap in part-time job in increasing, gender inequalities rise, depending on the length of working time in part-time and the quality of these part-time jobs. Part-time employment has an impact on gender wage gap. Countries in which the participation of women in the labour market is low, the gender wage gap is low because of selection bias of the profile of the working women (they are more educated and more involved in their career than the average worker).

The Overall Gender Earning Gap calculated by Eurostat[6] corresponds to the gender earnings gap for the whole population. This indicator combines on average the three elements of the monthly wage:

- Employment rate reflects the effective possibility for women not only to participate in the labour market but to have access to a job. In some countries, women's unemployment is higher than men's, even though since the recession that has deeply affected male employment, this gender gap decreased in most countries.

– Working time reflects the level of sexual division of labour and the difficulties to articulate work and family life that is persistently a women's issue.
– Hourly wage reflects the impact of vertical segregation (glass ceiling phenomena), horizontal segregation (sectors in which women are over represented are less-valued than sectors in which men are overrepresented) and the discrimination faced by women at the workplace.

Table 10.3 gives the results for countries under review. In countries where the gender overall earning gap is the lowest (below 30%), the gender gap in the three components is low (Finland, Portugal and Sweden). In Italy, the low female employment combined with the lowest working time of women compared to men explain most part of the gender overall earning gap, whereas in the Netherlands it is mainly explained by the fact that female part-time rate is high. In France, the gap (31.1%) is due gender gap in the three dimensions. In Germany, the gap is higher than in France and this is due to the greater gap in working time and in female employment rate.

Table 10.3 Gender overall earnings gap in 2014 in some European countries

Gender overall earnings gap in 2014 in some European countries							
	Average hourly wage (€)		Average number of hours paid per month		Employment rate for 15-64 y (%)		Overall gender wage gap
	Men	Women	Men	Women	Men	Women	
Finland	21,78	17,77	161	153	69,5	68	24,1
Portugal	8,08	6,88	168	161	65,8	59,6	26,1
Sweden	20,22	19,14	165	148	76,5	73,1	26,2
Belgium	20,49	19,15	162	139	65,8	59,6	27
France	18,78	15,87	154	140	67,3	60,4	31,1
Spain	12,76	10,86	162	145	60,7	51,2	35,7
Denmark	30,16	25,35	131	125	75,8	69,8	36,1
Ireland	26,2	22,55	149	129	68,3	58	36,67
Greece	10,07	8,81	164	155	58	41,1	41,4
Italy	15,85	14,88	175	145	64,7	46,8	43,7
Austria	17,55	13,65	167	133	75,2	66,9	44,9
UK	20,93	16,56	162	129	76,8	67,1	45
Germany	19,87	15,44	154	122	78,1	69,5	45,2
Netherlands	19,41	16,29	145	104	78,1	68,1	47,5

Source: Eurostat, structure of earnings survey (earn_ses_hourly) (earn_ses_monthly) (lfsa_ergaed) (teqges01)

The unbalanced repartition of part-time employment implies a persistence of the gender gap in income. The gender overall gap is higher in countries in which the female part-time employment rate is high. It is the case in Germany, the Netherlands, Austria or the United Kingdom.

3 Conclusion

The European strategy based on the sole overall employment rate led some countries to increase part-time job for women, which increased inequalities in terms of earnings. In order to structurally tackle gender inequalities, gender gap in employment rate should not be the only goal, and three major dimensions of labour market assimilation crucial for gender inequalities should also be taken into account: female employment rate, working time and hourly wage. Each of these dimensions concentrates the factors of gender inequalities. The employment strategies adopted by the member states are no longer bounded by a gender European framework. This leads to mitigate results in terms of the reduction in economic inequalities. Gender equality objective requires to be integrated in different dimensions of European policies. This objective requires a combination of quantitative and qualitative components to insure women's emancipation and gender equality in the European labour markets (Fagan and Rubery 2018). This demands a strong commitment of European Institutions to put gender back at the core of the EES.

Notes

1. We do not include Eastern European and Baltic countries that have recently joined the euro. These countries are at different stages of economic development and tend to have very different labour market institutions.
2. Results were virtually identical when age dummies were included in the regression, or if the interaction between education and age dummies was used. These results are available upon request.
3. http://europa.eu/rapid/press-release_MEMO-07-426_en.htm.

4. The objectives of Barcelona imply that member states provide childcare by 2010 to at least 90% of children between 3 years old and the mandatory school age and at least 33% of children under 3 years of age (Report from the Commission to the European Parliament, the Council, the European Economic and Social Committee and the Committee of the Regions, 2013).
5. http://ec.europa.eu/eurostat/web/europe-2020-indicators/europe-2020-strategy.
6. http://ec.europa.eu/eurostat/statistics-explained/index.php/Gender_statistics.

References

Addabbo, T., P. Rodríguez, and L. Gálvez. 2015. Gender Differences in Labor Force Participation Rates in Spain and Italy Under the Great Recession. *World Economy Journal* 41: 21–42.

Akgunduz, Y.E., and J. Plantenga. 2015. *Childcare Prices and Maternal Employment: A Meta-analysis*. Retrieved from https://core.ac.uk/download/files/153/6400130.pdf.

Allègre, G., and G. Verdugo. 2017. *Labour Force Participation and Job Polarization: Evidence from Europe During the Great Recession*. OFCE Working Paper, 1.

Bettio, F., J. Plantenga, and M. Smith. 2013. *Gender and the European Labour Market*. New York: Routledge. Retrieved from https://books.google.fr/books?id=nmVb1j8w5n0C&pg=PA147&lpg=PA147&dq=lisbon+strategy+gender&source=bl&ots=vTxe2uzPKS&sig=kBFbVxgSsBgjGBmPifQtQ4PifEY&hl=fr&sa=X&ved=0ahUKEwj2lq_GmLrbAhVLkRQKHXQfAvwQ6AEIaTAI#v=onepage&q=lisbon strategy gender&f=false.

Bredtmann, J., S. Otten, and C. Rulff. 2014. Husband's Unemployment and Wife's Labor Supply—The Added Worker Effect Across Europe. *Ruhr Economic Papers*. https://doi.org/10.4419/86788550.

Brilli, Y., D. Del Boca, and C.D. Pronzato. 2016. Does Child Care Availability Play a Role in Maternal Employment and Children's Development? Evidence from Italy. *Review of Economics of the Household* 14 (1): 27–51. https://doi.org/10.1007/s11150-013-9227-4.

Bryan, M., and S. Longhi. 2013. *Couples' Labour Supply Responses to Job Loss: Growth and Recession Compared*. IZA Discussion Paper (7775). https://doi.org/10.1111/manc.12186.

Carrasco, R., J.F. Jimeno, and A.C. Ortega. 2015. Returns to Skills and the Distribution of Wages: Spain 1995–2010. *Oxford Bulletin of Economics and Statistics* 77 (4): 542–565. https://doi.org/10.1111/obes.12077.

Ellina, C.A. 2003. *Promoting Women's Rights: The Politics of Gender in the European Union*. Routledge. Retrieved from https://www.routledge.com/Promoting-Womens-Rights-Politics-of-Gender-in-the-European-Union/Ellina/p/book/9780203506783.

Eydoux, A., A. Math, and H. Périvier. 2014. European Labour Markets in Times of Crisis a Gender Perspective. *Revue de l'OFCE* 133 (2). https://doi.org/10.3917/reof.133.0007.

Fagan, C., and J. Rubery. 2018. Advancing Gender Equality Through European Employment Policy: The Impact of the UK's EU Membership and the Risks of Brexit. *Social Policy and Society* 17 (2): 297–317. https://doi.org/10.1017/S1474746417000458.

González Gago, E., and M. Segales Kirzner. 2014. Women, Gender Equality and the Economic Crisis in Spain. In *Women and Austerity: The Economic Crisis and the Future for Gender Equality*, ed. M. Karamessini and J. Rubery, 228–248. New York/London: Routledge.

Gush, K., J. Scott, and H. Laurie. 2015. Households' Responses to Spousal Job Loss: "All Change" or "Carry on as Usual"? *Work, Employment & Society*. https://doi.org/10.1177/0950017014556411.

Heckman, J.J., and T.E. Macurdy. 1980. A Life Cycle Model of Female Labour Supply. *Review of Economic Studies* 47 (1): 47–74. https://doi.org/10.2307/2297103.

Hoskyns, C. 1996. Integrating Gender: Women, Law and Politics in the European Union. *Verso*. Retrieved from https://books.google.fr/books/about/Integrating_Gender.html?id=rjRu4M-zfH8C&redir_esc=y.

Karamessini, M., and F. Koutentakis. 2014. Labour Market Flows and Unemployment Dynamics by Sex in Greece During the Crisis. *Revue de l'O* 133: 216–239.

Karamessini, M., and J. Rubery, eds. 2013. *Women and Austerity: The Economic Crisis and the Future for Gender Equality*. Oxford: Routledge.

———. 2014. The Challenge of Austerity for Equality. *Revue de l'OFCE* 133 (2): 15. https://doi.org/10.3917/reof.133.0015.

Lewis, J. 1992. Gender and the Development of Welfare Regimes. *Journal of European Social Policy* 2 (3): 159–173. https://doi.org/10.1177/095892879200200301.

———. 2002. Gender and Welfare State Change. *European Societies* 4 (4): 331–357. https://doi.org/10.1080/1461669022000022324.

Lundberg, S. 1985. The Added Worker Effect. *Journal of Labor Economics* 3 (1): 11–37.

Mincer, J. 1962. Labor Force Participation of Married Women: A Study of Labor Supply. *Aspects of Labor Economics* 1 (06): 63–106. https://doi.org/10.1016/S1574-0692(06)01007-5.

Périvier, H. 2014. Men and Women During the Economic Crisis. Employments Trends in Eight European Countries. *Revue de l'OFCE* (133): 41. https://doi.org/10.3917/reof.133.0041.

———. 2018. Recession, Austerity and Gender: A Comparison of Eight European Labour Markets. *International Labour Review*. https://doi.org/10.1111/ilr.12032.

Rossilli, M. 1997. The European Community' s Policy on the Equality of Women. From the Treaty of Roma to the Present. *The European Journal of Women's Studies* 4 (1): 63–82.

Rubery, J. 1988. *Women and Recession*. London: Routledge.

———. 2015. Austerity and the Future for Gender Equality in Europe. *ILR Review* 68 (4): 715–741.

Smith, M., and P. Villa. 2014. The Long Tail of the Great Recession. Forgone Employment and Forgone Policies. *Revue de l'OFCE* 2008 (133): 85–119. https://doi.org/10.3917/reof.133.0085.

Stratigaki, M. 2004. The Cooptation of Gender Concepts in EU Policies: The Case of "Reconciliation of Work and Family". *Social Politics* 11 (1): 30–56+145. https://doi.org/10.1093/sp/jxh025.

Verashchagina, Alina, and Marina Capparucci. 2014. Living Through the Crisis in Italy: Labour Market Experiences of Men and Women. In *Women and Austerity: The Economic Crisis and the Future for Gender Equality*, ed. Maria Karamessini and Jill Rubery, 248–270. IAFFE Advances in Feminist Economics. Abingdon: Routledge.

Verdugo, G. 2014. The Great Compression of the French Wage Structure, 1969–2008. *Labour Economics* 28: 131–144. https://doi.org/10.1016/j.labeco.2014.04.009.

Villa, P., and M. Smith. 2013. Policy in a Time of Crisis. In *Women and Austerity: The Economic Crisis and the Future for Gender Equality*, vol. 11, 273. New York/London: Routledge.

Vuri, D. 2016. Do Childcare Policies Increase Maternal Employment? *IZA World of Labor*, March 1–10. https://doi.org/10.15185/izawol.241.

11

Building a Consistent European Climate-Energy Policy

Aurélien Saussay, Paul Malliet, Gissela Landa Rivera, and Frédéric Reynès

1 Introduction

Since the enactment of the Kyoto Protocol in 1997, the European Union (EU) has clearly taken a leadership position in the fight against climate change during the international negotiations. Its constant diplomatic efforts have strongly contributed to the signature of the Paris Agreement in December 2015. During the COP 21, the largest greenhouse gases (GHG) emitting countries have agreed to take drastic mitigation actions in order to limit the global temperature increase to 1.5 °C compared to pre-industrial level. Such an ambitious objective implies that global carbon neutrality should be achieved between 2055 and 2070 (UNEP 2014, p. XV).

A. Saussay (✉) • P. Malliet • G. Landa Rivera
OFCE, Sciences Po, Paris, France
e-mail: aurelien.saussay@sciencespo.fr

F. Reynès
NEO – Netherlands Economic Observatory, Rotterdam, Netherlands
OFCE, Sciences Po, Paris, France
TNO – Netherlands Organisation for Applied Scientific Research, The Hague, Netherlands

© The Author(s) 2018
J. Creel et al. (eds.), *Report on the State of the European Union*,
https://doi.org/10.1007/978-3-319-98364-6_11

Beyond their diplomatic efforts, EU member states have taken concrete actions to reduce their GHG emissions. The latter have decreased by more than 20% since 1990 showing a decoupling between EU economic growth and it environmental footprint.[1] Although advocated and ratified by the EU, the objectives defined in the Paris agreement remain challenging for its member states, which need to implement a rapid and major change in the structure of their supply and demand of energy.

A proactive EU climate policy is generally justified by its expected benefits. In addition to its environmental benefits, the transition to a sustainable energy system contributes to European energy security, since the continent has little fossil fuel resources. It is also rightly perceived as a tool to favor local economic activities and therefore to have a positive effect on the European economy. Despite these advantages, the EU has had difficulties in implementing a fully coherent climate policy. As we shall see, an important obstacle stems from the fact that most of the energy transition actually takes place at the member state level and not at the EU level. This multi-level governance often creates inconsistencies between general climate objectives and their actual implementations.

The second section provides a quantitative illustration of the various levels of governance managing energy transition projects through an analysis of the projects financed by the European Fund for Strategic Investments (EFSI). The third section investigates how the EU could bring more coherence into its climate actions. In addition to solving the current ambiguity between the EU policy and budget priorities, the EU could play an important coordination role through the use or improvements of its available instruments. The fourth section looks at the EU industrial prospects in the rising markets related to energy transition and how climate policy could support the EU current leading but fragile competitive advantage.

2 The Multiple Levels of Governance for the Energy Transition

Achieving the energy transition in the EU requires significant investments across a variety of economic sectors. In broad terms, these investments, which would span multiple decades, can be classified into three categories (European Commission 2017c):

- Production and distribution of energy (renewables and electrical network improvements);
- Refurbishment of existing capital (buildings and industrial facilities in particular);
- Transportation infrastructure (intercity rail and urban public transportation).

Projects in each of these categories are implemented across varying geographical scopes, ranging from the very local to the cross continental. Indeed, while retrofitting residential buildings to achieve improvements in energy efficiency is a local endeavor, interconnections between electrical networks can involve multiple countries and regulatory bodies. Accordingly, the choice of the most appropriate level of governance, at the city, regional, national or European level will vary with each type of project. The role of the EU in implementing the energy transition is both guided and constrained by this variety of scopes.

Yet, with the exception of network infrastructures in the energy and transportation sectors, we expect most of the project types listed above to be local in nature. This can be verified by identifying the share of energy transition-related projects conducted over different geographical scopes and financed by the EFSI. The EFSI is a joint fund set up by the EIB and the EIF. It is the main pillar in the Investment Plan for Europe started in 2015 to address the investment gap in the EU since the onset of the 2008 financial crisis. During its conception phase, the European Commission organized a call for proposals that would seek financing from this new fund to further several key priorities of the EU—including climate change mitigation. As such, the list of EFSI transactions offers a reasonable survey of current and future energy transition-related projects in Europe.

We collected a comprehensive listing of all 396 projects funded by the EFSI that had been signed or approved by June 1, 2018, and classified them across two dimensions. First, we found out whether the project was national, cross-border (involving two or more member countries) or European (concerning all EU member states). Second, we identified the main focus of the project, both in broad (energy transition, environmental

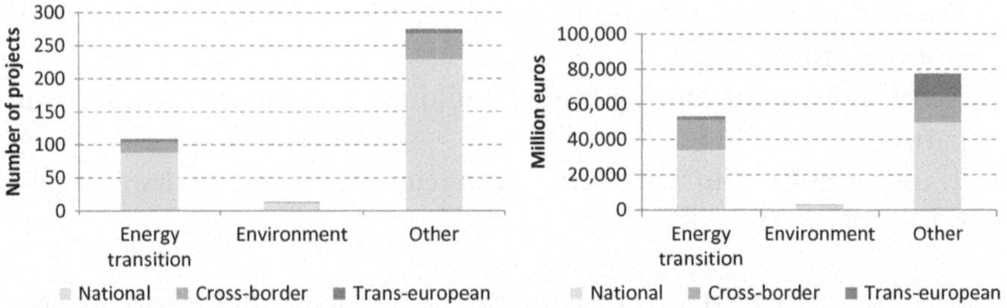

Fig. 11.1 Number and value of EFSI projects by sector and geographical scope

or other) and detailed terms (e.g. wind power, residential buildings retrofits, industrial energy efficiency, etc.). The results of this analysis are presented in Fig. 11.1.

We find that 31% of projects signed or approved under the EFSI are environment-related, with 27% concerning the energy transition proper. The overwhelming majority (81%) of these are national in scope, although this is not characteristic of energy transition projects. This finding is nuanced when considering the value of the projects financed, with the share of single-country projects decreasing to 64%. Still, according to both measures, very few projects concern the EU in its entirety.

However, analyzing the nature of the projects financed reveals that 97% of the value of cross-border energy transition related projects actually pertains to funds which are themselves dedicated to the financing of the energy transition. These funds are financial vehicles destined to support energy transition investments—they are not actual physical project themselves. In effect, in these instances, the EFSI finances another financer (Fig. 11.2).

This finding confirms the local character of the overwhelming majority of energy transition investments. With the exception of one project targeting energy efficiency improvements, all physical projects financed by the EFSI are circumscribed to a single member state.

This goes on to show that the EU is ill suited to lead energy transition projects that are implemented, and therefore best managed, at the local level. But this does not mean that the European level has no place in supporting climate mitigation in its member states. On the contrary, the EU

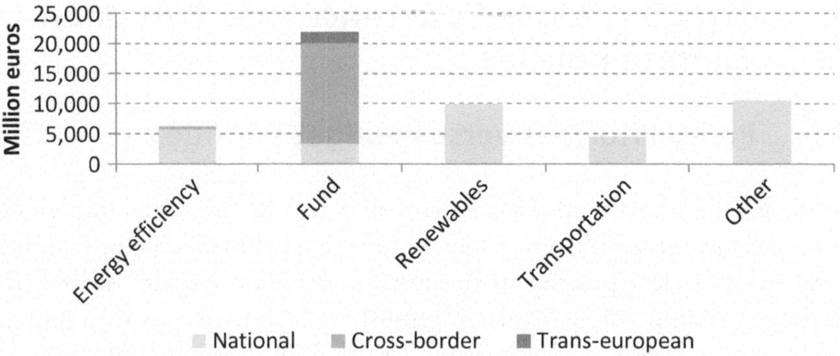

Fig. 11.2 EFSI energy transition projects value by focus and geographical scope. (Note: Fund designates funding vehicles set up to support energy transition investments that receive the financing from the EFSI; energy efficiency includes residential retrofits and industrial efficiency; renewables includes wind, solar power and biogas; transportation includes rail and public transportation; other includes in particular electric networks and smart metering)

can help with one of the key aspects of the energy transition, financing. By leveraging aggregation effects, bodies at the European level can raise financing more cheaply and efficiently than separate national organizations. Thus, while the implementation of energy transition projects would certainly benefit from governance commensurate with their geographical scale and location, their financing can benefit from European-scale coordination. While raising cheaper capital at the European level can be applied to any type of investments, the capital intensiveness of most energy transition projects (e.g. renewable electric capacities, buildings retrofits, public transportation infrastructure) makes it particularly relevant in this specific case.

In this respect, the EFSI offers an interesting example of what the EU could achieve to increase the financing available for the energy transition. The time horizon of the fund has already been extended from 2018 to 2020, increasing its target from €300 billion worth of projects co-financed to 500 billion across all sectors. However, the fund could provide an even larger contribution by financing slightly riskier projects in the climate mitigation field—thereby leveraging the financial backing that the European level can provide for the projects that need it the most.

3 Bringing More Coherence into European Climate Policies

3.1 Policy Priorities Versus Budget Priorities

While local and national governments may handle the actual implementation of the energy transition, the fight against climate change is rightly heralded as a clear priority in the European policy agenda. Indeed, the European Commission regularly publishes documents on this subject. Examples include the Green Paper entitled "A European Strategy for Sustainable, Competitive and Secure Energy" (European Commission 2006), the Communications entitled "An energy policy for Europe" (European Commission 2007) or "A policy framework for climate and energy in the period from 2020 to 2030" (European Commission 2014). These documents identify the main challenges and priorities regarding energy and climate policies, which are based on three pillars:

1. The fight against climate change by significantly reducing energy-related GHG emissions.
2. The improvement of energy security by reducing the dependency on extra-European imported energy sources.
3. The prospect of benefiting from the positive economic dividends of the energy transition thanks to the increase in activity generated by investments in energy savings, related jobs creations and a reduction in the exposure to rising and volatile energy prices.
4. Although these general political commitments for climate policy are voluntarist, several reports and studies have shown that their actual integration in existing policies is still limited (e.g. Kok and de Coninck 2007; Medarova-Bergstrom et al. 2011). A first reason is that the EU budget is relatively small, since it represents around 1% of the gross national income of its member states and only around 2% of EU public expenditure. Moreover, this share has declined over time.

Nevertheless, with about 20% of the total €1,000 billion EU budget allocated to climate action for the period 2014–2020 (European

Commission 2017b), the EU budget appears ambitious and aligned with policy priorities. At the same time, a large part of the funding disbursed by the EU is allocated to sectors that are large contributors to GHG emissions, in particular agriculture, transport and housing.

In theory, the Cohesion Policy funds (Cohesion Fund, European Regional Development Fund and European Social Fund) have the objective to promote the "shift towards a low-carbon economy". But in practice, a large part of these funds is controlled by member states and allocated to emission intensive infrastructures. For instance, €930 million of the 2014–2020 Structural Funds is earmarked to finance natural gas infrastructures. In some regions, households receive EU funds to replace their old domestic coal boilers with newer coal combustion systems. The Common Agricultural Policy is still largely supporting intensive farming system. The EU Cohesion Policy funding in the transport sector is heavily biased toward high-carbon transport and energy infrastructure: twice as much is invested into road infrastructure than into low-emission mobility solutions and only 7% goes to energy efficiency, renewables, electricity distribution, storage and smart grids.

Similar inconsistencies with official policy priorities also exist for the funds centrally managed by the European Commission. For instance, the Connecting Europe Facility, which is the largest energy, transport and ICT infrastructure investment fund, has allocated €1.1 billion to gas projects in the period 2014–2018. This is more than twice the amount allocated to electricity interconnection projects.

Climate change policy is determined by several levels of governance (EU, member state, regional, local). This represents a major challenge for policy integration and the development of a coherent climate policy framework. A necessary step to achieve a coherent European climate policy is to put the budget priorities in line with key policy objectives. As advocated by the High-Level Expert Group on Sustainable Finance (European Commission 2017a), the next Multiannual Financial Framework (MFF) 2021–2027 offers a good opportunity to amend the criteria governing the allocation of EU funding in order to increase the level of climate policy alignment above the current 20%. A first draft of the MFF has been presented by the EC on May 2, 2018.[2] With €1300 billion (1.14% of the EU gross national income), it appears as a compromise between the European Parliament's demand to increase the EU expenditure to 1.3% of EU's GNI and the Netherlands, Sweden, Denmark and Austria's opposition to any increase. Given the numerous criticisms voiced by member states on the current version of the budget,[3] one can already expect difficult and long negotiations. It is important that these negotiations deal also with the adaptation of the funding conditions in order to solve the current discrepancy between the stated EU policy priorities and the actual budget priorities. Ways to achieve such a major change are still largely unclear.

3.2 Strengthening and Harmonizing European Climate-Energy Policy Instruments

We cannot expect the budget of the EU to be sufficient to achieve the goals exposed above; however, it can have a role of coordination between national and European policies as they suffer a lack of coherence. The coordination between the national energy policies should be ensured at the EU level, defining common and not contradictory instruments. European energy-climate policies employ a mix of different policy instruments to influence actor's behavior by changing the economic incentive structure to reduce GHG emissions. The use of these main instruments in the EU can be classified into two types (Gorlach 2013):

- Non-market-based: command and control regulation, reporting requirement, technology support, removal of green-tech financial barriers and information, and voluntary approach.
- Marked-based: principally taxes, emissions trading and removal of perverse incentive

Although the EU is on the right path to achieve its goals of reducing its GHG emissions by 2020, reaching commitments for the following decade is not ensured in a context of economic recovery. New consumption needs and an absence of consensus between the member states to implement ambitious instruments could prevent the EU to reach the long-term commitment (reduction of 80 to 95% of its GHG emissions, in application of the Paris Agreement). For instance, there are opposite energy policies in a certain number of countries, particularly Germany, where energy transition has been driven by its decision to abandon and replace nuclear power by increasing the share of renewable. But this is not sufficient to offset an important production of coal, alert to an increase in CO_2 emissions in EU after 2020. In this situation, Germany is expected to miss its target of reducing GHG emissions by 40% by 2020 (Hedberg 2017).

Contradictory strategies can have negative effects, slow down the current trend in renewable capacity investments and therefore prevent the EU from meeting its National Determined Commitment (NDC). The role of the EU is to provide the necessary signals, by drawing on a specific roadmap, for path of emission reduction of each activity sector (transport, energy, industry, construction, agriculture, etc.) including coherent national policies with the goals in the Paris Agreement for 2050. The Clean Energy Package[4] is in discussion now, this type of instrument should be included in the debate.

EU measures to increase the cost of emissions are largely considered the best way to achieve decarbonization, but these have highlighted difficulties in their achievement due to opposition from some member states such as Poland and the member states that are the most dependent on fossil energies. The current revision of the EU-Energy Tax Directive[5] and the forthcoming proposal for an EU Budget 2021–2027 offers a great opportunity to strength current levels of taxation applied to motor fuels, heating fuels and electricity in line with the mid- and long-term Union's climate commitments.

The European Emissions Trading Scheme (EU-ETS) is the oldest and largest trading system for emission. Its implementation was done in three phases from 2005 to 2020 very inconclusively, due to the absence to create incentive for mitigation options, such as a shift from coal to gas, for long-term investments into low-carbon capital stocks and into research and development. Price of emission allowance, at around €5–10 for the last two years, and forecasts of future price are below the level to be necessary to drive transition toward a low-carbon economy. This trend will not change by the lately reform of the EU-ETS (phase IV, 2021–2028). This reform contributes with some improvement in the reduction of surplus quota with the creation of the market stability reserve, but without significant effect on the price to be expected. In this context, implementation of a carbon price floor in the EU-ETS could achieve decarbonization efficiently, but in the actual situation of political standoff, a minimum carbon price could be carried out at national level or between nearby countries that were willing to join. This alternative is supported by the French Government. A coalition of willing member states could be formed with France, Nederland, UK and the new German administration, and to broaden it over time.

4 Making Europe the Global Energy Transition Champion

Beyond budgetary concerns, the energy transition offers both a challenge and an opportunity for the entire economy. Overhauling our existing economic arrangements, which have been developed around the use of fossil fuels, necessitates a number of new technologies that present a significant economic opportunity. However, despite the ambition of its climate change policies, the EU has failed so far to capitalize on its early start and turn its policy leadership into a competitiveness asset.

4.1 Learning from Past Failures: Solar PV, CFLs and LEDs

Despite being at the vanguard of the climate change fight for several decades, Europe has experienced in the past years a sharp downturn in its domestic solar panel manufacturing industry. This is mainly due to the strong pressure exercised by Chinese companies, which now dominate the market.

While China's share in PV production was less than 1% in 2001, it now accounts for more than half of the world production. Conversely, Europe's global production share accounts for less than 4% in 2015[6] with a structural trade deficit in solar component of about €10 billion. This newfound Chinese dominance in the PV industry (spurring a dynamic of continuous declining cost of solar electricity production) has led the European Commission to address a protracted anti-dumping trade dispute against China's panel makers with the imposition of anti-dumping duties on EU imports of solar panels in June 2013. Eventually, parties reached an agreement less than two months later by imposing limits on volume and minimum price for module imports, but this event highlights the trade tensions on key sectors in the energy transition. However, this issue also addresses the unanticipated effects of uncoordinated economic push and pull policies (Voituriez and Wang 2015). Whereas the Chinese government was pursuing a supply-side support policy[7] to reduce the price of PVs (even below its cost of production), the EU was mainly using demand-side policies to incentivize the development of renewable energy.

4.2 Europe's Industrial Potential

Europe was the world region that invested the most in renewable energy R&D with $4.3 billion[8] in 2015 (of which $1.4 billion comes from government spending). It is also the main applicant for patents in Climate Change Mitigation Technologies (CCMT) (Rudyk et al. 2015). For the 1995–2011 period, 18% of CCMT inventions were made in Europe. This share rose to around 36%[9] for those considered highly valuable.[10] According to a report by the Industrial Innovation for Competitiveness Initiative (I24C and CapGemini 2016), Europe possesses a strong leadership in 3 out of 11 energy-related innovation areas, and at least an average position for 8 of them.

For instance, the automotive industry, historically dominated by developed countries, still represents a significant share of the European economy with about 4% of its total GDP. Its market is currently experiencing several disruptions, which could lead to a massive transformation of the market—possibly wiping out historical manufacturers. The emergence of new major players from different backgrounds (technology companies, manufacturers based in developing countries) as well as technological advances achieved in autonomous vehicles or electric engines prefigure a new, harsher business environment in which the major European car manufacturers will have to compete.

To mitigate this risk, the European Commission has created the GEAR working group (High Level Group on the Competitiveness and Sustainable Growth of the Automotive Industry in European Union 2017). This offers a signal that the EC is ready to take on this challenge with all automotive industry stakeholders and elaborate a supportive institutional framework. Securing and adapting an industrial leading position in sectors such as the automotive industry is certainly vital for European economic interests, but will not be sufficient to make Europe an economic champion of the energy transition. Several technologies (such as building energy efficiency, smart grids or energy storage) that are expected to be central in the progressive phasing-out fossil fuel use are still at the innovation stage, or at best at the very beginning of their commercialization. In the innovation cycle, success in the early phases does not necessarily translate into longer-term gains.[11] By easing the access to private capital, either through the development of risk-sharing mechanisms or by backing loans, European authorities could spur the deployment of CCMT.

5 Conclusion

By the scale of its impact on the entire economy, the energy transition requires a high level of coordination as well as a significant impulse from the public sector. The EU has been at the vanguard of climate change mitigation policy for the better part of two decades, but its effectiveness in fostering the implementation of the energy transition can be improved.

The overwhelming majority of energy transition investments are conducted at the local and national levels, which sets natural limits for the role the EU. However, for specific network infrastructure projects—particularly long-distance electrical interconnections—the EU offers the only relevant governance level. More importantly, leveraging aggregation effects can make the EU a powerful tool to rise low-cost financing for the energy transition, as exemplified by the EFSI.

Second, the EU can provide a platform to improve the coordination between each member state's energy policies. Transitioning to a low-carbon energy mix requires the cooperation of European countries, and to a certain extent to synchronize the pace of the decarbonization of their energy supply. This can only be accomplished through EU-mediated coordination. On a similar note, the EC should improve the coherence between EU-level policy and budgetary priorities regarding the energy transition.

Finally, the current leadership of Europe in terms of R&D for energy transition-related activities should not be considered as a perpetual advantage, which would ensure the development of domestic firms. In order to make the energy transition an inclusive and growth-oriented pathway, it is necessary for member states and European institutions to coordinate economic policies within their borders, but also with the rest of the world. In order to secure the European lead in R&D activities and reap the commercial fruits of Europe's ambitious climate change policies, the EU should increase its support for the commercialization of these new technologies.

Notes

1. http://ec.europa.eu/eurostat/statistics-explained/index.php/Greenhouse_gas_emission_statistics.
2. http://ec.europa.eu/budget/mff/figures/index_en.cfm.
   http://ec.europa.eu/regional_policy/cs/policy/evaluations/data-for-research/.
3. https://www.euractiv.com/section/future-eu/news/commissions-realistic-budget-criticised-by-member-states/?utm_term=Autofeed&utm_campaign=Echobox&utm_medium=Social&utm_source=Twitter#link_time=1525276571.
4. https://ec.europa.eu/energy/en/topics/energy-strategy-and-energy-union/clean-energy-all-europeans.
5. https://ec.europa.eu/info/consultations/evaluation-eu-framework-taxation-energy-products-and-electricity_en.
6. Similarly, the combined production share of United States and Japan, which represented 70% of the world production in 2001, was less than 10% in 2015.
7. Mainly through 50% corporate tax reduction and loan facilities.
8. Asia, excluding China and India, is the second region with $2.4 billion R&D investments.

9. In the fields of Transports, Carbon capture and Smart grids, this share rose even up to around 40%.
10. High-valuable patents are defined as those that have a patent protection in at least two jurisdictions.
11. The economic literature often refers to the concept of "valley of death" to describe the timespan between the initial research and the commercialization a product which can lead to business failures because first movers are not adequately capitalized.

References

European Commission. 2006. *Green Paper. A European Strategy for Sustainable, Competitive and Secure Energy*. Brussels.

———. 2007. An Energy Policy for Europe. Communication from the Commission to the European Council and the European Parliament. *Publication Office of the European Union*, 1–28.

———. 2014. A Policy Framework for Climate and Energy in the Period from 2020 to 2030. doi:COM(2014) 15 final COMMUNICATION.

———. 2017a. *Interim Report – Financing a Sustainable European Economy*. Brussels.

———. 2017b. Reflection Paper on the Future of European Defence. *European Commission COM*, 315.

———. 2017c. *Third Report on the State of the Energy Union*. Brussels.

Gorlach, Benjamin. 2013. *What Constitutes an Optimal Climate Policy Mix? Defining the Concept of Optimality, Including Political and Legal Framework Conditions*, No. CECILIA2050 WP1 Deliverable 1.1.

Hedberg, Annika. 2017. Germany's Energy Transition: Making It Deliver, No. October.

High Level Group on the Competiteness and Sustainable Growth of the Automotive Industry in European Union, European Commission. 2017. Gear 2030.

I24C, and CapGemini. 2016. Scaling up Innovation in the Energy Union to Meet New Climate, Competitiveness and Societal Goals – Scoping the Future in Light of the Past.

Kok, M.T.J., and H.C. de Coninck. 2007. Widening the Scope of Policies to Address Climate Change: Directions for Mainstreaming. *Environmental Science & Policy* 10 (7–8): 587–599. Elsevier.

Medarova-Bergstrom, Keti, Axel Volkery, Pernille Schiellerup, Sirini Withana, and David Baldock. 2011. Strategies and Instruments for Climate Proofing the EU Budget. *IEEP*. Brussels.

Rudyk, Ilja, Gerard Owens, Alessio Yolpe, Robert Ondhowe, and Antoine Dechezleprêtre. 2015. *Climate Change Mitigation Technologies in Europe – Evidence from Patent and Economic Data*. Brussels.

UNEP. 2014. *The Emissions Gap Report*. Retrieved from http://www.unep.org/publications/ebooks/emissionsgapreport2014/.

Voituriez, Tancrède, and Xin Wang. 2015. Real Challenges Behind the EU – China PV Trade Dispute Settlement. *Climate Policy* 15 (5): 670–677.

12

Toward a Well-Being Europe

Éloi Laurent

1 Introduction: Governing Numbers

No region of the world embodies better the emergence of data-driven societies than one of its most recent political organizations: the European Union (EU). The European Community (which became the EU in 1992) was founded in 1957, based—with good reason—on the mistrust of politics. Rereading French foreign minister Robert Schuman's declaration of May 9, 1950, there is little doubt that this EU founding father saw unabashed political power as a threat to peace. In his eyes, it was necessary to deprive European countries of the means to destroy their fragile post-war peace, even if this meant that democracy had to be constrained. The constraint in question came in the form of economic rules[1] embedded in the Treaty of Rome (1957), which morphed with the Maastricht

É. Laurent (✉)
OFCE, Sciences Po, Paris, France

School of Management and Innovation Sciences Po, Paris, France

Stanford University, Stanford, CA, USA
e-mail: eloi.laurent@sciencespo.fr

© The Author(s) 2018
J. Creel et al. (eds.), *Report on the State of the European Union*,
https://doi.org/10.1007/978-3-319-98364-6_12

Treaty (1992) into quantitative criteria used to constantly monitor and evaluate member states from the moment of their admission into the various circles of European integration.[2]

The EU is today largely governed by numbers. The Maastricht Treaty is the economic constitution of contemporary Europe,[3] and in it the political power of data is very tangible: ratios govern the admission of countries into the EU and the euro area and are supposed to guarantee the continent's stability, unity, and prosperity (see Chaps. 2 and 3)."

This project is officially motivated by the goal of paving the way for a better common future for European peoples, but the Stability Pact and the ECB statutes give priority to "price stability" and "fiscal sustainability," even if this means reducing governments' ability to deliver economic dynamism and employment expansion. Some indicators have been given prevalence over others out of political choice. But it is more and more clear that the intermediate objectives that prevail (fiscal balance, currency strength, price stability) are at odds in practice with the attainment of the ultimate social objectives (such as employment) that matter the most to populations.[4]

Countries belonging to the euro area, the most integrated part of the European project, have relied on these economic rules to govern their common policies. It can be said that the regulations have not served them well. If they have brought about an apparent culture of discipline, they were not able to create a lasting culture of cooperation: the "great recession" of 2008–2009 triggered a crisis that has, in recent years, turned into a lack of political trust among European citizens.[5] While economic discipline through numbers was supposed to ease peacetime relations, it has instead created divergence among nations and conflicts within their borders.

There is indeed a real European paradox regarding well-being indicators since the great recession: on the one hand, the EU has tried to capitalize on the discontent with standard economics and to embrace the "beyond GDP" agenda; on the other, it has become even more rigid in applying its ill-advised targets. The communication "GDP and Beyond: Measuring Progress in a Changing World," released in 2009 by the European Commission, described ways to improve indicators in order to better reflect societal concerns. The Commission's intent was to adjust and complement Gross Domestic Product (GDP) with indicators that monitored social and environmental progress.[6]

Yet, so far, the new strategy has not produced tangible results in changing European governance, which still relies heavily on conventional economic indicators. What is more, while the EU was putting forward these new indicators, it was also coercing the Greek government, from 2010 onward, into reaching European ratios in a time of recession, delaying the country's economic recovery by several years, imposing extremely difficult social conditions on the Greek population,[7] and creating perilous political tensions among member states.[8] As the European example makes clear, democracy ends up at risk when too much confidence is put by policymakers on too-narrow indicators.

This chapter advocates a two-step approach to reenchant the European project: first, put well-being and sustainability (not public finance discipline, growth, or finance) at the center of European policy; second, build a social-ecological state calibrated for the early twenty-first century where the inequality and ecological crises feed one another.

2 Embracing the Well-Being and Sustainability Transition

Conceived in the mid-1930s by Harvard development economist Simon Kuznets to take stock of the Great Depression and improved by a team of British economists around John Maynard Keynes in the midst of the war effort, GDP was crowned king of all economic data at the Bretton Woods conference in July 1944, when Western nations embraced it as their common currency of power and success. From then on, to be "developed" meant to have developed its GDP. It took three decades for the "beyond GDP" to emerge. In a series of papers published between 1972 and 1973, economists William Nordhaus and James Tobin suggested that "growth" (understood narrowly as the increase of GDP) had become "obsolete" and attempted for the first time to offer not just an ethical or theoretical alternative to growth, but an empirical one (Nordhaus and Tobin 1973).

This research and policy-making agenda has greatly expanded since then (see Gadrey and Jany-Catrice 2006), and gained momentum in the last decade, starting with the organization of the "Beyond GDP" conference under the auspices of the EU in December 2007, aimed at taking stock of existing alternative indicators to GDP.[9] Today, dozens of well-being indicators (i.e. well-being, resilience, and sustainability indicators) are being produced and updated each year.[10]

The EU has two very good reasons to embrace the well-being and sustainability transition: historically, it has built itself as a normative and post-materialistic power; in the current geopolitical context, it must take its "fate into its own hands" and depart from the US where the obsession of growth, profit, and finance is harming the well-being of citizens (a destruction tangible with the alarming degradation of inequality, health, trust in democracy, and environmental quality).

But, as I have just argued, the EU is currently suffering from values schizophrenia: it was the first major power to embrace the "Beyond GDP" agenda (in 2007) and has tried since then to integrate well-being indicators into its policies (e.g. the EU 2020 strategy), several of its member states being the most advanced countries on the planet with regards to social justice and sustainability policy. But it continues to govern itself with the outdated Maastricht criteria, which are doubly misleading: they focus on discipline and not cooperation and are expressed in percentage of GDP.

Why is a well-being transition needed? Because the twenty-first-century challenges cannot be understood let alone addressed with twentieth-century policy indicators such as growth of GDP conceived in the mid-1930s. To put it differently, while policymakers govern with numbers and data, they are as well governed by them. These data thus should be relevant and accurate. Such is no longer the case of GDP. Consider the crisis of inequality (the growing gap between the haves and the have-nots) and the crisis of the Biosphere (the alarming degradation of climate, ecosystems, and biodiversity that threatens human well-being). Neither can be analyzed or mitigated with growth (of GDP) simply because GDP was not designed to assess either. As a result, focusing on growth leads to analytical and policy mistakes: policymakers neglect equality and distributional issues, confusing growth with social progress, and degrade ecosystems for short-term economic gains, harming human well-being while believing to improve it. Policy ends up divorcing from citizens' aspirations and scientific knowledge. But there is nothing inevitable about this: we can change what we measure to reform what we manage and put human well-being back at the center of policy at all levels of governance.

What is well-being?[11] It stems from an eternal question: what are the real drivers of human development and success beside material conditions? Exploring human well-being means articulating a multidimensional vision of human welfare casually referred to as "quality of life." Human well-being can be assessed at different geographic scales, objectively (via measures of health status or educational attainments), subjectively (through the assessment of happiness or trust), but it is in all cases a static metric that tells us nothing about its evolution over time.

For a dynamic approach that sheds light not only on the current state of well-being but also on its future, one has to turn to the concepts of resilience and sustainability. The questions asked by citizens and policymakers then become substantially more complex: "Can we project our well-being over time?" Resilience is a first step in this direction, as it tries to determine if well-being can resist and survive shocks. More precisely, it assesses the ability of a community, a territory, a nation, or the whole planet to cope with economic, social, or environmental shocks and their capacity to return afterward to their pre-shock level of well-being without seeing it degraded or destroyed. One typical, pressing resilience issue is how human communities around the world can adapt to climate change.

The measurement of sustainability is even more ambitious, in that it seeks to evaluate well-being in the long run, both after the occurrence of shocks and during normal times. Attempting to assess sustainability is about trying to understand how these stocks can be maintained or even increased over time, such as how services freely provided by ecosystems can continue benefiting future generations. (Consider, for example, pollination, on which 75% of the world's crops at least partially depend.) From this perspective, resilience can be understood as the short-run horizon of sustainability: resilience is concerned with shocks and sustainability with stocks.

Instead of growth and public finance discipline, well-being (human flourishing), resilience (resisting shocks), and sustainability (caring about the future) should become the collective horizons of EU member states. The challenge is to make those alternative indicators performative, and not just descriptive. This does not depend only on their technical quality but, much more importantly, on their embedment in public debate and the democratic process.

The basic course of action is to make visible what matters for humans and then make it count. Unmeasurability means invisibility: "What is not measured is not managed." As the saying goes. Conversely, as we have argued, measuring is governing: indicators determine policies and actions. Measuring, done properly, can produce positive social meaning. It does not mean that everything should be monetized or marketed but understanding how what matters to humans can be accounted for is the first step to valuing and taking care of what really counts. There is no accountability without accounting.

A key distinction should be made here among quantification, monetization, and commodification (or marketization). We certainly argue for quantification of invisible value so that it is not ignored or blindly destroyed (this is the example of health in the US and happiness in China). But this quantification should not necessarily imply monetization. And this monetization, when necessary, does not lead inevitably to commodification.

Consider food labeling. If the only dimension of food resources that receives recognition is their monetary cost, the health dimension will never be reflected in production and/or consumption behavior. Appropriate labeling on the other hand (such as the one being implemented currently in France in the form of a Nutri-score ranging from A to E), will inform the consumer about important aspects of the food that manufacturers may have an interest in concealing, such as the presence of chemical additives, the total caloric value, or its salt or fat content.

Or consider ecosystems valuation. To destroy a wetland rich in biodiversity on the basis of the economic value of the housing that can be built on it is to rely on one value (the immediate economic one) against all the others that have just as much bearing on human well-being. Revealing the plural values of biodiversity or ecosystems, monetized or not, amounts in this case to protecting them from blind destruction.

In fact, the performative power of well-being indicators does not depend only on the technical quality but, much more importantly, on their embedment in public debate and the democratic process.

This can be done by integrating indicators in policy through representative democracy, regulatory democracy, and participatory democracy. Applied carefully by private and public decision makers, well-being indicators can foster genuine progress.

For instance, we should be rethinking the way we vote the budget. Most Parliaments members around the world, including in the European Parliament, know very little about the true state of their country apart from aggregate macroeconomic indicators when they make key decisions on public finance. In an old democracy like France, the statistical information given to MPs amounts to GDP and its components. It would not to be difficult to select well-being indicators in key dimensions relevant for public finance, starting with inequality, and embed those indicators in the budgetary procedure so that they are made public and discussed prior to voting. A permanent parliamentary body could even be created that could become a place of continuing deliberation on public choice impacting well-being, bringing together experts and citizens to mobilize the right indicators on the right issues in order to provide policymakers with the relevant information to make their choices. This could take place at the national level as well as the regional level (e.g. the EU).

The EU should in fact design and organize, within the European semester, a debate in the European Parliament and all member states parliaments on well-being and sustainability indicators, conform to European values and national priorities, and give those indicators priority over public finance criteria at the time of budget voting.

The second reform concerns regulatory democracy and, more precisely, the reform of economic instruments used routinely by the executive branch of EU member states governments to design public policies once laws have been adopted. Public policies today too often rely on simplistic models framed by cost-benefit analysis (CBA). CBA evaluates the efficiency (and profitability) of a project by calculating the net worth or net benefits it produces, that is, the amount of potential benefit less the costs associated with the project. The only dimensions to enter the analysis are economic flows (benefits and costs) that can be monetized. It would be much more interesting to systematically replace these methods with a multicriteria analysis where the financial cost or benefit is not the sole reference and where intangible effects are considered alongside tangible ones—or at least to perform sensitivity tests to evaluate the impact of alternative parameters, especially social discount rates, on CBA results.

Finally, participatory democracy must strengthen these reforms of the legislative and executive branch. Democracy is not just one dimension of well-being, but also the method that must govern its definition and governance: it is at once an outcome and an input. An example of participatory method is "citizens' conferences," a setting that includes a panel of citizens, experts, and decision makers discussing the respective importance of different dimensions of well-being and agreeing on a common dashboard to be implemented (such method was implemented in the French region of Nord-Pas-de-Calais in 2010). It is of crucial importance to build tangible transitions in the EU at the local level, since well-being is best measured where it is actually experienced. The well-being transition is, in the words of Elinor Ostrom (2010), a "polycentric transition": each level of government can seize this opportunity to reform policy without waiting for the impetus to come from above.

3 Building the European Social-Ecological State

Going beyond growth as a social project does not only mean complementing and eventually replacing GDP with indicators of well-being, resilience, and sustainability. It also implies linking those three objectives in a new shared, positive narrative and building robust institutions to sustain it.

This new European narrative cannot rely in the twenty-first century exclusively on economic prosperity and monetary credibility, as has been the case for the last six decades. Because social protection and sustainability have become two strong pillars of the European identity, it should instead be based on the sustainability-justice nexus: our societies will be more just if they are more sustainable and more sustainable if they are more just (see Boyce 2002, 2013). In other words, it makes environmental sense to mitigate our social crisis and social sense to mitigate our environmental crises. This is the basic statement of the social-ecological approach (Laurent 2011a, b) and it can be a starting point to revive the European project building on its own history.

The first arrow of causality, which runs from inequality to environmental degradation, can be labeled "integrative social-ecology," as it shows that the gap between the rich and the poor and the interaction of the two groups leads to the worsening of environmental degradations and ecological crises that affect every member of a given community (e.g. greater inequality leads to a lesser adaptation capacity).

The reciprocal arrow of causality that goes from ecological crises to social injustice can be labeled "differential social-ecology," as it shows that the social impact of ecological crises is not the same for different individuals and groups, given their socioeconomic status (the most vulnerable socially are "ecological sentinels" in the sense that they are first and foremost affected by current ecological crises).

In other words, the social-ecological approach considers the reciprocal relationship between social and environmental issues, demonstrating how social logics determine environmental damage and crises and exploring the reciprocal relation, that is, the consequences of these damages on social inequality. Environmental risk is certainly a collective and global horizon, but it is socially differentiated. Who is responsible for what and with what consequences for whom? Such is the social-ecological approach, and it calls for social-ecological policy.

The development of a social-ecological policy requires prior identification and analysis of the associated and sometimes inextricable character of the social and the environmental dimensions: there is a need to recognize the ecological stakes within social issues, as well as to reveal the social stakes of ecological issues, at the national as well as European level (the social-ecological dimension of carbon taxation for instance is a national and European policy matter). This approach can be formalized using a social-ecological matrix (see Fig. 12.1).

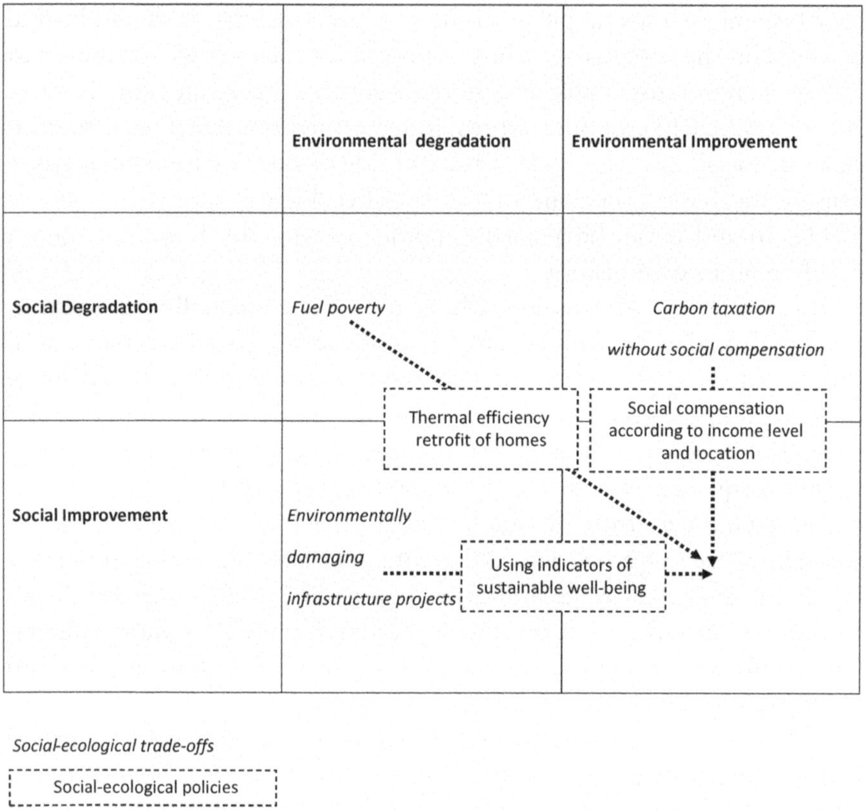

Fig. 12.1 Social-ecological trade-offs and synergies

Reading of Fig. 12.1

Each quadrant represents a combined assessment of the social and environmental outcome of a given situation or policy. In the top left quadrant, fuel poverty results both in monetary poverty and energy over-consumption. Thermal insulation (home weatherization) allows for a reduction in energy consumption (and thus lower related greenhouse gas emissions, triggering environmental improvement), which translates into lower expenditure devoted to energy by fuel poor households, allowing for social progress.

In the top right quadrant, carbon taxation without social compensation is both socially regressive, as it hurts the poorest more because of their higher income share devoted to energy consumption, and environmentally efficient, because it reduces greenhouse emissions by pricing carbon. Introducing social compensation based on income level but also location (rural areas versus urban areas, suburban areas vs. urban centers, etc.) maintains the environmental efficiency of the policy measure (compensation should not be understood as exoneration) but eases its social impact and therefore its political acceptability.

Finally, the bottom left quadrant takes the example of CBA applied to infrastructure projects, for instance housing. When biodiversity and ecosystems are not or only partially taken into consideration, building a residential complex on a wetland increases human well-being while at the same time destroying ecosystems and biodiversity. The social-ecological policy in this case is conceptual: it consists in changing indicators used to decide or not to implement the policy by integrating the social value of ecosystems and biodiversity. When a correct assessment based on comprehensive wealth analysis including benefits derived from natural capital is carried out, the infrastructure project will be moved to a better/less harmful location, resulting in both environmental and social progress.

Implementation of a social-ecological policy requires active awareness of the interplay of social issues and environmental challenges so as to enable progress in both of these dimensions simultaneously (as in the case of housing insulation). Yet there are numerous cases in which to envisage and devise a social-ecological policy is to recognize the need for arbitration between the social question and the environmental question as a prerequisite for finding appropriate solutions (e.g. carbon taxation which, if one is not careful, can entail harmful social consequences).

Going further, what could be the purpose of a social-ecological state? The modern welfare state was devised in the 1880s in unified Germany to forge a new alliance between labor and capital, and was built upon the idea that human beings are entitled to receive protection against the hazards of nature and social life. "Social security"—currently guaranteed to fewer than 30% of the world's population in about half of the planet's countries—is already a considerable extension of the "civil security" that Hobbes entrusted to the Leviathan in the mid-1600s.

The next stage for European member states consists in moving on from social security to social-ecological security by acknowledging that the nature of social risk underwent a fundamental change at the end of the twentieth century. A state fit for the twenty-first century should aim at forging a new alliance between social issues and environmental challenge. Because social risk today includes a major environmental dimension (floods, heat waves, hurricanes, storms, pollutions, etc.), citizens are entitled to expect public authorities to develop and put in place adequate means of protection. Because the well-being of individuals and groups is increasingly determined by environmental conditions, it is legitimate for social policy to include environmental dimension. Environmental crises, in other words, should be considered as social risks and therefore call for insurance.

What might be the role of a European social-ecological state? It would be no different from that fulfilled by the welfare state through its functions of allocation, redistribution, and stabilization, but these functions would be applied to environmental issues.

The allocation function of the social-ecological state means revealing the hidden social costs of ecological crises—such as respiratory diseases, strokes, etc. caused by air pollution in European urban centers—in order to reduce them and the inequality that they compound. Numerous reports indeed stress the beneficial effect of environmental regulations on health and well-being (such as the Clean Air Act in the US or the Montreal Protocol on the ozone layer at the global level). The social cost of ecological crises must be made visible in order to reveal the misguided allocation of resources to which the current economic systems lead. A key notion in this respect is environmental inequality.

From the proven importance of environmental factors in the health of citizens arises the ethical and political question concerning the socially differentiated exposure and vulnerability of individuals and groups. To understand why environmental inequalities may be unjust, one must adopt a notion grounded in an explicit theory of justice. One possibility is to base environmental justice on the capability-building and human development framework developed by Amartya Sen.

The capability approach recommends that well-being be assessed beyond material conditions and reflects also the quality of life of a given person. Among the determinants of quality of life, environmental conditions appear of great importance.

Based on this analytical framework, we can define environmental inequality: an environmental inequality, which may be the simple empirical observation of a difference or disparity, results in an injustice or is unjust if the well-being and capabilities of a particular population are disproportionately affected by its environmental conditions of existence. The environmental conditions of existence consist of, negatively, exposure to pollution and risks, and, positively, access to amenities and natural resources (water, air, food). The particular character of the population in question can be defined according to different criteria: social, demographic, territorial, and so on. Yet, environmental justice does not imply that environmental conditions must be equal for all citizens or groups, but that they should not disproportionately affect their well-being and capabilities with respect to the rest of the population.

Environmental justice, which originally initiated in the US, therefore can be said, for EU member states and institutions, to aim at identifying, measuring, and correcting environmental inequalities that result in social injustice. It implies the adoption of an effective arsenal of public policies grounded on scientific research.

Let us now consider the function of stabilization. In its traditional meaning, this consists of governments' bringing into play automatic stabilizers and discretionary policy in order to cushion an economic shock and prevent a recession from degenerating into a depression. The stabilization function thus increases resilience. The social-ecological stabilization function is, by the same logic, aimed at enabling individuals to deal with ecological shocks (e.g. the heatwave of 2003) by preserving their well-being.

Finally, when it comes to redistribution, tax systems should be reformed to penalize the excessive use of natural resources, starting with fossil fuels. The EU member states should embark on a third tax revolution, after the taxation of income at the beginning of the twentieth century and of consumption in the 1950s. Currently, on average, environmental taxation represents 6% of total taxation and has declined since 2002 (when it represented 7%).

4 Conclusion: Two Transitions in One

Indicators of well-being and sustainability need the social-ecological narrative to become performative. The social-ecological state could not operate without new indicators of well-being and sustainability.

Social-ecological accounting, risk, and insurance could end up reinventing social policy in the face of socially unequal environmental crises just as public policy was reinvented in the last 100 years to mutualize, prevent, and ultimately reduce major social risks for hundreds of millions of people. This revolution started in Europe. The well-being and social-ecological transitions should as well.

Notes

1. Brennan and Buchanan (1988).
2. See Dani (2005) and Maduro (1998).
3. This conception was formally advanced by Finn Kydland and Edward Prescott (1977), who intended to develop and legitimize, on behalf of individual freedoms and the effectiveness of public policy, an economic constitutional order constraining the state's power. According to this perspective, public policies ought to be governed by principles with which the state cannot interfere.
4. Le Cacheux and Laurent (2015).
5. "The New Sick Man of Europe: the European Union," Pew Research Center Commentary, May 13, 2013, http://www.pewglobal.org/2013/05/13/the-new-sick-man-of-europe-the-european-union/.
6. The communication identified five key actions for the short to medium term: complement GDP with environmental and social indicators (environmental index and quality of life and well-being); provide near real-time information for decision-making; report more accurately on distribution and inequalities; develop a European sustainable development scoreboard (including thresholds for environmental sustainability); and extend national accounts to environmental and social issues.
7. *The Lancet* reported that the health of the Greek population had suffered tremendously during the worst of the austerity policy, and even talked about a "Greek public health tragedy." HIV incidence in injectable-drug users rose more than tenfold from 2009 to 2012 and tuberculosis incidence in this population more than doubled in 2013; state funding for mental health decreased by 55% between 2011 and 2012; major depression grew to two and a half times its 2008 rate by 2011; suicides increased by 45% between 2007 and 2011; and infant mortality jumped by 43% between 2008 and 2010. See Kentikelenis et al. (2014).

8. By the same token, in July 2016, the EU triggered the sanction mechanisms of the Stability Pact against Portugal and Spain for failing to respect deficit reduction targets, while the two countries were still economically and politically very weak.
9. Proceedings of this conference can be found here: http://ec.europa.eu/environment/beyond_gdp/2007_conference_en.html.
10. A good place to keep track of this production is the news section of the Beyond GDP blog maintained by the EU: http://ec.europa.eu/environment/beyond_gdp/news_en.html as well as the Wikiprogress website http://wikiprogress.org/.
11. See Laurent (2018).

References

Boyce, J.K. 2002. *The Political Economy of the Environment*. Cheltenham: Edward Elgar.

———. 2013. *Economics, the Environment and Our Common Wealth*. Cheltenham: Edward Elgar.

Brennan, G., and J.M. Buchanan. 1988. *The Reason of Rules: Constitutional Political Economy*. New York: Cambridge University Press.

Dani, M. 2005. *Economic Constitutionalism(s) in a Time of Uneasiness: Comparative Study on the Economic Constitutional Identities of Italy, the WTO and the EU*. Jean Monnet Working Paper 08/05. New York: New York University.

Gadrey, J., and F. Jany-Catrice. 2006. *The New Indicators of Well-Being and Development*. Basingstoke: Palgrave Macmillan.

Kentikelenis, A., et al. 2014. Greece's Health Crisis: From Austerity to Denialism. *The Lancet* 383 (9918): 748–753.

Kydland, F.E., and E.C. Prescott. 1977. Rules Rather than Discretion: The Inconsistency of Optimal Plans. *Journal of Political Economy* 85 (3): 473–491.

Laurent, É. 2011a. *Social-écologie*. Paris: Flammarion.

———. 2011b. Issues in Environmental Justice Within the European Union. *Ecological Economics* 70 (11): 1846–1853.

———. 2018. *Measuring Tomorrow: Accounting for Well-being, Resilience and Sustainability in the 21st century*. Oxford/Princeton: Princeton University Press.

Le Cacheux, J., and É. Laurent. 2015. *Report on the State of the European Union*. Vol. 4, *Is Europe Sustainable?* Basingstoke: Palgrave Macmillan.

Nordhaus, W., and J. Tobin. 1973. Is Growth Obsolete? In *The Measurement of Economic and Social Performance*, ed. Milton Moss. New York: National Bureau of Economic Research.

Ostrom, E. 2010. Beyond Markets and States: Polycentric Governance of Complex Economic Systems. *American Economic Review* 100 (3): 641–672.

Poiares Maduro, M. 1998. *We the Court: The European Court of Justice and the European Economic Constitution*. Oxford: Hart Publishing.

13

A Currency Democratically Shared Among Democracies

Maxime Parodi

The European Union has long been accused of suffering from a democratic deficit. This is nevertheless an ambivalent reproach. For some, this simply amounts to a matter of worrying about the distance between the ordinary citizen and Europe's institutions, a gap that results in a high abstention rate in European elections and a clear lack of interest in European issues. For others, it is a question of pointing to the weakness of national debates and the impotence of national parliaments in the face of decisions taken at the EU level, which seem to fall on nations like arbitrary decrees. For still others, the best illustration of the absence of democracy at the European level is the poverty of the European debate and the lack of transnational dialogue, whereas action is needed that is strong and legitimate at this level, particularly with respect to macroeconomic governance in the euro zone.

Behind these criticisms, everyone is trying to come up with their own answer to the problem of the absence of one European people to give shape to a European democracy. Can there be a democracy at the EU

M. Parodi (✉)
OFCE, Sciences Po, Paris, France
e-mail: maxime.parodi@sciencespo.fr

© The Author(s) 2018

J. Creel et al. (eds.), *Report on the State of the European Union*,
https://doi.org/10.1007/978-3-319-98364-6_13

level without a European demos? Some believe that it is necessary to use forceps to bring about this European people by creating a European government and parliament and more or less reproducing the institutional system of this or that European country. Others hold that it is on the contrary imperative to protect the existing demos at the national level by opposing the EU's undemocratic interference, at the risk of losing democracy at every level. These two obviously irreconcilable camps traverse the political spectrum of most European nations and are today helpless in the face of the challenge being posed by the ever greater intermingling of European societies and their interests.

And yet, this cleavage ignores the essential question for the European Union: can a multitude of demos coexist democratically? And if so, how? What principles would common institutions have to respect? And is a common currency possible under these principles?

1 The Two Concepts of Democracy

The challenge is above all conceptual: modern democracy was first thought of in the framework of the nation-state, that is to say, in a specific political format where a sovereign reigns over a territory considered as closed, as if the collective destiny depended only on the sovereign's decisions and not on what happens beyond the border. In this context, democracy is simply defined from the notion of popular sovereignty: all powers are granted by and for the people. The political form is therefore imposed: to have a democracy, there must be one people, and only one. And the current alternative of the European Union can be readily summed up: either we count on the revolutionary emergence of the European people to democratize the Union, which simply becomes a nation replacing the present nations; or we keep the existing nations and acknowledge that a Union of peoples cannot be democratic.

It is possible, however, to define democracy differently than in terms of sovereignty. Indeed, the quality of sovereignty immediately reduces the political question of living together to that of giving oneself a king—as if politics consisted solely in designating who makes lawful decisions in the here and now. But politics is also about being able to debate public affairs and to strive to found just laws and institutions. In this broader context, democracy no longer consists in associating people and government by diverse means, but resides more crucially in the vitality of the public debate and the participation of everyone, the weak and the powerful, in this debate. Democracy then consists of redistributing the power to speak to the public, so that the arguments and positions of all the people are taken into account in public decisions and in establishing the rules, laws and institutions. The point is to ensure that the debate, and its consequences for everyday life, are not taken over by the powerful or by those who claim to speak in the name of a fantasized and instrumentalized "people".

With this second definition, the debate on democracy can be extracted from nationalist channels. Furthermore, a retreat into nationalism could now be in contradiction with citizens' democratic aspirations. Given the fact that European societies are more and more open to each other and that the continent's citizens have interests and are engaged in projects that do not stop at national borders, such a retreat would drastically limit people's horizons. Brexit offers an illustration: the English worker employed in an Opel assembly plant is not asking to build 100% English cars, but to enjoy the opportunity offered by long-term collaboration within a network of companies specializing in the automotive industry. With this rise of transnational interests and joint projects in Europe, it is ever more necessary to broaden the democratic debate beyond national borders.

There are, however, several ways that this broadening could be handled. First, the idea could be advanced of a cosmopolitan or post-national democracy that would be based on transnational debates conducted by citizens who are strongly involved in civil society. Governance within the EU would become democratized because of its citizens' active engagement in argumentation and deliberation. From this perspective, the EU would reduce its democratic deficit through the activities of international institutions and non-governmental organizations. What matters would be the citizens' own activity, expressed through vigorous transnational associations. In this deliberative form, power is dispersed among various institutions and associations that must, therefore, collaborate by communicating within diverse networks.

This perspective does however raise a number of doubts (Bohman 2005), among which are two main criticisms. First, the deliberative approach probably overestimates the power of argumentation within the EU. Transnational activism will not suffice to render the EU's organization democratic, even if such activism is desirable. Second, this kind of democratization will remain very limited, since it does not affect the general public, but is confined to the most committed citizens in active associations.

2 The Principle of a Demoicracy

Another conceptual approach consists of not rejecting either of these two notions of democracy, but instead trying to conceive of the rights of the national peoples and the rights of Europe's citizens together. This idea is being proposed today under the neologism of demoicracy, which insists on a plurality of demos. Philippe Van Parijs had originally come up with this term to criticize the de facto primacy of the peoples over the Union (Van Parijs 1997). But other authors have given it a positive sense (see Nicolaïdis 2012; Cheneval and Schimmelfennig 2012). For them, demoicracy means recognizing the plurality of the peoples and States, but doing this while respecting the fundamental rights of the citizens of other EU countries.

In this respect, it is possible to define the principle of this demoicratic approach by following a parallel with the theory of John Rawls (1971), as Francis Cheneval has proposed (2011). Rawls advances a model of reasoning that is valid within a nation-state. In this model, every citizen must reason behind a veil of ignorance to judge whether a law or an institution is just or unjust. Because of this veil, everyone ignores their social position and is therefore led to reason about social cooperation by worrying about the fairness of treatment between all social positions, since an individual could occupy any of these positions. This model can however be readily extended to the case of cooperation between citizens of different nations. Suffice it to say that each of the citizens thinks about the proper cooperation between the citizens of a number of nations, but without knowing to which nation they themselves belong. In this model, the citizens of each of the peoples open themselves up to the reasoning of other peoples. And, at the same time, the plurality of nationalities maintains the possibility that the institutions and rules are not the same for all. The citizens can opt for a uniform solution where the institutions and rules are similar throughout the EU, which would amount to unifying a European nation, but this is more of a borderline case. The model actually provides an opportunity to maintain national differences, and in all likelihood, such opportunities would be exploited in many areas.

What we see here is a principle of argumentation that is able to organize cooperation democratically between multiple democracies. It sheds light on what one can expect from deliberations in a pluri-national forum, without denying the citizens' national membership while obliging them to show impartiality among all the participants.

From a demoicratic point of view, it is also necessary to consider the distribution of powers at the institutional level so that the scope of this principle is as broad as possible. The coexistence of the national and the transnational has to be organized. Thus, it is a matter, on the one hand, of recognizing the plurality of peoples, constituted as so many nation-states, and, on the other hand, of assuming the fact that these peoples are generally open to each other and because of this they share a number of common goods and, to some extent, a common destiny.

A double institutional necessity thus emerges. First, there must be European institutions that embody the citizens' aspirations for a demoicracy and defend their rights. There must be a representation of the citizens—a European Parliament—that allows the citizens to be heard with regard both to what they expect from fair European cooperation and to the political orientations they consider legitimate at the European level. The citizens must be able to discuss intergovernmental negotiations by testing their argumentative value according to demoicratic principles. Transnational or cosmopolitan interests and arguments must be allowed, meaning that it is no longer possible to limit international cooperation to State-to-State or government-to-government negotiations. Democracy requires more than international institutions like the United Nations.

But, on the other hand, it is also necessary to maintain, at least ultimately, European nations' right of veto in order to ensure that no European partner is politically dominated. Each people thus has the right to leave the Union and retains its constituent power over its legal and political order. However, while this is necessary in order to guarantee the principle that the Union will not politically dominate any European people, this right is only a last resort and serves above all to guarantee that all nations will be heard in debates. The same holds for the constituent power: while it is a consequence of the right to leave, it must nevertheless be exercised in a spirit that is compatible with demoicracy, and therefore, unless a country is seeking to leave, it must take into account the neighbouring European legal and political order in its decisions. This does not, moreover, exclude nations from transferring authority to common authorities in limited areas. Countries may, for example, unanimously recognize the authority of the European Court of Justice and have to submit to it without a veto, except to decide to withdraw entirely from the Union, as envisaged by Britain with Brexit. Tomorrow, this could be the case for some police powers, or the establishment of common taxation rules.

This dual institutional necessity finally imposes the idea that the distribution of power within the European Union cannot be hierarchical. It can only be a heterarchy, a concept that is found in particular in the latest writings by Habermas (2015), which expresses the idea that no power centre dominates and that decisions can be taken only in common.

The EU can be considered as the incomplete achievement of a demoicracy. In broad terms, it more or less respects several major principles that it is right to expect (see Cheneval and Schimmelfennig 2012). The well-known democratic deficit of the European Union is then more relative than absolute: it is undoubtedly due to the lack of links between the expectations expressed by neighbouring nations and national debates and, consequently, to the weakness of the European Parliament. But this could also arise from ambiguity concerning the intentions of European construction. Is the intention to establish a hierarchy, which is a way of understanding the principle of subsidiarity? Or on the contrary to stick to the necessities of a common life within the Union? Indeed, the deficit is not found only at the level of the Union, but also translates at national level into debates that never directly address the question of the consequences of our policies and laws for neighbouring nations, and vice versa. However, judging over a long time frame, a change is emerging:

citizens increasingly think of their State as a Member State of a Union rather than as a nation whose destiny will be shaped by its hands alone (Bickerton 2012).

3 The Single Currency and Its Deficits in Governance

A single currency is a particular challenge for a demoicracy.[1] It is a common good that can be managed in different ways, fairly or unfairly, efficiently or inefficiently, by distributing the macroeconomic risks and benefits unequally between the countries and the citizens of each country. Faced with this challenge, an economic government of the euro often seems to be a necessity in order to respond effectively to the functional needs of a single currency. But this seems incompatible with demoicratic principles for at least two reasons. First, this supranational government would be hierarchically above the national governments, at least as regards the major topics in financing the economy, which would contradict the heterarchical principle and, therefore, the principle of the non-domination of peoples. Second, granting budget capacity to this government means that it could make significant financial transfers between the Member States or the citizens in order to ensure the macroeconomic regulation of the euro zone. But the citizens are clearly not ready to accept such transfers, which are already sources of conflict at the regional level.[2]

It is therefore necessary to retreat from this requirement of an economic government of the euro zone, or at least not to think about it on the model of our national governments. But again, one must ask whether such a government is as necessary as it is supposed to be, and whether the current teaming of governments, as they are, is not sufficient. Indeed, while everyone expects cooperation to be effective, it is not the first priority; the first priority is that cooperation benefits everyone and, to this end, the governance of the euro cannot bypass the requirement of the non-domination of the peoples.

Basically, the European Union faces three deficits in governance (Nicolaïdis & Watson, 2016). First, a cohesion deficit related to the impunity of the stowaway. In the absence of a central State with coercive resources, how can we ensure that all Member States play the game of cooperation? Then comes the deficit in macroeconomic regulation. In the absence of a substantial central budget, how can macroeconomic imbalances between the Union's different regions be managed? Finally, the social justice deficit. Without a European welfare state, how can the risks and benefits to be accorded to Europe's citizens be distributed, especially during a serious economic crisis such as that of 2008?

These deficits do not however mean that the euro is a currency without a State. In reality, it is a currency shared by States and, as such, it is very different from a currency like bitcoin. These States can thus, if necessary, act in concert as a single State would. The whole question, from a demoicratic perspective, is to know how a voluntary coordination of the States can cope with the aforesaid deficits while not using coercive means except as a last resort since—as is one of the foundations of any democracy—coercion must not be more common than reason.

3.1 A Demoicratic Perspective for the Common Currency

To the extent possible, it would be better to leave the hands of the countries free to manage their economic problems and conduct their trade-offs, but while not failing to include among the issues discussed the externalities and systemic problems that a particular national policy might pose for its European neighbours (and even beyond). The strategy of the stowaway is thus not prohibited at this stage, but it would become more visible. It is not easy for national politicians to justify this kind of strategy to their citizens. For the citizens, this means publicly accepting that a situation has an undue advantage. This has of course never prevented the Swiss from defending their banking secrecy or the Irish from keeping their low corporate tax rate, but criticism of the externalities of these policies is not as ineffective as one might think. By shining a light on their illegitimacy, criticism weakens and, in the more or less long term, condemns non-cooperative policies like these. A more direct initiative against the stowaway from a supranational authority could, on the contrary, awaken nationalistic reactions and mobilize citizens against European interference. This means that, in the fight against the stowaway, circumventing national democracy is not a good strategy. And while there must be a supranational authority to fight against forms of non-cooperation, this can be established only with the consent of each of the democracies. In this case too, it is necessary first to raise awareness about the mutual costs of externalities.

The absence of a substantial European budget is a problem from the moment when the budgetary competence of the Member States has been limited. In this case, of course, the possibility of pursuing a counter-cyclical fiscal policy at the European level is compromised. But the solution is not necessarily to increase the European budget. Furthermore, a central government would have to be able to spend this budget freely, and this is a clear political obstacle: Margaret Thatcher's "I want my money back!" was not just an English buzz phrase, it imposed a strong constraint on the budget, and proposals to increase the European budget by earmarking spending, for example, for the ecological transition, will not get around this. Moreover, if the principle of heterarchy is accepted, the budget must be discussed by the European partners; this means lengthy debates and endless negotiations, which is incompatible with the idea of a reactive European fiscal capacity capable of pursuing a counter-cyclical policy.

This is why greater fiscal freedom for the Member States may be more relevant for macroeconomic policy across Europe. Such an approach involves getting rid of the discipline imposed by the Maastricht criteria or, at present, the European Fiscal Compact (in the Treaty on Stability, Coordination and Governance—the TSCG). Once again, it is a question of putting the emphasis on the responsibility of the States, which will take over the recommendations of the European Commission that they consider relevant (e.g. during the debates in the European Semester). As before, fiscal coordination involves everyone's voluntary participation, discussing externalities and systemic issues. The States retain fiscal and budgetary autonomy as well as a capacity to take on debt.

All this means maintaining the principle of no bailout of the States, which is the counterpart of this budgetary and fiscal responsibility. Similarly, a State must be able to default on its debt. It must also be able to leave the euro, although not as hurriedly as in the case of a default. In this respect, a default on debt should not imply leaving the euro. In the case of a national currency, the destinies of the national debt and the currency are in fact linked through the banking system: the default risk causes the currency to devalue. But in the case of a shared currency, there is a certain ambivalence, which must be removed by dissociating the two events. A State must be able to fail without pulling down the entire banking system in its wake, in such a way that the citizens of the failed State do not find themselves dispossessed of their currency because they have shared it. To do this, the European Central Bank (ECB) must be able to support part of the banking system while prohibiting the system from financing the debt of the bankrupt State.

The fact remains that these scenarios are not desirable, for anyone, and the famous moral hazard is probably exaggerated, since the risk of an economic collapse is not covered (because while the help of the partners is not prohibited by the principle of no bailout, it is never guaranteed). On these bases, supranational discipline is advantageously replaced by self-discipline.

Finally, the sharing of the European currency must benefit all the partners, which means discussing the sharing of risks resulting from this cooperation and the fact of at least partially pooling them. The difference principle of Rawls can serve as a guide in this area (Rawls 1971). In the Rawlsian model, which deals only with solidarity within a nation, the point is to ensure that cooperation benefits everyone, and especially that it benefits the most disadvantaged as much as possible (because the norm of reciprocity is strong within a nation). In the demoicratic model, a similar principle would require that there is concern about what cooperation brings to the most disadvantaged citizen of the most disadvantaged nation (Cheneval 2011). The sense of reciprocity is certainly weaker than within a nation, but it is sufficiently strong that everyone guarantees to the others that their nation should not see its relative position deteriorate to the point where its most disadvantaged citizens would have an interest in leaving for other nations. The Greek case serves as an illustration. If the country is sacrificed and the new generations see their future condemned under the burden of debt, they will have an interest in leaving their country (even further increasing the burden for those who remain). But no one would agree to wind up in such a situation. There is therefore a European solidarity that must guarantee that everyone can certainly try their luck in another country but also that they can flourish in their country of origin. This means that no nation should be sacrificed on the altar of "efficient" cooperation with the others. The most disadvantaged nation must therefore have a real possibility of reaching the economic level of the others.

4 Two Readings of the Incompleteness of the Euro

In the words of many economists and European Commission officials, the current reform spirit aims to "complement" the euro by endowing it with an ad hoc technical-political structure that would be a functional equivalent of a European State (Report of the five Presidents, "Completing the European Economic and Monetary Union", 22 June 2015). However, the resulting proposals for reform struggle to reconcile economic demands with political expectations, such as proposals that pretend that a European people will emerge from the economic crisis and that an economic government in the euro zone is attainable through reform. So too technocratic proposals that wish to regulate the euro using econometric models to circumvent policy. The same holds for proposals that are more symbolic than anything else and act as if the EU were going to provide new guarantees or social protections beyond those provided by the countries: for example, the European unemployment insurance projects or the banking union. These kinds of projects, though intended to move the European project forward, generally wind up being stripped of their substance because they do not correspond to the political expectations of many European partners. To take a conflictual aspect within the euro zone, the northern countries fear that solidarity measures are a one-way street and serve purely and simply to finance the southern countries, which they consider poorly managed.

The feeling that the single currency is functioning poorly cannot in and of itself justify just any old proposal. Wanting to "complete the euro" therefore leads to a political impasse. This impasse exists only because everyone wants to take everyone else in a direction that the latter are rejecting. It would be better to recognize the differences between perspectives and expectations about the Union and to learn how to deal with these.

In this respect, it is possible to interpret the problem of the incompleteness of the currency otherwise, by trying this time to link each of the States to the currency. There is indeed reason to be concerned that the European currency is able to function as a foreign currency for each of the euro zone States, taken one by one. Economists know how dangerous it is for a society to give up its monetary sovereignty and to abandon any form of regulation over its currency. States that have done so in the course of history, by adopting a foreign currency in their domestic market or by taking on debt in foreign currencies, have generally fared poorly. In most cases, these States have fallen into serious debt problems because they no longer have the financial instruments needed to respond adequately to an economic crisis. This is the main criticism opponents of the euro have made against the euro.

But instead of trying to build a European leviathan to tame the single currency, we could also consider building the link between the common currency and each of the States closest to the Member States of the euro zone. To do this, it is not necessary to give up the single currency and return to the national currencies. As with the path proposed in the first part, where we refused to choose between a democracy based on a European people to the exclusion of national peoples or national democracies that exclude any European horizon, the point here is about defending a common currency that has close ties with every country.

If the euro is the equivalent of a foreign currency for each of the member countries, it is primarily because of the mistrust of the other euro zone members. From the very outset, everyone tried with the famous Maastricht criteria to regulate their partners' budgetary policy—as if they were irresponsible. Nor have we ever really left behind this state of mind since then: what dominates is the fear of having to bail out failed States and a suspicion of moral hazard, which would incite everyone to indiscriminately take on debt because they would be assured of being covered by their partners.

But the Greek episode showed that these fears were unfounded. Europe has reacted too slowly, but during the process, the real architecture of the common currency has come to light. On the one hand, the ECB ended up playing the role, State by State, of lender of last resort. On the other hand, the question of a default or bail out was the subject of consultation between the partner countries about both the assistance to be accorded and the mechanisms likely to provide the most reactive response in light of the Greek case, subject of course to certain conditions (the European Solidarity Mechanism and TSCG).

The Greek episode shows that a State can (partially) default without leaving the euro, with a restructured debt and a risk premium on its government bonds. Two lessons can be learned. First, there is no insurance that a failed State will be saved in full by the other euro zone members, so there is no moral hazard. Second, the organic link between State and currency, which is implicit in countries with a national currency, has been replaced by the combination of the ECB's unstinting support for the currency and the way the bankrupt State has been handled politically. There has been an effort to explain the new link between the State and the currency in a demoicratic framework.

This new architecture has not arisen by accident, but rather reflects a balance between what the different partners are willing to accept in a situation of crisis. Future reforms, if they prove necessary, must continue in this direction, on the one hand, by carrying forward the effort to clarify the link between Member States and the common currency in a demoicratic spirit and, on the other hand, by figuring out how to connect the ECB, which in this instance seized on the sovereignty on the euro, with a demoicratic spirit. On this last point, it should be emphasized that the ECB does not take only "technical" decisions, but also commits the citizens of the euro zone through its decisions to buy sovereign or quasi-sovereign securities. Even as an independent institution, it cannot avoid having to account for its positions sooner or later.

5 Conclusion

The trap in the debates about the European Union is to think about democracy at the EU level based on our own national democratic experiences. But the European political space is quite specific: it is composed of a multitude of peoples who are very open to each other, interacting massively together, and thus subject to transnational conflicts of interest that need peaceful solutions. Democracy must therefore take a different form to take account of this specificity. The neologism "demoicracy" was developed to insist precisely on this specificity, on the need to democratize relations between multiple democracies.

The single currency poses a particular challenge because it forces us to cooperate politically, which was not necessarily self-evident when everyone had their currency and tried to use it to get an advantage against their neighbours. Henceforth, central institutions like the ECB are needed, but in light of the principle of non-domination, it is also necessary to give the countries a relatively large amount of autonomy by relying more on voluntary cooperation that is aware of externalities and systemic risks than on a central authority lacking in legitimacy. The democratization of the EU can be guaranteed only by bringing together several sources of legitimacy, national and European, and getting away from the hierarchical principle as much as possible. The ultimate goal is to find the right institutional arrangement, the one that will best advance the arguments that conform to the demoicratic principle, by bringing into our national debates the externalities and systemic risks that the States impose on their neighbours. These are the grounds on which the European Parliament and other means of mobilizing Europe's citizens can advance demoicracy.

Notes

1. It will simply be noted here that the plurality of national currencies within a single market was another type of challenge, where a lack of unity weakened each of the currencies and also raised questions of justice and economic efficiency. The great extent to which the economies are intertwined is the real cause of the need to rethink the European monetary area.
2. As we can observe in Catalonia, Belgium, northern Italy and so on... These transfers can also be pure fantasies, which does not prevent them from fueling identity conflicts that, in general, were pre-existing.

References

Bickerton, Chris. 2012. *European Integration: From Nation-States to Member States*. Oxford: Oxford University Press.

Bohman, John. 2005. From Demos to Demoi: Democracy Across Borders. *Ratio Juris* 18 (3): 293–314.

Cheneval, Francis. 2011. *The Government of the Peoples. On the Idea and Principles of Multilateral Democracy*. Houndmills: Palgrave Macmillan.

Cheneval, Francis, and Frank Schimmelfennig. 2012. The Case for Democracy in the European Union. *Journal of Common Market Studies* 51 (2): 1–17.

Habermas, Jürgen. 2015. *The Lure of Technocracy*. Cambridge: Polity Press.

Nicolaïdis, Kalypso. 2012. The Idea of European Democracy. In *Philosophical Foundations of European Union Law*, ed. Julie Dickson and Pavlos Eleftheriadis, 247–274. Oxford: Oxford University Press.

Nicolaïdis, Kalypso, and Max Watson. 2016. Sharing the Eurocrats' Dream: A Democratic Approach to EMU Governance in the Post-Crisis Era. In *The End of the Eurocrat's Dream*, ed. Damian Markus Jachtenfuchs Chalmers and Christian Joerges, 50–77. Cambridge: Cambridge University Press.

Rawls, John. 1971. *A Theory of Justice*. Harvard: Harvard University Press.

Van Parijs, Philippe. 1997. Should the EU Become More Democratic? In *Democracy and the European Union*, ed. Andreas Follesdal and Peter Koslowski, 287–301. Berlin: Springer.

14

Conclusion: Where Is the Compass Pointing to?

Jérôme Creel, Éloi Laurent, and Jacques Le Cacheux

Gentle breeze or hurricane? Moving or stalled? And if moving, where to? The period leading to the May 2019 European Parliament elections is going to be a crucial year for the European Union (EU): the elections for

J. Creel (✉)
OFCE, Sciences Po, Paris, France

ESCP Europe, Paris, France
e-mail: jerome.creel@sciencespo.fr

É. Laurent
OFCE, Sciences Po, Paris, France

School of Management and Innovation Sciences Po, Paris, France

Stanford University, Stanford, CA, USA
e-mail: eloi.laurent@sciencespo.fr

J. Le Cacheux
Université de Pau et des Pays de l'Adour, Pau, France

Ecole Nationale des Ponts et Chaussées, Marne-la-Vallée, France

Sciences Po, Paris, France
e-mail: jacques.lecacheux@sciencespo.fr

© The Author(s) 2018
J. Creel et al. (eds.), *Report on the State of the European Union*,
https://doi.org/10.1007/978-3-319-98364-6_14

the European Parliament will take place in a political context that dramatically differs from the one of the previous ballot, held in May 2014. As already pointed out in the introduction of this volume, populism has been rising in the EU in recent years, and actually acceding to power in national governments in a number of member states. Even in countries, such as Germany, where populist parties are not in the governing coalition, they exert a significant influence on the agenda and on positions taken by some coalition members. On July 1, 2018, Austria, led by a right-wing and far-right government, took over the EU rotating presidency for six months: during the second half of the year, the council of Ministers of Home Affairs will be chaired by a minister from the overtly nationalist and populist party FPO.

The March 2018 wave of Eurobarometer (Eurostat 2018), already mentioned in the introduction, probably gives better indications on the mood of European citizens than the composition of national governments, so heavily influenced by specifically national political institutions; comparing it to that conducted in March 2013, one year ahead of the previous European general election, is instructive: whereas then immigration and terrorism were ranking relatively low among EU citizens' concerns, with respectively 10% and 7% of the polled placing them as top priorities, they now dominate, with respectively 38% and 29%, while the economic situation regarded back then as the top priority by 48% of respondents, is now ranking third, with a bare 18%. On the other hand, positive opinions on the euro, trust in EU institutions and the feeling that "my voice counts" in EU are all on the rise, but with large differences across countries, low levels of positive opinions being observed in Greece, France, and Italy and high levels in Portugal, Denmark, Ireland, and for the latter item, Germany.

This contrasted snapshot of the European political situation is to be confronted with the economic situation. Compared to five years ago, the improvement is perceptible everywhere, even in countries, such as Greece, that are still way below what they had known prior to the Great Recession and the sovereign debt crisis. Unemployment is still high in Southern Europe, but slowly decreasing; per capita incomes are still below pre-crisis levels, but slightly rising again. Is it not time to fix what has not worked, and "repair the roof when the sun is shining" (iAGS 2017)?

By mid-2018, it seems that not all member states' national governments share the sense of urgency or the same priorities. Not surprisingly, given their relative prosperity, Northern European members of the Euro Area in general appear to be content with overall existing arrangements and fear that any progress toward fiscal integration will lead to permanent fiscal transfers to Southern European members. National stances on upcoming negotiations on important items of the European agenda or external events reflect these differences and the distribution of perceived present and expected future gains and losses for the countries.

Hence, after forming a relatively united front to negotiate Brexit and to respond to President Trump first round of tariff hikes on aluminum and steel imports, member states may find it much more difficult to find agreement on a number of crucial decisions facing them in the coming months. Foremost among these challenges is the attitude toward Russia and the USA. The sanctions imposed on Russia after its annexation of Crimea in 2014 have been prolonged recently; but there is mounting opposition to this EU policy stemming from national governments of countries where populist parties are in power or exert strong influence. And the announcement by President Trump of a wave of tariff hikes, this time hitting automobile imports, may trigger divergent reactions, with countries, like Germany, massively exporting these goods to the US market, trying to reach a compromise, while others would rather choose sanctions.

On immigration, the divide is blurred by the strong pressure of public opinions. The relatively open position of such countries as Germany and Sweden is now weakened by internal tensions, whereas the number of national governments now in favor of stricter rules or even closed borders has been increasing. In the Council meeting on June 28, 2018, populist governments now in power in a significant number of member states have obtained an effective repeal of the so-called "Dublin Regulation", whereby migrants are supposed to stay in the country where they first entered the EU territory and can be sent back to this country whenever they are caught as illegal aliens in other EU member states. The common EU policy vis à vis migrants and asylum seekers is to be redefined and strengthened, but clearly in the direction of stricter criteria and stronger border controls, as well as closed camps in the EU and in neighboring countries for entering migrants.

On this particular issue, the Council supports the proposal made by the Commission in the next Multiannual Financial Framework (2021–2027) to increase the funds allocated to border controls (FRONTEX). But the rest of the proposed EU budget is likely to raise heated controversies among member states, in particular on the reduction of expenditures for agriculture and structural funds, but also on the proposed, very modest, new own resources from carbon emission permit sales and, even more contentious, from a levy on the currently discussed Common Consolidated Corporate Tax Base (CCCTB). Although the Council reaffirms its will to fight tax avoidance and better tax multinationals, there are still very strong oppositions from some member states on the proposed solutions.

Regarding the future of the Euro Area and its governance, the high hopes entertained in some quarters after Macron's Sorbonne speech have been showered by recent German reactions, and even more so by its virtual disappearance from the latest Council meeting conclusions. The Franco-German compromise reached in Meseberg on June 19, 2018 (German and French Governments 2018) contains only a few indications on a future Euro Area budget, in the framework of the EU budget and probably from the same funding, small and exclusively dedicated to investment in new technologies and human capital, far from the ambitious French plans of a stabilization budget. Corporate taxation as well as other issues are mentioned in the joint declaration, but only to be dealt with in a future common "roadmap".

But even this modest progress in the direction of strengthening the Euro Area has immediately raised opposition from other member states, some resenting the Franco-German leadership per se, others because their perceived national interest is felt threatened. Hence the likelihood that the EU and the Euro Area get stalled again until the next crisis comes and forces action is high.

References

Eurostat. 2018. *Eurobarometer March 2018*. http://ec.europa.eu/commfrontoffice/publicopinion/index.cfm/Survey/getSurveyDetail/instruments/STANDARD/surveyKy/2180.

iAGS. 2017. *Repair the Roof When the Sun Is Shining*. 6th Report of the Independent Annual Growth Survey. https://www.iags-project.org/.

German and French Governments. 2018. *Meseberg Declaration*, June 19. https://www.pubaffairsbruxelles.eu/meseberg-declaration-german-federal-chancellors-office-press/.

Index[1]

[1] Note: Page numbers followed by 'n' refer to notes.

© The Author(s) 2018
J. Creel et al. (eds.), *Report on the State of the European Union*,
https://doi.org/10.1007/978-3-319-98364-6

The manufacturer's authorised representative in the EU is Springer Nature Customer Service Centre GmbH, Europaplatz 3, 69115 Heidelberg, Germany. If you have any concerns regarding our products, please contact ProductSafety@springernature.com

Printed and bound by CPI Group (UK) Ltd, Croydon, CR0 4YY
30/09/2026
02225434-0004